BEST PLAYS BY CHEKHOV

The Sea Gull

Uncle Vanya

The Three Sisters

The Cherry Orchard

BEST PLAYS BY

CHEKHOV

The Sea Gull

Uncle Vanya

The Three Sisters

The Cherry Orchard

Translated and with an introduction by

STARK YOUNG

THE MODERN LIBRARY · NEW YORK

Library of Congress Catalog Card Number: 56–8837

Random House IS THE PUBLISHER OF *The Modern Library*

Manufactured in the United States of America

CONTENTS

Introduction   vii

The Sea Gull   1

Uncle Vanya   71

The Three Sisters   137

The Cherry Orchard   225

INTRODUCTION

by STARK YOUNG

It was my intention to begin this preface with some discussion, however brief, of Chekhov's qualities as a dramatist. But one way or another through the numerous translations, and very often through some of the theatrical performances, there has gathered around his name the greatest variety of impressions, or conceptions, of him. He may be put down as morbid or as having something too much of the "Russian soul"; it may be said that his plays lack plot, that his speeches are often too involved, that he is depressing, that he provides little spice or action for the players, and so on and so on, according to the critic in each case.

In fact, when I made a translation for Miss Lynn Fontanne and Mr. Alfred Lunt some seasons ago, there were a good many people who always spoke of it as an "adaptation," meaning to praise my effort and at the same time to indicate their relief from too much of this Russian dramatist.

On the other hand, a note came to me, unrequested, from Dr. Nicholas Rumanceff, for thirty years a member of the Moscow Art Theatre, sometime chairman of its

Board of Directors, and a well known scholar: "After
reading the reviews I might have concluded that *The Sea
Gull* had been rearranged for a better understanding and
response on the part of American audiences. Knowing
the other translations and knowing the play, I could
easily have believed that this new version, to be thus successful, must be an adaptation. But such was not the case.
I found almost word for word Chekhov's characteristic,
it seemed to me, in Mr. Young's translation. The reason
the American public loves and understands the play is
that it is like Chekhov in English."

With half a dozen translations of Chekhov's plays
available, plus the dictionary, we could hardly say that
most of the bare meanings are not close enough to hand.
A great part of the mischance that has fallen to Chekhov's
lines has not, however, been a matter of mere vocabulary.
The vocabulary could hardly be simpler than it is in
Chekhov. In fact the directors of the theatre where his
plays were to be given wondered "what to do about utter-
ing these simplest of phrases simply." And Stanislavsky
has told us in writing that when he came to producing
The Sea Gull, he did not know any way to proceed; he
found the words too simple. That was in 1896. Of all the
dramatists Chekhov least deserves the muddle of the various styles that have been foisted on him in English—the
involved, for instance, or the elevated, or the psycho-
logical-gloomy, or the turgid-soulful, or the flat, or the
lacking in lyricism or in wit.

We can get a hint of what can happen to him even in
the young lady's speech to her adored author. In the
Russian she says, "You work too hard and have no time
left to feel your own importance"; the translated young
lady says, "You are overworked and you have not the

leisure nor the desire to appreciate your own significance." In one translation this same young lady, instead of saying that "evidently the play is not going on," soars into "apparently there's to be no continuation." And the remark that "every one writes as he wants to and as he can" becomes "every one writes in accordance with his desire and his capacity." Mr. Brooks Atkinson has exactly the right word for it when he speaks of how *opaque* some of the translations are that we have taken for granted.

I must cite one or two among many instances where the translator clearly prefers his own style to Chekhov's. For example, what the speech says in Russian is, "I fall always more and more behind, like a peasant missing his train, and the upshot is I can write only landscape and in all the rest I am false and false to the marrow of my bones." The translator undertakes to improve on that: "I am left behind them like a peasant missing his train at a station and finally I come back to the conclusion that all I am fit for is to describe landscapes, and that whatever else I attempt rings abominably false." If that seems unbelievable, it is less so perhaps than when Sonia's lovely line in *Uncle Vanya,* "We shall see the whole sky all diamonds," is turned into "We shall see all Heaven lit with radiance."

Chekhov has many dramatic devices—repetitions, parallels, balances and so on—which are caught or missed according to the translator. There is, too, the matter of sayability, that possibility of speaking the lines on the stage, as many an actor to his joy or sorrow has found out. There are plentiful illustrations of this in various translations, but short examples will make the point just as well. In *The Sea Gull,* Chekhov's actress shouts at the farm manager—and this is the exact order, number of words, and punctuation of her speech—"What horses? How should I know? What horses!" One translation has it, "What horses? How can I tell which?" That may seem a simple change but try and shout it. Or where the farm manager in a rage has to shout back at her, "You don't know what a farm means!" try shouting, "You don't know what the management of an estate involves!" Why such renderings are preferred to Chekhov's simple lines would be hard to explain.

Comparisons among the four plays in this volume are, of course, possible and not hard to make. Critics have noted that a play of Chekhov's is not a mixture of the spirit of comedy and the spirit of tragedy; it can fall only within some softer, less sharply defined mood. Chekhov's most impressive creation in the art of the drama consists in his power to create such a mood. I should say that in the creation of this particular mood, wit *per se* played a great part, the rest being mostly played by Chekhov's lyricism—the music of his profound and gentle humanity. This mood is most evident in *The Three Sisters* and *The Cherry Orchard,* and causes them to be for many people the best beloved of his plays. They have more fragrance, as it were, more of that fanciful recklessness and those impetuous springs of emotion that so many people have come to think of and love as Chekhov. *Uncle Vanya* may be deeper in its creation and portrayal of the characters, which here are passionately seen and as passionately to be acted. Certainly it has more of a dramatic line running through it than the other two plays. *The Sea Gull,* coming earlier, in 1896, is no doubt less fully Chekhov than the later plays. It has more of the qualities and moti-vations to be found in European drama generally. It is also more immediately actable than the three other plays and is closer to the taste of our theatre in the West.

In Chekhov the thought is not so often in one speech only; it is in the combination of speeches. And the sequence of the speeches is part of the whole idea or dramatic movement. Chekhov's subtlety needs constant watching by the actors and the director; there is a deceptive economy in every speech or emotional reference or transition. They are elusive and at times seemingly vague but they are also as exact as the beating of your pulse. This dramatic writing is diffused, and is lighter than down, is suddenly dark and pathetic, is all at once luminous and beautiful. A hovering life lies over the scenes, and a strange and living pressure emerges. Chekhov is like a wise, evenly balanced doctor who takes all in his stride. He can portray the human scene without bitterness, harsh theories or sentimental indulgence. For this very reason—the fact that life is so vividly apparent and expressed in him—Chekhov should never seem to be really depressing.

Biographical Note

Anton Chekhov was born in Taganrog, an old port on the Sea of Azov, on January 17, 1860. He was of Russian peasant stock, but his grandfather had bought the freedom of the family. During his student days at the University of Moscow, from which he received his degree in medicine in 1884, he began writing short stories under the pen name of Antosha Chekhonté.

Early in his career he became interested in writing for the theatre, and his first efforts were such one-act plays as *On the Road* (1884), *The Swan Song* (1886), *The Bear* (1888), *The Proposal* (1889), and *The Wood Demon* (1889), which was to be rewritten ten years later as *Uncle Vanya*.

In 1887, Chekhov wrote *Ivanov,* his first full-length play, but it was not a success when produced in Moscow and St. Petersburg. In 1896, *The Sea Gull* was produced in St. Petersburg as part of an occasion in honor of an admired comedienne; poorly performed, it was a sorry failure. The following season, however, when the play was produced by the newly organized Moscow Art Theatre, it was an overwhelming success. It was in fact a furor. Nevertheless, for all the furor and ovation, the house was half empty, and the excitement did not imply any wide immediate acceptance of the play. The truth is that none of Chekhov's plays won any real triumph until the second season, and, even after that, it was necessary to wait a long time before they drew full houses.

In 1899 *Uncle Vanya* was produced by the Moscow Art Theatre, followed in 1901 by *The Three Sisters* and in 1904 by *The Cherry Orchard*. During this period, Chekhov lived in the Crimea, to which he had gone for his health, making occasional trips to Moscow to supervise the production of his plays. He died on July 2, 1904, at Badenweiler, a German health resort in the Black Forest, and was buried in Moscow.

Among the worth-while readings on Chekhov are David Magarshack's *Chekhov: A Life,* Maxim Gorky's *Reminiscences of Tolstoi, Chekhov, and Andreyev,* and Eric Bentley's essay on Chekhov in *In Search of Theater.*

Among the earlier translations of Chekhov's plays we may list those by Constance Garnett, Julius West, George Calderon, Marian Fell, and S. S. Koteliansky.

For advice and assistance in my translations I must thank Mrs. Catherine Burland, a widely read Russian lady living in this country.

The Sea Gull

CHARACTERS

IRINA NIKOLAEVNA ARKADINA, MADAME TREPLEFF, *an actress*

KONSTANTINE GAVRILOVICH TREPLEFF, *her son*

PETER NIKOLAEVICH SORIN, *her brother*

NINA MIKHAILOVNA ZARYECHNY, *a young girl,
the daughter of a wealthy landowner*

ILYA AFANASEVICH SHAMREYEFF, *a retired lieutenant,
Sorin's steward*

PAULINE ANDREEVNA, *his wife*

MASHA (MARIA ILYINISHNA), *his daughter*

BORIS ALEXEEVICH TRIGORIN, *a literary man*

EUGENE SERGEEVICH DORN, *a doctor*

SEMYON SEMYONOVICH MEDVEDENKO, *a schoolmaster*

YAKOV, *a laborer*

COOK

Two housemaids

ACT ONE

A section of the park on SORIN's *estate. The wide avenue leading away from the spectators into the depths of the park toward the lake is closed by a platform hurriedly put together for private theatricals, so that the lake is not seen at all. To left and right of the platform there are bushes. A few chairs, a small table.*

The sun has just set. On the platform behind the curtain are YAKOV *and other workmen; sounds of coughing and hammering are heard.* MASHA *and* MEDVEDENKO *enter on the left, returning from a walk.*

MEDVEDENKO: Why do you always wear black?

MASHA: I am in mourning for my life. I'm unhappy.

MEDVEDENKO: You unhappy? I can't understand it. Your health is good, and your father is not rich but he's well enough off. My life is much harder to bear than yours. I get twenty-three roubles a month, and that's all, and then out of that the pension fund has to be deducted, but I don't wear mourning.

(They sit down.)

MASHA: It isn't a question of money. Even a beggar can be happy.

MEDVEDENKO: Yes, theoretically he can, but not when you come right down to it. Look at me, with my mother, my two sisters and my little brother, and my salary twenty-three roubles in all. Well, people have to eat and drink, don't they? Have to have tea and sugar? Have tobacco? So it just goes round and round.

MASHA (*Glancing toward the stage*): The play will begin soon.

MEDVEDENKO: Yes. The acting will be done by Nina Zaryechny and the play was written by Konstantine Gavrilovich. They are in love with each other, and today their souls are mingled in a longing to create some image both can share and true to both. But my soul and your soul can't find any ground to meet on. You see how it is. I love you; I can't stay at home because I keep wishing so for you; and so every day I walk four miles here and four miles back and meet with nothing but indifference on your part. That's only natural. I've got nothing, we're a big family. Who wants to marry a man who can't even feed himself?

MASHA: Fiddlesticks! (*She takes snuff*) Your love touches me, but I can't return it, that's all. (*Offers him snuff*) Help yourself.

MEDVEDENKO: I'd as soon not.

(*A pause.*)

MASHA: My, how close it is! It must be going to storm tonight. All you do is philosophize or talk about money. You think the worst misery we can have is poverty. But I think it's a thousand times easier to go ragged and beg for bread than. . . . But you'd never understand that . . .

(*Enter* SORIN, *leaning on his walking stick, and* TREPLEFF.)

SORIN: For some reason, who knows, my dear boy, the country's not my style. Naturally. You can't teach an old horse new tricks. Last night I went to bed at ten o'clock, and at nine this morning I awoke feeling as if my brain stuck to my skull, and so on. (*Laughing*) And then on top of all that I fell asleep after dinner just the same. And so now I'm a wreck, I'm still lost in a nightmare, and all the rest of it . . .

TREPLEFF: That's true, Uncle, you really ought to live in town. (*Sees* MASHA *and* MEDVEDENKO) Look, my friends, we'll call you when the play starts, but don't stay here now. I'll have to ask you to go.

SORIN (*To* MASHA): Maria Ilyinishna, won't you kindly ask your father to leave that dog unchained, to stop that howling? All last night again my sister couldn't sleep.

MASHA: You'll have to tell my father yourself. I shan't do it, so please don't ask me to. (*To* MEDVEDENKO) Let's go.

MEDVEDENKO: Then you'll let us know before the play starts.

(MASHA *and* MEDVEDENKO *go out.*)

SORIN: That just means the dog will howl all night again. You see how 'tis; in the country I have never had what I wanted. It used to be I'd get leave for twenty-eight days, say, and come down here to recoup, and so on; but they plagued me so with one silly piece of nonsense after another that the very first day I wanted to be out of it. (*Laughs*) I've always left here with relish . . . Well, now that I'm retired, I have nowhere to go and all the rest of it. Like it—like it not, I live . . .

YAKOV: We're going for a swim, Konstantine Gavrilovich.

TREPLEFF: So long as you are back in ten minutes. (*Looks at his watch*) We're about to begin.

YAKOV: Yes, sir.

TREPLEFF: Here's your theatre. The curtain, then the first wing, then the second wing, and still further open space. No scenery at all. You see what the background is—it stretches to the lake and on to the horizon. And the curtain will go up at 8:30, just when the moon's rising.

SORIN: Magnificent!

TREPLEFF: If Nina's late, then, of course, the whole effect will be spoilt. It's time she was here now. But her father and stepmother watch her so she can hardly get out of the house, it's like escaping from prison. (*Straightening his uncle's tie*) Uncle, your hair and beard are rumpled up—you ought to have them trimmed . . .

SORIN (*Combing his beard*): It's the tragedy of my life. I always look as if I'd been drunk, even when I was young I did—and so on. Women never have loved me. (*Sits down*) Why is my sister in such bad humor?

TREPLEFF: Why? Bored. (*Sits down by* SORIN) Jealous. She's set against me, against the performance and against my play, because Nina's going to act in it and she's not. She's never read my play but she hates it.

SORIN: You (*Laughing*) imagine things, really . . .

TREPLEFF: Yes, she's furious because even on this little stage it's Nina will have a success and not she. (*Looks at his watch*) A psychological case, my mother. She's undeniably talented, intelligent, capable of sobbing over a novel; she recites all of Nekrasov's poetry by heart; she nurses the sick like an angel; but you just try praising Duse to her; oh, ho! You praise nobody but her, write about her, rave about her, go into ecstasies over her marvelous performance in *La Dame Aux Camélias* or in *The Fumes of Life*. But all that is a drug she can't get in the country, so she's bored and cross. We are all her enemies—it's all our fault. And then she's superstitious, afraid of three candles or number thirteen. She's stingy. She's got seventy thousand roubles in an Odessa bank—I know that for a fact. But ask her for a loan, she'll burst into tears.

SORIN: You've got it into your head your play annoys your mother, and that upsets you, and so on. Don't worry, your mother worships the ground you walk on.

TREPLEFF (*Picking petals from a flower*): Loves me—loves me not, loves me—loves me not, loves me—loves me not. (*Laughing*) You see, my mother doesn't love me, of course not. I should say not! What she wants is to live, and love, and wear pretty clothes; and here I am twenty-five years old and a perpetual reminder that she's no longer young. You see, when I'm not there she's only thirty-two, and when I am she's forty-three . . . and for that she hates me. She knows too that I refuse to admit the theatre. She loves the theatre; it seems to her that she's working for humanity, for holy art. But to my thinking her theatre today is nothing but routine, convention. When the curtain goes up, and by artificial light in a room with three walls, these great geniuses, these priests of holy art, show how people eat, drink, make love, move about and wear their jackets; when they try to fish a moral out of these flat pictures and phrases, some sweet little bit anybody could understand and any fool take home; when in a thousand different dishes they serve me the same thing over and over, over and over, over and over—well, it's then I run and run like Maupassant from the Eiffel Tower and all that vulgarity about to bury him.

SORIN: But we can't do without the theatre.

TREPLEFF: We must have new forms. New forms we must have, and if we can't get them we'd better have nothing at all. (*He looks at his watch*) I love my mother, I love her very much; but she leads a senseless life, always making a fuss over this novelist, her name forever chucked about in the papers . . . it disgusts me. It's merely the simple egotism of an ordinary mortal, I suppose, stirring me up sometimes that makes me wish I had somebody besides a famous actress for a mother, and fancy if she had been an ordinary woman I'd have been happier. Uncle, can you imagine anything more hopeless than my position is in her house? It used to be she'd entertain, all famous people . . . actors and authors—and among them all I was the only one who was nothing, and they put up with me only because I was her son. Who am I? What am I? I left the university in my third year, owing to circumstances, as they say, for which the editors are not responsible; I've no talent at all, not a kopeck on me; and according to my passport I am—a burgher of Kiev. My father, as you know, was a burgher of Kiev, though he was also a famous actor. So when these actors and writers of hers bestowed on me their gracious attentions, it seemed to me their eyes were measuring my insignificance—I guessed their thoughts and felt humiliated.

SORIN: By the by, listen, can you please tell me what sort of man this novelist is? You see, I can't make him out. He never opens his mouth.

TREPLEFF: He's an intelligent man, he's simple, apt to be melancholy. Quite decent. He's well under forty yet but he's already celebrated, he's had more than enough of everything. As for his writings . . . well, we'll say charming, full of talent, but after Tolstoi or Zola, of course, a little of Trigorin goes a long way.

SORIN: My boy, I'm fond of writers, you know. Once there were two things I wanted passionately. To marry and to be an author. I never succeeded in doing either. It must be pleasant being a minor writer even, and all the rest of it.

TREPLEFF: I hear footsteps. (*Embraces his uncle*) I can't live without her. Just the sound of her footsteps is lovely. (*Going to meet* NINA ZARYECHNY *as she enters*) I'm insanely happy! My enchantress! My dream!

NINA: I'm not late. . . . Surely I'm not late . . .

TREPLEFF (*Kissing her hands*): No, no, no.

NINA: All day I worried, was so frightened. . . . I was so afraid father wouldn't let me come. But at last he's gone out. He went out just now with my stepmother. The sky has turned red, the moon will soon be up, and I raced the horse, raced him. (*Laughs*) But I'm so happy. (*Warmly shaking* SORIN's *hand.*)

SORIN (*Laughing*): You've been crying, I see by your little eyes. That's not fair.

NINA: That's so. You can see how out of breath I am. Do let's hurry. I've got to go in half an hour. I must. Don't ask me to stay, my father doesn't know I'm here.

TREPLEFF: It's time to begin anyhow. . . . I'll go call them.

SORIN: I'll go. I'll go this minute. (*Begins to sing "The Two Grenadiers," then stops*) Once I started singing like that and a deputy who was standing by said, "Your Excellency has a very strong voice" . . . then he thought awhile and said, "Strong but unpleasant." (*Exits, laughing.*)

NINA: My father and his wife won't let me come here; they say it's Bohemia. They are afraid I'll go on the stage. But I am drawn here to this lake like a sea gull. My heart is full of you.

TREPLEFF: We're alone.

NINA: Isn't that someone over there?

TREPLEFF: No, nobody. (*Kisses her.*)

NINA: What kind of tree is that?

TREPLEFF: It's an elm.

NINA: Why does it look so dark?

TREPLEFF: Because it's evening and everything looks darker. Don't go away early, please don't.

NINA: I must.

TREPLEFF: But if I should follow you, Nina? I'll stand all night in the garden, looking up at your window.

NINA: Oh, no! You mustn't. The watchman would see you and Treasure doesn't know you yet, he'd bark.

TREPLEFF: I love you.

NINA: Ssh . . . !

TREPLEFF: Who's that? . . . You, Yakov?

YAKOV (*From behind stage*): Yes, sir.

TREPLEFF: You must get to your seats, it's time to begin. The moon's coming up.

YAKOV: Yes, sir.

TREPLEFF: Have you got that methylated spirits? Is the sulphur ready? (*To* NINA) You see when the red eyes appear there must be a smell of sulphur around. You'd better go now, everything's ready. Do you feel nervous?

NINA: Yes, awfully. It's not that I'm afraid of your mother so much, it's Boris Trigorin terrifies me, acting before him, a famous author like him. Tell me, is he young?

TREPLEFF: Yes.

NINA: What marvelous stories he writes!

TREPLEFF (*Coldly*): I don't know. I don't read them.

NINA: It's hard to act in your play. There are no living characters in it.

TREPLEFF: Living characters! I must represent life not as it is and not as it should be, but as it appears in my dreams.

NINA: In your play there's no action; it's all recitation. It seems to me a play must have some love in it.

(*They go out by way of the stage. Enter* PAULINE ANDREEVNA *and* DORN.)

PAULINE: It's getting damp, go back and put on your galoshes.

DORN: I'm hot.

PAULINE: You don't take any care of yourself and it's just contrariness. You're a doctor and know very well how bad damp air is for you, but you like to make me miserable. You sat out on that terrace all last evening on purpose.

DORN (*Sings low*): Oh, never say that I . . .

PAULINE: You were so enchanted by Madame Arkadina's conversation you didn't even notice the cold . . . You may as well own up—she charms you . . .

DORN: I'm fifty-five.

PAULINE: Fiddlesticks! What's that for a man, it's not old. You're still young enough looking, women still like you.

DORN (*Gently*): Tell me, what is it you want?

PAULINE: Before an actress you are all ready to kiss the ground. All of you!

DORN (*Sings low*): Once more I stand before thee. . . . If society does make a fuss over actors, treats them differently from, say shopkeepers—it's only right and natural. That's the pursuit of the ideal.

PAULINE: Women have always fallen in love with you and hung on your neck. Is that the pursuit of the ideal too?

DORN (*Shrugs his shoulders*): Why? In the relations women have had with me there has been a great deal that was fine. What they chiefly loved in me was the fact that I was a first-class doctor for childbirths. Ten or fifteen years ago, you remember, I was the only decent accoucheur they had in all this part of the country. Besides, I've always been an honorable man.

PAULINE (*Clasping his hand*): My dear!

DORN: Ssh . . . here they come!

(*Enter* MADAME ARKADINA *on* SORIN'S *arm,* TRIGORIN, SHAMREYEFF, MEDVEDENKO *and* MASHA.)

SHAMREYEFF: In '73 at the Poltava Fair . . . pure delight . . . I can assure you she was magnificent, ah, magnificent! Pure delight! But tell me if you know where Chadin, Paul Semyonovich, the comedian, is now? Take his Raspluyef . . . 'twas better than Sadovsky's, I can assure you, most esteemed lady. But what's become of him?

ARKADINA: You keep asking me about someone before the flood . . . how should I know? (*Sits down.*)

SHAMREYEFF: Ah. (*Sighs*) Paulie Chadin! Nobody like that now. The stage is not what it was, Irina Nikolaevna, ah no! In those days there were mighty oaks, now we have nothing but stumps.

DORN: There are not many brilliant talents nowadays, it's true, but the general average of the acting is much higher.

SHAMREYEFF: I can't agree with you there. However, that's a matter of taste, *De gustibus aut bene, aut nihil.*

(TREPLEFF *comes out from behind the stage.*)

ARKADINA: My dear son, when does it begin?

TREPLEFF: Please be patient. It's only a moment.

ARKADINA (*Reciting from* Hamlet): My son!
"Thou turnst mine eyes into my very soul,
  And there I see such black and grained spots
  As will not leave their tinct."

TREPLEFF (*Paraphrasing from* Hamlet): Nay, but to live
in wickedness, seek love in the depths of sin. . . . (*Behind the stage a horn blows.*) Ladies and gentlemen,
we begin! I beg your attention. (*A pause*) I begin.
(*Tapping the floor with a stick. In a loud voice*)
Harken ye mists, out of ancient time, that drift by
night over the bosom of this lake, darken our eyes with
sleep and in our dream show us what will be in 200,000
years.

SORIN: In 200,000 years nothing will be.

TREPLEFF: Then let them present to us that nothing.

ARKADINA: Let them. We are asleep.

(*The curtain rises. Vista opens across the lake. Low
on the horizon the moon hangs, reflected in the
water.* NINA ZARYECHNY *all in white, seated on a
rock.*)

NINA: Men and beasts, lions, eagles and partridges, antlered deer, mute fishes dwelling in the water, starfish
and small creatures invisible to the eye . . . these and
all life have run their sad course and are no more.
Thousands of creatures have come and gone since there
was life on the earth. Vainly now the pallid moon doth
light her lamp. In the meadows the cranes wake and
cry no longer; and the beetles' hum is silent in the
linden groves. Cold, cold, cold. Empty, empty, empty!
Terrible, terrible, terrible. (*A pause*) Living bodies
have crumbled to dust, and Eternal Matter has changed

them into stones and water and clouds and there is one soul of many souls. I am that soul of the world. . . . In me the soul of Alexander the Great, of Cæsar, of Shakespeare, of Napoleon and of the lowest worm. The mind of man and the brute's instinct mingle in me. I remember all, all, and in me lives each several life again.

(*The will-o'-the-wisps appear.*)

ARKADINA (*In a stage whisper*): We're in for something decadent.

TREPLEFF (*Imploring and reproaching*): Mother!

NINA: I am alone. Once in a hundred years I open my lips to speak, and in this void my sad echo is unheard. And you, pale fires, you do not hear me. . . . Before daybreak the putrid marsh begets you, and you wander until sunrise, but without thought, without will, without the throb of life. For fear life should spring in you the father of Eternal Matter, the Devil, causes every instant in you, as in stones and in water, an interchange of the atoms, and you are changing endlessly. I, only, the world's soul, remain unchanged and am eternal. (*A pause*) I am like a prisoner cast into a deep, empty well, and know not where I am nor what awaits me. One thing only is not hidden from me: in the stubborn, savage fight with the Devil, the principle of material forces, I am destined to conquer; and when that has been, matter and spirit shall be made one in the shadow of my soul forever. And lo, the kingdom of universal will is at hand. But that cannot be before long centuries of the moon, the shining dog star, and the earth, have run to dust. And till that time horror shall be, horror, horror, horror! (*A pause; upon the background of the lake appear two red spots*) Behold, my mighty adversary, the Devil, approaches. I see his awful, blood-red eyes.

ARKADINA: I smell sulphur, is that necessary?

TREPLEFF: Yes, it is.

ARKADINA (*Laughing*): Yes, it's a stage effect!

TREPLEFF: Mother!

NINA: But without man he is lost. . . .

PAULINE (*To* DORN): You're taking your hat off. Put it on, you'll catch cold.

ARKADINA: The doctor has taken off his hat to the Devil, the father of Eternal Matter?

TREPLEFF (*Blazing up, in a loud voice*): The play's over! That's enough! Curtain!

ARKADINA: Why are you angry?

TREPLEFF: That's enough. Curtain! Drop the curtain! (*Stamping his foot*) Curtain! (*The curtain falls*) You must excuse me! I don't know how it was but I forgot somehow that only a chosen few can write plays and act them. I was infringing on a monopoly. . . . My . . . I . . . (*Instead of saying more he makes a gesture of having done with it and goes out to the left.*)

ARKADINA: What's the matter with him?

SORIN: Irina, my dear, you mustn't treat a young man's pride like that.

ARKADINA: Now what have I said?

SORIN: You've hurt his feelings.

ARKADINA: But he told us beforehand it was all in fun, that's the way I took it . . . of course.

SORIN: All the same . . .

ARKADINA: And now it appears he's produced a master-piece. Well, I declare! Evidently he had no intention of amusing us, not at all; he got up this performance and fumigated us with sulphur to demonstrate to us how plays should be written and what's worth acting in. I'm sick of him. Nobody could stand his everlasting digs and outbursts. He's an unruly, conceited boy.

SORIN: He was only hoping to give you some pleasure.

ARKADINA: Yes? I notice he didn't choose some familiar sort of play, but forced his own decadent raving on us. I can listen to raving. I don't mind listening to it, so long as I'm not asked to take it seriously; but this of his is not like that. Not at all, it's introducing us to a new epoch in art, inaugurating a new era in art. But to my mind it's not new forms or epochs, it's simply bad temper.

TRIGORIN: Everyone writes as he wants to and as he can.

ARKADINA: Well, let him write as he wants to and as he can, so long as he leaves me out of it.

DORN: Great Jove angry is no longer Jove.

ARKADINA: I'm not Jove, I'm a woman. (*Lighting a cigarette*) I'm not angry . . . I'm merely vexed to see a young man wasting his time so. I didn't mean to hurt him.

MEDVEDENKO: Nobody has any grounds for separating matter from spirit, for it may be this very spirit itself is a union of material atoms. (*Excitedly, to* TRIGORIN) You know, somebody ought to put in a play, and then act on the stage, how we poor schoolmasters live. It's a hard, hard life.

ARKADINA: That's so, but we shan't talk of plays or atoms. The evening is so lovely. Listen . . . they're singing! (*Pausing to listen*) How good it is!

PAULINE: It's on the other side of the lake.

(*A pause.*)

ARKADINA: Sit down by me here. (*To* TRIGORIN) You

know, ten or fifteen years ago we had music on this
lake every night almost. There were six big country
houses then around the shore; and it was all laughter,
noise, shooting and lovemaking . . . making love
without end. The *jeune premier* and the idol of all six
houses was our friend here, I must present (*Nods toward* DORN) Doctor Eugene Sergeevich. He's charming
now, but then he was irresistible. Why did I hurt my
poor boy's feelings? I'm worried about him. (*Calls*)
Kostya! Son! Kostya!

MASHA: I'll go look for him.

ARKADINA: Would you, my dear?

MASHA (*Calling*): Ah-oo! Konstantine. Ah-oo! (*She goes
out.*)

NINA (*Coming from behind the stage*): Evidently we're
not going on, so I may as well come out. Good evening!
(*Kisses* MADAME ARKADINA *and* PAULINE ANDREEVNA.)

SORIN: Bravo! Bravo!

ARKADINA: Bravo! Bravo! We were all enchanted. With
such looks and such a lovely voice, it's a sin for you to
stay here in the country. You have talent indeed. Do
you hear? You owe it to yourself to go on the stage.

NINA: Oh, that's my dream. (*Sighing*) But it will never
come true.

ARKADINA: Who can tell? Let me present Boris Alexeevich Trigorin.

NINA: Oh, I'm so glad . . . (*Much embarrassed*) I'm always reading your . . .

ARKADINA (*Drawing* NINA *down beside her*): Don't be
shy, dear. He may be a famous author, but his heart's
quite simple. Look, he's embarrassed too.

DORN: I suppose we may raise the curtain now. This way
it's frightening.

SHAMREYEFF (*Loudly*): Yakov, my man, raise the curtain!

(*The curtain is raised.*)

NINA (*To* TRIGORIN): It's a strange play, isn't it?

TRIGORIN: I didn't understand a word of it. However, I enjoyed watching it. You acted with so much sincerity and the scenery was so lovely. (*A pause*) I dare say there are quantities of fish in this lake.

NINA: Yes.

TRIGORIN: I love fishing. I can think of no greater pleasure than to sit along towards evening by the water and watch a float.

NINA: But, I'd have thought that for anyone who had tasted the joy of creation, no other pleasures could exist.

ARKADINA (*Laughing*): Don't talk like that. When people make him pretty speeches he simply crumples up.

SHAMREYEFF: I remember one evening at the Opera in Moscow when the celebrated Silva was singing, how delighted we were when he took low C. Imagine our surprise . . . it so happened the bass from our church choir was there and all at once we heard "Bravo Silva" from the gallery a whole octave lower . . . like this . . . "Bravo Silva." The audience was thunderstruck.

(*A pause.*)

DORN: The angel of silence is flying over us.

NINA: Oh, I must go. Good-by.

ARKADINA: Where to? Where so early? We won't allow it.

NINA: Papa is waiting for me.

ARKADINA: What a man, really! (*Kissing her*) Well, there's no help for it. It's too sad losing you.

NINA: If you only knew how I don't want to go.

ARKADINA: Somebody must see you home, child.

NINA (*Frightened*): Oh, no, no.

SORIN (*Imploring her*): Don't go.

NINA: I must, Peter Nikolaevich.

SORIN: Stay an hour more, and so on. Come now, really . . .

NINA (*Hesitating with tears in her eyes*): I can't! (*She shakes hands and hurries out.*)

ARKADINA: Now there's a really poor, unfortunate girl. They say her mother when she died willed the husband all her immense fortune, everything to the very last kopeck, and now this little girl is left with nothing, since her father has already willed everything he has to the second wife. That's shocking.

DORN: Yes, her papa is rather a beast, I must grant him that.

SORIN (*Rubbing his hands to warm them*): What do you say, we'd better go in too, it's getting damp. My legs ache.

ARKADINA: It's like having wooden legs, you can hardly walk on them. Come on, you poor old patriarch. (*She takes his arm.*)

SHAMREYEFF (*Offering his arm to his wife*): Madame?

SORIN: There's that dog howling again. (*To* SHAMREYEFF) Be good enough, Ilya Afanasevich, to tell them to let that dog off the chain.

SHAMREYEFF: It can't be done, Peter Nikolaevich, or we'll be having thieves in the barn, and the millet's there. (*To* MEDVEDENKO, *walking beside him*) Yes, a whole octave lower. "Bravo Silva"! And not your concert singer, mind you, just ordinary church choir.

MEDVEDENKO: And what salary does a church singer get? (*All except* DORN *go out.*)

DORN (*Alone*): I don't know . . . maybe I'm no judge, I

may be going off my head, but I liked that play. There's something in it. When the girl spoke of the vast solitude, and afterward when the Devil's eyes appeared, I could feel my hands trembling. It was all so fresh and naïve. But here he comes. I want to say all the nice things I can to him.

(*Enter* TREPLEFF.)

TREPLEFF: They've all gone.

DORN: I'm here.

TREPLEFF: Masha's been hunting for me all over the park. Unbearable creature!

DORN: Konstantine Gavrilovich, I admired your play extremely. It's a curious kind of thing and I haven't heard the end, but still it made a deep impression on me. You've got great talent. You must keep on! (KON-STANTINE *presses his hand and embraces him impulsively*) Phew, what a nervous fellow! Tears in his eyes! What I wanted to say is you chose your subject from the realm of abstract ideas, and that's right . . . a work of art should express a great idea. There is no beauty without seriousness. My, you are pale!

TREPLEFF: So you think I ought to go on?

DORN: Yes. But write only of what is profound and eternal. You know how I have lived my life, I have lived it with variety and choiceness; and I have enjoyed it; and I am content. But if ever I had felt the elevation of spirit that comes to artists in their creative moments I believe I should have despised this body and all its usages, and tried to soar above all earthly things.

TREPLEFF: Forgive me, where's Nina?

DORN: And another thing. In a work of art there must be a clear, definite idea. You must know what your object is in writing, for if you follow that picturesque road without a definite aim, you will go astray and your talent will be your ruin.

TREPLEFF (*Impatiently*): Where is Nina?

DORN: She's gone home.

TREPLEFF (*In despair*): What shall I do? I want to see her. I must see her. I'm going . . .

(MASHA *enters.*)

DORN: Calm yourself, my friend!

TREPLEFF: But all the same I'm going. I must go.

MASHA: Konstantine Gavrilovich, come indoors. Your mother wants you. She's anxious.

TREPLEFF: Tell her I've gone . . . and please . . . all of you let me alone! Don't follow me around.

DORN: Come, come, come, boy, you mustn't act like this . . . it won't do.

TREPLEFF (*In tears*): Good-by, Doctor . . . and thank you . . . (*Exits.*)

DORN (*Sighing*): Ah, youth, youth . . .

MASHA: When there is nothing else left to say, people always say, "Ah, youth, youth." (*Takes a pinch of snuff.*)

DORN (*Takes snuffbox out of her hand and flings it into the bushes*): It's disgusting. (*A pause*) There in the house they seem to be playing. We'd better go in.

MASHA: No, no, wait a minute.

DORN: What is it?

MASHA: Let me talk to you . . . I don't love my father, I can't talk to him, but I feel with all my heart that you are near me. . . . Help me . . . help me . . . (*Starts to sob*) or I shall do something silly, I'll make my life a mockery, ruin it . . . I can't keep on . . .

DORN: How? Help you how?

MASHA: I'm tortured. No one, no one knows what I'm
suffering . . . (*Laying her head on his breast, softly*)
I love Konstantine.

DORN: How nervous they all are! How nervous they all
are! And so much love! O magic lake! (*Tenderly*)
What can I do for you, child? What, what?

Curtain

ACT TWO

*A croquet lawn. In the background on the right is the
house with a large terrace; on the left is seen the lake, in
which the blazing sun is reflected. Flowerbeds. Noon.
Hot. On one side of the croquet lawn, in the shade of an
old linden tree,* MADAME ARKADINA, DORN *and* MASHA *are
sitting on a garden bench.* DORN *has an open book on his
knees.*

ARKADINA (*To* MASHA): Here, let's stand up. (*They both
stand up*) Side by side. You are twenty-two and I am
nearly twice that. Doctor Dorn, tell us, which one of us
looks the younger?

DORN: You, of course.

ARKADINA: There you are . . . you see? . . . And why is
it? Because I work, I feel, I'm always on the go, but
you sit in the same spot all the time, you're not living. I
make it a rule never to look ahead into the future. I let
myself think neither of old age nor of death. What will
be will be.

MASHA: But I feel as if I were a thousand, I trail my life

along after me like an endless train. . . . Often I have no wish to be living at all. (*Sits down*) Of course that's all nonsense. I ought to shake myself and throw it all off.

DORN (*Sings softly*): Tell her, pretty flowers . . .

ARKADINA: Then I'm correct as an Englishman. I'm always dressed and my hair always *comme il faut*. Would I permit myself to leave the house, even to come out here in the garden, in a dressing gown or with my hair blowzy? Never, I should say not! The reason I have kept my looks is because I've never been a frump, never let myself go, as some do. (*Arms akimbo, she walks up and down the croquet green*) Here I am, light as a bird. Ready to play a girl of fifteen any day.

DORN: Well, at any rate, I'll go on with my reading. (*Takes up the book*) We stopped at the corn merchants and the rats.

ARKADINA: And the rats. Go on. (*Sits*) Let me have it, I'll read. It's my turn anyhow. (*She takes the book and looks for the place*) And the rats . . . here we are . . . (*Reads*) "And certainly, for people of the world to pamper the romantics and make them at home in their houses is as dangerous as for corn merchants to raise rats in their granaries. And yet they are beloved. And so when a woman has picked out the author she wants to entrap, she besieges him with compliments, amenities and favors." Well, among the French that may be, but certainly here with us there's nothing of the kind, we've no set program. Here with us a woman before she ever sets out to capture an author is usually head over heels in love with him herself. To go no further, take me and Trigorin . . .

    (*Enter* SORIN, *leaning on a stick, with* NINA *at his*

side. MEDVEDENKO *follows him, pushing a wheel chair.*)

SORIN (*Caressingly, as if to a child*): Yes? We're all joy, eh? We're happy today after all. (*To his sister*) We're all joy. Father and Stepmother are gone to Tver, and we are free now for three whole days.

NINA (*Sits down beside* ARKADINA *and embraces her*): I am so happy! I belong now to you.

SORIN (*Sitting down in the wheel chair*): She looks lovely today.

ARKADINA: Beautifully dressed, intriguing . . . that's a clever girl. (*She kisses* NINA) We mustn't praise her too much. It's bad luck. Where's Boris Alexeevich?

NINA: He's at the bathhouse fishing.

ARKADINA: You'd think he'd be sick of it. (*She begins reading again.*)

NINA: What is that you have?

ARKADINA: Maupassant's "On the Water," darling. (*Reads a few lines to herself*) Well, the rest is uninteresting and untrue. (*Shutting the book*) I'm troubled in my soul. Tell me, what's the matter with my son? Why is he so sad and morose. He spends day after day on the lake and I hardly ever see him any more.

MASHA: His heart's troubled. (*To* NINA, *timidly*) Please, Nina, read something out of his play, won't you?

NINA (*Shrugging her shoulders*): You really want me to? It's so uninteresting.

MASHA (*With restrained eagerness*): When he recites anything his eyes shine and his face grows pale. He has a beautiful sad voice, and a manner like a poet's.

(*Sound of* SORIN's *snoring.*)

DORN: Pleasant dreams.

ARKADINA (*To* SORIN): Petrusha!

SORIN: Eh?

ARKADINA: Are you asleep?

SORIN: Not at all.

(*A pause.*)

ARKADINA: You are not following any treatment for yourself, that's not right, brother.

SORIN: I'd be glad to follow a treatment, but the doctor
won't give me any.

DORN: Take care of yourself at sixty!

SORIN: Even at sixty a man wants to live.

DORN (*Impatiently*): Bah! Take your valerian drops.

ARKADINA: I'd think it would do him good to take a cure
at some springs.

DORN: Well . . . he might take it. He might not take it.

ARKADINA: Try and understand that!

DORN: Nothing to understand. It's all clear.

(*A pause.*)

MEDVEDENKO: Peter Nikolaevich ought to give up smoking.

SORIN: Fiddlesticks!

DORN: No, it's not fiddlesticks! Wine and tobacco rob
us of our personality. After a cigar or a vodka, you're
not Peter Nikolaevich, you're Peter Nikolaevich plus
somebody else; your ego splits up, and you begin to see
yourself as a third person.

SORIN: Fine (*Laughs*) for you to argue! You've lived
your life, but what about me? I've served the Depart-
ment of Justice twenty-eight years, but I've never lived,
never seen anything, and all the rest of it, so naturally
I want to have my life. You've had your fill and that's
why you turn to philosophy. I want to live, and that's
why I turn to sherry and smoking cigars after dinner,
and so on. And that's that.

DORN: One must look seriously at life, but to go in for cures at sixty and regret the pleasures you missed in your youth, is, if you'll forgive me, frivolous.

MASHA (*Gets up*): It must be time for lunch. (*Walking slow and hobbling*) My foot's gone to sleep. (*Exits.*)

DORN: She'll down a couple of glasses before lunch.

SORIN: The poor thing gets no happiness of her own.

DORN: Fiddlesticks, your Excellency.

SORIN: You argue like a man who's had his fill.

ARKADINA: Oh, what can be duller than this darling country dullness is! Hot, quiet, nobody ever does anything, everybody philosophizes. It's good to be here with you, my friends, delightful listening to you, but . . . sitting in my hotel room, all by myself, studying my part . . . how much better!

NINA (*Ecstatically*): Good! I understand you.

SORIN: Of course, in town's better. You sit in your study, the footman lets nobody in without announcing them, there's the telephone . . . on the street, cabs and so on . . .

DORN (*Singing sotto voce*): Tell her, my flowers . . .
    (*Enter* SHAMREYEFF, *behind him* PAULINE.)

SHAMREYEFF: Here they are. Good morning! (*Kisses* MADAME ARKADINA's *hand, then* NINA's) Very glad to see you looking so well. (*To* MADAME ARKADINA) My wife tells me you are thinking of driving into town with her today. Is that so?

ARKADINA: Yes, we are thinking of it.

SHAMREYEFF: Hm! That's magnificent, but what will you travel on, my most esteemed lady? Today around here we are hauling rye, all the hands are busy. And what horses would you take, may I ask?

ARKADINA: What horses? How should I know . . . what horses!

SORIN: There are carriage horses here!

SHAMREYEFF (*Flaring up*): Carriage horses? But where do I get the harness? Where do I get the harness? It's amazing. It's incomprehensible! Most esteemed lady! Excuse me, I am on my knees before your talent, I'd gladly give ten years of my life for you, but I cannot let you have the horses!

ARKADINA: But what if I have to go? A fine business this is!

SHAMREYEFF: Most esteemed lady! You don't know what a farm means.

ARKADINA (*Flaring up*): The same old story! In that case I'll start for Moscow today. Order me horses from the village, or I'll walk to the station.

SHAMREYEFF (*Flaring up*): In that case I resign my position! Find yourself another steward! (*Exits*)

ARKADINA: Every summer it's like this, every summer here they insult me! I'll never put my foot here again! (*Goes out in the direction of the bath-house. Presently she is seen going into the house.* TRIGORIN *follows, with fishing rods and a pail.*)

SORIN (*Flaring up*): This is insolent! The devil knows what it is! I'm sick of it, and so on. Bring all the horses here this very minute!

NINA (*To* PAULINE): To refuse Irina Nikolaevna, the famous actress! Any little wish of hers, the least whim, is worth more than all your farm. It's simply unbelievable!

PAULINE (*In despair*): What can I do? Put yourself in my shoes, what can I do?

SORIN (*To* NINA): Let's go find my sister. We'll all beg
her not to leave us. Isn't that so? (*Looking in the direction* SHAMREYEFF *went*) You insufferable man!
Tyrant!

NINA (*Prevents his getting up*): Sit still, sit still. We'll
wheel you. (*She and* MEDVEDENKO *push the wheel chair*)
Oh, how awful it is!

SORIN: Yes, yes, it's awful. But he won't leave, I'll speak
to him right off.

(*They go out.* DORN *and* PAULINE *remain.*)

DORN: People are certainly tiresome. Really the thing to
do, of course, is throw that husband of yours out by
the neck; but it will all end by this old woman, Peter
Nikolaevich and his sister's begging him to pardon
them. See if they don't.

PAULINE: He has put the carriage horses in the fields,
too. And these misunderstandings happen every day.
If you only knew how it all upsets me. It's making me
sick; you see how I'm trembling. I can't bear his
coarseness. (*Entreating*) Eugene, my darling, light of
my eyes . . . take me with you. Our time is passing,
we're not young any longer; if . . . if only we could
. . . for the rest of our lives at least . . . stop conceal-
ing things, stop pretending.

(*A pause.*)

DORN: I am fifty-five, it's too late to change now.

PAULINE: I know, you refuse me because there are other
women close to you. It's impossible for you to take
them all with you. I understand. I apologize! Forgive
me, you are tired of me.

(NINA *appears before the house, picking a bunch
of flowers.*)

DORN: No, not all that.

PAULINE: I am miserable with jealousy. Of course you are a doctor. You can't escape women. I understand.

DORN (*To* NINA, *as she joins them*): What's happening?

NINA: Irina Nikolaevna is crying and Peter Nikolaevich having his asthma.

DORN (*Rising*): I must go and give them both some valerian drops.

NINA (*Giving him the flowers*): Won't you?

DORN: *Merci bien.* (*Goes toward the house.*)

PAULINE: What pretty flowers! (*Nearing the house, in a low voice*) Give me those flowers! Give me those flowers!

(*He hands her the flowers, she tears them to pieces and flings them away. They go into the house.*)

NINA (*Alone*): How strange it is seeing a famous actress cry, and about such a little nothing! And isn't it strange that a famous author should sit all day long fishing? The darling of the public, his name in the papers every day, his photograph for sale in shop windows, his book translated into foreign languages, and he's delighted because he's caught two chub. I imagined famous people were proud and distant, and that they despised the crowd, and used their fame and the glamour of their names to revenge themselves on the world for putting birth and money first. But here I see them crying or fishing, playing cards, laughing or losing their tempers, like everybody else.

(TREPLEFF *enters, without a hat, carrying a gun and a dead sea gull.*)

TREPLEFF: Are you here alone?

NINA: Alone. (TREPLEFF *lays the sea gull at her feet.*) What does that mean?

TREPLEFF: I was low enough today to kill this sea gull. I lay it at your feet.

NINA: What's the matter with you? (*Picks up sea gull and looks at it.*)

TREPLEFF (*Pause*): It's the way I'll soon end my own life.

NINA: I don't even recognize you.

TREPLEFF: Yes, ever since I stopped recognizing you. You've changed toward me. Your eyes are cold. You hate to have me near you.

NINA: You are so irritable lately, and you talk . . . it's as if you were talking in symbols. And this sea gull, I suppose that's a symbol, too. Forgive me, but I don't understand it. (*Lays the sea gull on the seat*) I'm too simple to understand you.

TREPLEFF: This began that evening when my play failed so stupidly. Women will never forgive failure. I've burnt it all, every scrap of it. If you only knew what I'm going through! Your growing cold to me is terrible, unbelievable; it's as if I had suddenly waked and found this lake dried up and sunk in the ground. You say you are too simple to understand me. Oh, what is there to understand? My play didn't catch your fancy, you despise my kind of imagination, you already consider me commonplace, insignificant, like so many others. (*Stamping his foot*) How well I understand it all, how I understand it. It's like a spike in my brain, may it be damned along with my pride, which is sucking my blood, sucking it like a snake. (*He sees TRIGORIN, who enters reading a book*) Here comes the real genius, he walks like Hamlet, and with a book too. (*Mimicking*) "Words, words, words." This sun has hardly reached you, and you are already smiling, your glance is melting in his rays. I won't stand in your way. (*He goes out.*)

TRIGORIN (*Making notes in a book*): Takes snuff and drinks vodka, always wears black. The schoolmaster in love with her.

NINA: Good morning, Boris Alexeevich!

TRIGORIN: Good morning. It seems that things have taken a turn we hadn't expected, so we are leaving today. You and I aren't likely to meet again. I'm sorry. I don't often meet young women, young and charming. I've forgotten how one feels at eighteen or nineteen, I can't picture it very clearly, and so the girls I draw in my stories and novels are mostly wrong. I'd like to be in your shoes for just one hour, to see things through your eyes, and find out just what sort of a little person you are.

NINA: And how I'd like to be in your shoes!

TRIGORIN: Why?

NINA: To know how it feels being a famous genius. What's it like being famous? How does it make you feel?

TRIGORIN: How? Nohow, I should think. I'd never thought about it. (*Reflecting*) One of two things: either you exaggerate my fame, or else my fame hasn't made me feel it.

NINA: But if you read about yourself in the papers?

TRIGORIN: When they praise me I'm pleased; when they abuse me, I feel whipped for a day or so.

NINA: It's a marvelous world! If you only knew how I envy you! Look how different different people's lots are! Some have all they can do to drag through their dull, obscure lives; they are all just alike, all miserable;

others . . . well, you for instance . . . have a bright, interesting life that means something. You are happy.

TRIGORIN: I? (*Shrugging his shoulders*) Hm . . . I hear you speak of fame and happiness, of a bright, interesting life, but for me that's all words, pretty words that . . . if you'll forgive my saying so . . . mean about the same to me as candied fruits, which I never eat. You are very young and very kind.

NINA: Your life is beautiful.

TRIGORIN: I don't see anything so very beautiful about it. (*Looks at his watch*) I must get to my writing. Excuse me, I'm busy. . . . (*Laughs*) You've stepped on my pet corn, as they say, and here I am, beginning to get excited and a little cross. At any rate let's talk. Let's talk about my beautiful, bright life. Well, where shall we begin? (*After reflecting a moment*) You know, sometimes violent obsessions take hold of a man, some fixed idea pursues him, the moon for example, day and night he thinks of nothing but the moon. Well, I have just such a moon. Day and night one thought obsesses me: I must be writing, I must be writing, I must be . . . I've scarcely finished one novel when somehow I'm driven on to write another, then a third, and after the third a fourth. I write incessantly, and always at a breakneck speed, and that's the only way I can write. What's beautiful and bright about that, I ask you? Oh, what a wild life! Why now even, I'm here talking to you, I'm excited, but every minute I remember that the story I haven't finished is there waiting for me. I see that cloud up there, it's shaped like a grand piano . . . instantly a mental note . . . I must remember to put that in my story . . . a cloud sailing by . . . grand piano. A whiff of heliotrope. Quickly I make note of it:

cloying smell, widow's color . . . put that in next time I describe a summer evening. Every sentence, every word I say and you say, I lie in wait for it, snap it up for my literary storeroom . . . it might come in handy. . . . As soon as I put my work down, I race off to the theatre or go fishing, hoping to find a rest, but not at all . . . a new idea for a story comes rolling around in my head like a cannon ball, and I'm back at my desk, and writing and writing and writing. And it's always like that, everlastingly. I have no rest from myself, and I feel that I am consuming my own life, that for the honey I'm giving to someone in the void, I rob my best flowers of their pollen, I tear up those flowers and trample on their roots. Do I seem mad? Do my friends seem to talk with me as they would to a sane man? "What are you writing at now? What shall we have next?" Over and over it's like that, till I think all this attention and praise is said only out of kindness to a sick man . . . deceive him, soothe him, and then any minute come stealing up behind and pack him off to the madhouse. And in those years, my young best years, when I was beginning, why then writing made my life a torment. A minor writer, especially when he's not successful, feels clumsy, he's all thumbs, the world has no need for him; his nerves are about to go; he can't resist hanging around people in the arts, where nobody knows him, or takes any notice of him, and he's afraid to look them straight in the eyes, like a man with a passion for gambling who hasn't any money to play with. I'd never seen my readers but for some reason or other I pictured them as hating me and mistrusting me, I had a deathly fear of the public, and when my first play was produced it seemed to me all the dark eyes in the audience were looking at it with hostility and all the light eyes with frigid indifference. Oh how awful that was! What torment it was!

NINA: But surely the inspiration you feel and the creation itself of something must give you a moment of high, sweet happiness, don't they?

TRIGORIN: Yes. When I'm writing I enjoy it and I enjoy reading my proofs, but the minute it comes out I detest it; I see it's not what I meant it to be; I was wrong to write it at all, and I'm vexed and sick at heart about it. (*Laughs*) Then the public reads it. "Yes, charming, clever. . . . Charming but nothing like Tolstoi: A very fine thing, but Turgenev's *Fathers and Sons* is finer." To my dying day that's what it will be, clever and charming, charming and clever . . . nothing more. And when I'm dead they'll be saying at my grave, "Here lies Trigorin, a delightful writer but not so good as Turgenev."

NINA: Excuse me, but I refuse to understand you. You are simply spoiled by success.

TRIGORIN: What success? I have never pleased myself. I don't like myself as a writer. The worst of it is that I am in a sort of daze and often don't understand what I write. . . . I love this water here, the trees, the sky, I feel nature, it stirs in me a passion, an irresistible desire to write. But I am not only a landscape painter, I am a citizen too, I love my country, the people, I feel that if I am a writer I ought to speak also of the people, of their sufferings, of their future, speak of science, of the rights of man, and so forth, and I speak of everything, I hurry up, on all sides they are after me, are annoyed at me, I dash from side to side like a fox the hounds are baiting, I see life and science getting always farther and farther ahead as I fall always more and more behind, like a peasant missing his train, and the upshot is I feel that I can write only landscape, and in all the rest I am false and false to the marrow of my bones.

NINA: You work too hard, and have no time and no wish to feel your own importance. You may be dissatisfied with yourself, of course, but other people think you are great and excellent. If I were such a writer as you are I'd give my whole life to the people, but I should feel that the only happiness for them would be in rising to me; and they should draw my chariot.

TRIGORIN: Well, in a chariot . . . Agamemnon am I, or what? (*They are smiling.*)

NINA: For the happiness of being an author or an actress I would bear any poverty, disillusionment, I'd have people hate me. I'd live in a garret and eat black bread, I'd endure my own dissatisfaction with myself and all my faults, but in return I should ask for fame . . . real resounding fame. (*Covers her face with her hands*) My head's swimming. . . . Ouf!

ARKADINA (*From within the house*): Boris Alexeevich!

TRIGORIN: She's calling me. I dare say, to come and pack. But I don't feel like going away. (*He glances at the lake*) Look, how beautiful it is! Marvelous!

NINA: Do you see over there, that house and garden?

TRIGORIN: Yes.

NINA: It used to belong to my dear mother. I was born there. I've spent all my life by this lake and I know every little island on it.

TRIGORIN: It's all very charming. (*Seeing the sea gull*) What is that?

NINA: A sea gull. Konstantine shot it.

TRIGORIN: It's a lovely bird. Really, I don't want to leave here. Do try and persuade Irina Nikolaevna to stay. (*Makes a note in his book.*)

NINA: What is it you're writing?

TRIGORIN: Only a note. An idea struck me. (*Putting the notebook away*) An idea for a short story: a young girl, one like you, has lived all her life beside a lake; she loves the lake like a sea gull and is happy and free like a sea gull. But by chance a man comes, sees her, and out of nothing better to do, destroys her, like this sea gull here.

(*A pause.* MADAME ARKADINA *appears at the window.*)

ARKADINA: Boris Alexeevich, where are you?

TRIGORIN: Right away! (*Goes toward the house, looking back at* NINA. MADAME ARKADINA *remains at the window*) What is it?

ARKADINA: We're staying.

(TRIGORIN *enters the house.*)

NINA (*Coming forward, standing lost in thought*): It's a dream!

Curtain

ACT THREE

The dining room in SORIN'S *house. On the right and left are doors. A sideboard. A medicine cupboard. In the*

*middle of the room a table. A small trunk and hatboxes,
signs of preparations for leaving.*

TRIGORIN *is at lunch,* MASHA *standing by the table.*

MASHA: I tell you this because you're a writer. You
    might use it. I tell you the truth: if he had died when
    he shot himself I wouldn't live another minute. Just
    the same I'm getting braver; I've just made up my
    mind to tear this love out of my heart by the roots.

TRIGORIN: How will you do it?

MASHA: I'm going to get married. To Medvedenko.

TRIGORIN: Is that the schoolmaster?

MASHA: Yes.

TRIGORIN: I don't see why you must do that.

MASHA: Loving without hope, waiting the whole year
    long for something . . . but when I'm married I
    won't have any time for love, there'll be plenty of new
    things I'll have to do to make me forget the past. Any-
    how it will be a change, you know. Shall we have
    another?

TRIGORIN: Haven't you had about enough?

MASHA: Ah! (*Pours two glasses*) Here! Don't look at
    me like that! Women drink oftener than you imagine.
    Not so many of them drink openly like me. Most of
    them hide it. Yes. And it's always vodka or cognac.
    (*Clinks glasses*) Your health. You're a decent sort,
    I'm sorry to be parting from you.
        (*They drink.*)

TRIGORIN: I don't want to leave here myself.

MASHA: You should beg her to stay.

TRIGORIN: She'd never do that now. Her son is behaving himself very tactlessly. First he tries shooting himself and now, they say, he's going to challenge me to a duel. But what for? He sulks, he snorts, he preaches new art forms . . . but there's room for all, the new and the old . . . why elbow?

MASHA: Well, and there's jealousy. However, that's not my business.

> (*Pause.* YAKOV *crosses right to left with a piece of luggage.* NINA *enters, stops near window.*)

MASHA: That schoolmaster of mine is none too clever, but he's a good man and he's poor, and he loves me dearly. I'm sorry for him, and I'm sorry for his old mother. Well, let me wish you every happiness. Think kindly of me. (*Warmly shakes his hand*) Let me thank you for your friendly interest. Send me your books, be sure to write in them. Only don't put "esteemed lady," but simply this: "To Maria, who not remembering her origin, does not know why she is living in this world." Good-by. (*Goes out.*)

NINA (*Holding out her hand closed to* TRIGORIN): Even or odd?

TRIGORIN: Even.

NINA (*Sighing*): No. I had only one pea in my hand. I was trying my fortune: To be an actress or not. I wish somebody would advise me.

TRIGORIN: There's no advice in this sort of thing.

> (*A pause.*)

NINA: We are going to part . . . I may never see you again. Won't you take this little medal to remember me? I've had it engraved with your initials and on the other side the title of your book: *Days and Nights.*

TRIGORIN: What a graceful thing to do! (*Kisses the medal*) It's a charming present.

NINA: Sometimes think of me.

TRIGORIN: I'll think of you. I'll think of you as I saw you that sunny day . . . do you remember . . . a week ago when you had on your white dress . . . we were talking . . . a white sea gull was lying on the bench beside us.

NINA (*Pensive*): Yes, the sea gull. (*A pause*) Someone's coming . . . let me see you two minutes before you go, won't you? (*Goes out on the left as* MADAME ARKADINA *and* SORIN, *in full dress, with a decoration, enter, then* YAKOV, *busy with the packing.*)

ARKADINA: Stay at home, old man. How could you be running about with your rheumatism? (*To* TRIGORIN) Who was it just went out? Nina?

TRIGORIN: Yes.

ARKADINA: *Pardon!* We intruded. (*Sits down*) I believe everything's packed. I'm exhausted.

TRIGORIN: *Days and Nights,* page 121, lines eleven and twelve.

YAKOV (*Clearing the table*): Shall I pack your fishing rods as well?

TRIGORIN: Yes, I'll want them again. But the books you can give away.

YAKOV: Yes, sir.

TRIGORIN (*To himself*): Page 121, lines eleven and twelve. What's in those lines? (*To* ARKADINA) Have you my works here in the house?

ARKADINA: Yes, in my brother's study, the corner book-case.

TRIGORIN: Page 121. (*Exits.*)

ARKADINA: Really, Petrusha, you'd better stay at home.

SORIN: You're going away. It's dreary for me here at home without you.

ARKADINA: But what's there in town?

SORIN: Nothing in particular, but all the same. (*Laughs*) There's the laying of the foundation stone for the town hall, and all that sort of thing. A man longs, if only for an hour or so, to get out of this gudgeon existence, and it's much too long I've been lying around like an old cigarette holder. I've ordered the horses at one o'clock, we'll set off at the same time.

ARKADINA (*After a pause*): Oh, stay here, don't be lonesome, don't take cold. Look after my son. Take care of him. Advise him. (*A pause*) Here I am leaving and so shall never know why Konstantine tried to kill himself. I have a notion the main reason was jealousy, and the sooner I take Trigorin away from here the better.

SORIN: How should I explain it to you? There were other reasons besides jealousy. Here we have a man who is young, intelligent, living in the country in solitude, without money, without position, without a future. He has nothing to do. He is ashamed and afraid of his idleness. I love him very much and he's attached to me, but he feels just the same that he's superfluous in this house, and a sort of dependent here, a poor relation. That's something we can understand, it's pride of course.

ARKADINA: I'm worried about him. (*Reflecting*) He might go into the service, perhaps.

SORIN (*Whistling, then hesitatingly*): It seems to me the best thing you could do would be to let him have a little money. In the first place he ought to be able to dress himself like other people, and so on. Look how he's worn that same old jacket these past three years; he runs around without an overcoat. (*Laughs*)

Yes, and it wouldn't harm him to have a little fun . . . he might go abroad, perhaps . . . it wouldn't cost much.

ARKADINA: Perhaps I could manage a suit, but as for going abroad . . . no. Just at this moment I can't even manage the suit. (*Firmly*) I haven't any money! (SORIN *laughs*) I haven't. No.

SORIN (*Whistling*): Very well. Forgive me, my dear, don't be angry. You're a generous, noble woman.

ARKADINA (*Weeping*): I haven't any money.

SORIN: Of course if I had any money, I'd give him some myself, but I haven't anything, not a kopeck. (*Laughs*) My manager takes all my pension and spends it on agriculture, cattle-raising, bee-keeping, and my money goes for nothing. The bees die, the cows die, horses they never let me have.

ARKADINA: Yes, I have some money, but I'm an actress, my costumes alone are enough to ruin me.

SORIN: You are very good, my dear. I respect you. Yes. . . . But there again something's coming over me. . . . (*Staggers*) My head's swimming. (*Leans on table*) I feel faint, and so on.

ARKADINA (*Alarmed*): Petrusha! (*Trying to support him*) Petrusha, my darling! (*Calls*) Help me! Help! (*Enter* TREPLEFF, *his head bandaged, and* MEDVEDENKO.)

ARKADINA: He feels faint.

SORIN: It's nothing, it's nothing. . . . (*Smiles and drinks water*) It's gone already . . . and so on.

TREPLEFF (*To his mother*): Don't be alarmed, Mother, it's not serious. It often happens now to my uncle. Uncle, you must lie down a little.

SORIN: A little, yes. All the same I'm going to town

. . . I'm lying down a little and I'm going to town
. . . that's clear. (*He goes, leaning on his stick.*)

MEDVEDENKO (*Gives him his arm*): There's a riddle: in
the morning it's on four legs, at noon on two, in the
evening on three.

SORIN (*Laughs*): That's it. And on the back at night.
Thank you, I can manage alone.

MEDVEDENKO: My, what ceremony! (*He and* SORIN *go
out.*)

ARKADINA: How he frightened me!

TREPLEFF: It's not good for him to live in the country.
He's low in his mind. Now, Mother, if you'd only
have a burst of sudden generosity and lend him a
thousand or fifteen hundred, he could spend a whole
year in town.

ARKADINA: I haven't any money. I'm an actress, not a
banker.

(*A pause.*)

TREPLEFF: Mother, change my bandage. You do it so
well.

ARKADINA (*Takes bottle of iodoform and a box of band-
ages from cupboard*): And the doctor's late.

TREPLEFF: He promised to be here at ten, but it's already noon.

ARKADINA: Sit down. (*Takes off bandage*) You look as
if you were in a turban. Some man who came by the
kitchen yesterday asked what nationality you were.
But it's almost entirely healed. What's left is nothing.
(*Kisses him on the head*) While I'm away, you won't
do any more click-click?

TREPLEFF: No, Mother. That was a moment when I was
out of my head with despair, and couldn't control
myself. It won't happen again. (*Kisses her fingers*)

You have clever fingers. I remember long, long ago when you were still playing at the Imperial Theatre . . . there was a fight one day in our court, and a washerwoman who was one of the tenants got beaten almost to death. Do you remember? She was picked up unconscious . . . you nursed her, took medicines to her, bathed her children in the washtub. Don't you remember?

ARKADINA: No. (*Puts on fresh bandage.*)

TREPLEFF: Two ballet dancers were living then in the same house we did, they used to come and drink coffee with you.

ARKADINA: That I remember.

TREPLEFF: They were very pious. (*A pause*) Lately, these last days, I have loved you as tenderly and fully as when I was a child. Except for you, there's nobody left me now. Only why, why do you subject yourself to the influence of that man?

ARKADINA: You don't understand him, Konstantine. He's a very noble character.

TREPLEFF: Nevertheless, when he was told I was going to challenge him to a duel this nobility didn't keep him from playing the coward. He's leaving. Ignominious retreat!

ARKADINA: Such tosh! I myself beg him to leave here.

TREPLEFF: Noble character! Here we both are nearly quarreling over him, and right now very likely he's in the drawing room or in the garden laughing at us . . . developing Nina, trying once and for all to convince her he's a genius.

ARKADINA: For you it's a pleasure . . . saying disagreeable things to me. I respect that man and must ask you not to speak ill of him in my presence.

TREPLEFF: And I don't respect him. You want me too to think he's a genius, but, forgive me, I can't tell lies . . . his creations make me sick.

ARKADINA: That's envy. People who are not talented but pretend to be have nothing better to do than to disparage real talents. It must be a fine consolation!

TREPLEFF (*Sarcastically*): Real talents! (*Angrily*) I'm more talented than both of you put together, if it comes to that! (*Tears off the bandage*) You two, with your stale routine, have grabbed first place in art and think that only what you do is real or legitimate; the rest you'd like to stifle and keep down. I don't believe in you two. I don't believe in you or in him.

ARKADINA: Decadent!

TREPLEFF: Go back to your darling theatre and act there in trashy, stupid plays!

ARKADINA: Never did I act in such plays. Leave me alone! You are not fit to write even wretched vaudeville. Kiev burgher! Sponge!

TREPLEFF: Miser!

ARKADINA: Beggar! (*He sits down, cries softly*) Nonentity! (*Walks up and down*) Don't cry! You mustn't cry! (*Weeps. Kisses him on his forehead, his cheeks, his head*) My dear child, forgive me! Forgive me, your wicked mother! Forgive miserable me!

TREPLEFF (*Embracing her*): If you only knew! I've lost everything. She doesn't love me, now I can't write. All my hopes are gone.

ARKADINA: Don't despair. It will all pass. He's leaving right away. She'll love you again. (*Dries his tears*) That's enough. We've made it up now.

TREPLEFF (*Kissing her hands*): Yes, Mother.

ARKADINA (*Tenderly*): Make it up with him, too. You don't want a duel. You don't, do you?

TREPLEFF: Very well, only, Mother, don't let me see him. It's painful to me. It's beyond me. (TRIGORIN *comes in*) There he is. I'm going. (*Quickly puts dressings away in cupboard*) The doctor will do my bandage later.

TRIGORIN (*Looking through a book*): Page 121 . . . lines eleven and twelve. Here it is. (*Reads*) "If you ever, ever need my life, come and take it."

(TREPLEFF *picks up the bandage from the floor and goes out.*)

ARKADINA (*Looking at her watch*): The horses will be here soon.

TRIGORIN (*To himself*): If you ever, ever need my life, come and take it.

ARKADINA: I hope you are all packed.

TRIGORIN (*Impatiently*): Yes, yes. . . . (*In deep thought*) Why is it I seem to feel sadness in that call from a pure soul, and my heart aches so with pity? If you ever, ever need my life, come and take it. (*To* MADAME ARKADINA) Let's stay just one more day. (*She shakes her head.*)

TRIGORIN: Let's stay!

ARKADINA: Darling, I know what keeps you here. But have some self control. You're a little drunk, be sober.

TRIGORIN: You be sober, too, be understanding, reasonable, I beg you; look at all this like a true friend. . . . (*Presses her hand*) You are capable of sacrificing. Be my friend, let me be free.

ARKADINA (*Excited*): Are you so infatuated?

TRIGORIN: I am drawn to her! Perhaps this is just what I need.

ARKADINA: The love of some provincial girl? Oh, how little you know yourself!

TRIGORIN: Sometimes people talk but are asleep. That's how it is now . . . I'm talking to you but in my dream see her. I'm possessed by sweet, marvelous dreams. Let me go . . .

ARKADINA (*Trembling*): No, no, I'm an ordinary woman like any other woman, you shouldn't talk to me like this. Don't torture me, Boris. It frightens me.

TRIGORIN: If you wanted to, you could be far from ordinary. There is a kind of love that's young, and beautiful, and is all poetry, and carries us away into a world of dreams; on earth it alone can ever give us happiness. Such a love I still have never known. In my youth there wasn't time, I was always around some editor's office, fighting off starvation. Now it's here, that love, it's come, it beckons me. What sense, then, is there in running away from it?

ARKADINA (*Angry*): You've gone mad.

TRIGORIN: Well, let me!

ARKADINA: You've all conspired today just to torment me. (*Weeps.*)

TRIGORIN (*Clutching at his breast*): She doesn't understand. She doesn't want to understand.

ARKADINA: Am I so old or ugly that you don't mind talking to me about other women? (*Embracing and kissing him*) Oh, you madman! My beautiful, my marvel . . . you are the last chapter of my life. (*Falls on knees*) My joy, my pride, my blessedness! (*Embracing his knees*) If you forsake me for one hour even, I'll never survive it, I'll go out of my mind, my wonderful, magnificent one, my master.

TRIGORIN: Somebody might come in. (*Helps her to rise.*)

ARKADINA: Let them, I am not ashamed of my love for you. (*Kisses his hands*) My treasure! You reckless boy, you want to be mad, but I won't have it, I won't let you. (*Laughs*) You are mine . . . you are mine. This brow is mine, and the eyes mine, and this beautiful silky hair, too, is mine. You are all mine. You are so talented, so intelligent, the best of all modern writers; you are the one and only hope of Russia . . . you have such sincerity, simplicity, healthy humor. In one stroke you go to the very heart of a character or a scene; your people are like life itself. Oh, it's impossible to read you without rapture! Do you think this is only incense? I'm flattering you? Come, look me in the eyes. . . . Do I look like a liar? There you see, only I can appreciate you; only I tell you the truth, my lovely darling . . . You are coming? Yes? You won't leave me?

TRIGORIN: I have no will of my own . . . I've never had a will of my own. Flabby, weak, always submitting! Is it possible that might please women? Take me, carry me away, only never let me be one step away from you.

ARKADINA (*To herself*): Now he's mine. (*Casually, as if nothing had happened*) However, if you like you may stay. I'll go by myself, and you come later, in a week. After all, where would you hurry to?

TRIGORIN: No, let's go together.

ARKADINA: As you like. Together, together then. (*A pause.* TRIGORIN *writes in notebook*) What are you writing?

TRIGORIN: This morning I heard a happy expression:

"Virgin forest." It might be useful in a story. (*Yawns*)
So, we're off. Once more the cars, stations, station
buffets, stews and conversations!

(SHAMREYEFF *enters.*)

SHAMREYEFF: I have the honor with deep regret to an-
nounce that the horses are ready. It's time, most esteemed lady, to be off to the station; the train arrives
at five minutes after two. So will you do me the favor, Irina Nikolaevna, not to forget to inquire about
this: Where's the actor Suzdaltsev now? Is he alive?
Is he well? We used to drink together once upon a
time. In *The Stolen Mail* he was inimitable. In the
same company with him at Elisavetgrad, I remember,
was the tragedian Izmailov, also a remarkable personality. Don't hurry, most esteemed lady, there are
five minutes still. Once in some melodrama they were
playing conspirators, and when they were suddenly
discovered, he had to say "We are caught in a trap,"
but Izmailov said, "We are traught in a clap."
(*Laughs*) Clap!

(YAKOV *is busy with luggage.* MAID *brings* ARKA-
DINA'S *hat, coat, parasol, gloves. All help her put
them on. The* COOK *peers through door on left, as
if hesitating, then he comes in. Enter* PAULINE,
SORIN *and* MEDVEDENKO.)

PAULINE (*With basket*): Here are some plums for the
journey. They are sweet ones. In case you'd like some
little thing.

ARKADINA: You are very kind, Pauline Andreevna.

PAULINE: Good-by, my dear: If anything has been not
quite so, forgive it. (*Cries.*)

ARKADINA (*Embracing her*): Everything has been charming, everything's been charming. Only you mustn't cry.

PAULINE: Time goes so.

ARKADINA: There's nothing we can do about that.

SORIN (*In a greatcoat with a cape, his hat on and his stick in his hand, crossing the stage*): Sister, you'd better start if you don't want to be late. I'll go get in the carriage. (*Exits.*)

MEDVEDENKO: And I'll walk to the station . . . to see you off. I'll step lively.

ARKADINA: Good-by, my friends. If we are alive and well next summer we'll meet again. (*The* MAID, COOK *and* YAKOV *kiss her hand*) Don't forget me. (*Gives* COOK *a rouble*) Here's a rouble for the three of you.

COOK: We humbly thank you, Madame. Pleasant journey to you. Many thanks to you.

YAKOV: God bless you!

SHAMREYEFF: Make us happy with a letter. Good-by, Boris Alexeevich.

ARKADINA: Where's Konstantine? Tell him I'm off now. I must say good-by to him. Well, remember me kindly. (*To* YAKOV) I gave the cook a rouble. It's for the three of you.

> (*All go out. The stage is empty. Offstage are heard the usual sounds when people are going away. The* MAID *comes back for the basket of plums from the table and goes out again.*)

TRIGORIN (*Returning*): I forgot my stick. It's out there on the terrace, I think. (*As he starts to go out by the door on the left, he meets* NINA *coming in*) Is it you? We are just going . . .

NINA: I felt we should meet again. (*Excited*) Boris

Alexeevich, I've come to a decision, the die is cast. I am going on the stage. Tomorrow I shall not be here. I am leaving my father, deserting everything, beginning a new life. I'm off like you . . . for Moscow . . . we shall meet there.

TRIGORIN (*Glancing around him*): Stay at Hotel Slavyansky Bazaar. Let me know at once. Molchanovka, Groholsky House. I must hurry.

(*A pause.*)

NINA: One minute yet.

TRIGORIN (*In a low voice*): You are so beautiful. . . . Oh, how happy to think we'll be meeting soon. (*She puts her head on his breast*) I shall see those lovely eyes again, that ineffably beautiful, tender smile . . . those gentle features, their pure, angelic expression . . . my darling . . .

(*A long kiss.*)

Curtain

(*Two years pass between the Third and Fourth Acts.*)

ACT FOUR

One of the drawing rooms in SORIN'S *house, turned by* KONSTANTINE TREPLEFF *into a study. On the right and left, doors leading into other parts of the house. Facing us, glass doors on to the terrace. Besides the usual furniture of a drawing room, there is a writing table in the corner to the right; near the door on the left, a sofa, a bookcase full of books, and books in the windows and on the chairs.*

*Evening. A single lamp with a shade is lighted. Semi-
darkness. The sound from outside of trees rustling and
the wind howling in the chimney. The night watchman
is knocking.* MEDVEDENKO *and* MASHA *come in.*

MASHA: Konstantine Gavrilovich! Konstantine Gavrilovich! (*Looking around*) Nobody here. Every other
minute all day long the old man keeps asking where's
Kostya, where's Kostya? He can't live without him.

MEDVEDENKO: He's afraid to be alone. (*Listening*) What
terrible weather! It's two days now.

MASHA (*Turning up the lamp*): Out on the lake there
are waves. Tremendous.

MEDVEDENKO: The garden's black. We ought to have
told them to pull down that stage. It stands all bare
and hideous, like a skeleton, and the curtain flaps in
the wind. When I passed there last night it seemed to
me that in the wind I heard someone crying.

MASHA: Well, here . . . (*Pause.*)

MEDVEDENKO: Masha, let's go home.

MASHA (*Shakes her head*): I'm going to stay here tonight.

MEDVEDENKO (*Imploring*): Masha, let's go. Our baby
must be hungry.

MASHA: Nonsense. Matriona will feed it.

(*A pause.*)

MEDVEDENKO: It's hard on him. He's been three nights
now without his mother.

MASHA: You're getting just too tiresome. In the old
days you'd at least philosophize a little, but now it's
all baby, home, baby, home . . . and that's all I can
get out of you.

MEDVEDENKO: Let's go, Masha.

MASHA: Go yourself.

MEDVEDENKO: Your father won't let me have a horse.

MASHA: He will if you just ask him.

MEDVEDENKO: Very well, I'll try. Then you'll come to-morrow.

MASHA (*Taking snuff*): Well, tomorrow. Stop bothering me.

(*Enter* TREPLEFF *and* PAULINE; TREPLEFF *carries pillows and a blanket,* PAULINE *sheets and pillowcases. They lay them on the sofa, then* TREPLEFF *goes and sits down at his desk.*)

MASHA: Why's that, Mama?

PAULINE: Peter Nikolaevich asked to sleep in Kostya's room.

MASHA: Let me . . . (*She makes the bed.*)

PAULINE (*Sighing*): Old people, what children. . . . (*Goes to the desk. Leaning on her elbows she gazes at the manuscript. A pause.*)

MEDVEDENKO: So I'm going. Good-by, Masha. (*Kisses her hand*) Good-by, Mother. (*Tries to kiss her hand.*)

PAULINE (*With annoyance*): Well, go if you're going.

MEDVEDENKO: Good-by, Konstantine Gavrilovich.

(TREPLEFF, *without speaking, gives him his hand.* MEDVEDENKO *goes out.*)

PAULINE (*Gazing at the manuscript*): Nobody ever thought or dreamed that some day, Kostya, you'd turn out to be a real author. But now, thank God, the magazines send you money for your stories. (*Passing her hand over his hair*) And you've grown handsome . . . dear, good Kostya, be kind to my little Masha.

MASHA (*Making the bed*): Let him alone, Mama.

PAULINE: She's a sweet little thing. (*A pause*) A woman,

Kostya, doesn't ask much . . . only kind looks. As I well know.

(TREPLEFF *rises from the desk and without speaking goes out.*)

MASHA: You shouldn't have bothered him.

PAULINE: I feel sorry for you, Masha.

MASHA: Why should you?

PAULINE: My heart aches and aches for you. I see it all,

MASHA: It's all foolishness! Hopeless love . . . that's only in novels. No matter. Only you mustn't let yourself go, and be always waiting for something, waiting for fine weather by the sea. If love stirs in your heart, stamp it out. Now they've promised to transfer my husband to another district. As soon as we get there . . . I'll forget it all . . . I'll tear it out of my heart by the roots.

(*Two rooms off is heard a melancholy waltz.*)

PAULINE: Kostya is playing. That means he's feeling sad.

MASHA (*Waltzes silently a few turns*): The great thing, Mama, is to be where I don't see him. If only my Semyon could get his transfer, I promise you I'd forget in a month. It's all nonsense.

(*Door on left opens.* DORN *and* MEDVEDENKO *come in, wheeling* SORIN *in his chair.*)

MEDVEDENKO: I have six souls at home now. And flour at seventy kopecks.

DORN: So it just goes round and round.

MEDVEDENKO: It's easy for you to smile. You've got more money than the chickens could pick up.

DORN: Money! After practicing medicine thirty years, my friend, so driven day and night that I could never call my soul my own, I managed to save up at last two thousand roubles; and I've just spent all that on a trip abroad. I've got nothing at all.

MASHA (*To her husband*): Aren't you gone yet?

MEDVEDENKO (*Apologizing*): How can I, when they won't let me have a horse?

MASHA (*Under her breath angrily*): I wish I'd never lay eyes on you again.

> (SORIN'S *wheel chair remains left center.* PAULINE, MASHA *and* DORN *sit down beside him.* MEDVEDENKO *stands to one side gloomily.*)

DORN: Look how many changes they have made here! The drawing room is turned into a study.

MASHA: Konstantine Gavrilovich likes to work in here. He can go into the garden whenever he likes and think.

> (*A watchman's rattle sounds.*)

SORIN: Where's my sister?

DORN: She went to the station to meet Trigorin. She'll be right back.

SORIN: If you thought you had to send for my sister, that shows I'm very ill. (*Reflecting*) Now that's odd, isn't it? I'm very ill, but they won't let me have any medicine around here.

DORN: And what would you like? Valerian drops? Soda? Quinine?

SORIN: So it's more philosophy, I suppose. Oh, what an affliction! (*He motions with his head toward the sofa*) Is that for me?

PAULINE: Yes, for you, Peter Nikolaevich.

SORIN: Thank you.

DORN (*Singing sotto voce*): The moon drifts in the sky tonight.

SORIN: Listen, I want to give Kostya a subject for a

story. It should be called: "The Man Who Wanted To". . . . *L'homme qui a voulu.* In my youth long ago wanted to become an author . . . and never became one; wanted to speak eloquently . . . and spoke execrably (*Mimicking himself*) and so on and so forth, and all the rest of it, yes and no, and in the résumé would drag on, drag on, till the sweat broke out; wanted to marry . . . and never married; wanted always to live in town . . . and now am ending up my life in the country, and so on.

DORN: Wanted to become a State Counselor . . . and became one.

SORIN (*Laughing*): For that I never longed. That came to me of itself.

DORN: Come now, to be picking faults with life at sixty-two, you must confess, that's not magnanimous.

SORIN: How bullheaded you are! Can't you take it in? I want to live.

DORN: That's frivolous, it's the law of nature that every life must come to an end.

SORIN: You argue like a man who's had his fill. You've had your fill and so you're indifferent to living, it's all one to you. But at that even you will be afraid to die.

DORN: The fear of death . . . a brute fear. We must overcome it. The fear of death is reasonable only in those who believe in an eternal life, and shudder to think of the sins they have committed. But you in the first place don't believe, in the second place what sins have you? For twenty-five years you served as State Counselor . . . and that's all.

SORIN (*Laughing*): Twenty-eight.

(TREPLEFF *enters and sits on the stool beside* SORIN.
MASHA *never takes her eyes off his face.*)

DORN: We are keeping Konstantine Gavrilovich from
his work.

TREPLEFF: No, it's nothing.

(*A pause.*)

MEDVEDENKO: Permit me to ask you, Doctor, what town
in your travels did you most prefer?

DORN: Genoa.

TREPLEFF: Why Genoa?

DORN: Because of the marvelous street crowd. When
you go out of your hotel in the evening you find the
whole street surging with people. You let yourself
drift among the crowd, zigzagging back and forth,
you live its life, its soul pours into you, until finally
you begin to believe there might really be a world
spirit after all, like that Nina Zaryechny acted in your
play. By the way, where is Nina just now? Where is
she and how is she?

TREPLEFF: Very well, I imagine.

DORN: I've been told she was leading rather an odd
sort of life. How's that?

TREPLEFF: It's a long story, Doctor.

DORN: You can shorten it.

(*A pause.*)

TREPLEFF: She ran away from home and joined
Trigorin. That you knew?

DORN: I know.

TREPLEFF: She had a child. The child died. Trigorin
got tired of her, and went back to his old ties, as
might be expected. He'd never broken these old ties
anyhow, but flitted in that backboneless style of his
from one to the other. As far as I could say from what

I know, Nina's private life didn't quite work out.

DORN: And on the stage?

TREPLEFF: I believe even worse. She made her debut in Moscow at a summer theatre, and afterward a tour in the provinces. At that time I never let her out of my sight, and wherever she was I was. She always attempted big parts, but her acting was crude, without any taste, her gestures were clumsy. There were moments when she did some talented screaming, talented dying, but those were only moments.

DORN: It means, though, she has talent?

TREPLEFF: I could never make out. I imagine she has. I saw her, but she didn't want to see me, and her maid wouldn't let me in her rooms. I understood how she felt, and never insisted on seeing her. (*A pause*) What more is there to tell you? Afterward, when I'd come back home here, she wrote me some letters. They were clever, tender, interesting; she didn't complain, but I could see she was profoundly unhappy; there was not a word that didn't show her exhausted nerves. And she'd taken a strange fancy. She always signed herself the sea gull. In *The Mermaid* the miller says that he's a crow; the same way in all her letters she kept repeating she was a sea gull. Now she's here.

DORN: How do you mean, here?

TREPLEFF: In town, staying at the inn. She's already been here five days, living there in rooms. Masha drove in, but she never sees anybody. Semyon Semyonovich declares that last night after dinner he saw her in the fields, a mile and a half from here.

MEDVEDENKO: Yes, I saw her. (*A pause*) Going in the opposite direction from here, toward town. I bowed to her, asked why she had not been out to see us. She said she'd come.

TREPLEFF: Well, she won't. (*A pause*) Her father and stepmother don't want to know her. They've set watchmen to keep her off the grounds. (*Goes toward the desk with* DORN) How easy it is, Doctor, to be a philosopher on paper, and how hard it is in life!

SORIN: She was a beautiful girl.

DORN: How's that?

SORIN: I say she was a beautiful girl. State Counselor Sorin was downright in love with her himself once for a while.

DORN: You old Lovelace!

(*They hear* SHAMREYEFF's *laugh.*)

PAULINE: I imagine they're back from the station.

TREPLEFF: Yes, I hear Mother.

(*Enter* MADAME ARKADINA *and* TRIGORIN, SHAMREYEFF *following.*)

SHAMREYEFF: We all get old and fade with the elements, esteemed lady, but you, most honored lady, are still young . . . white dress, vivacity . . . grace.

ARKADINA: You still want to bring me bad luck, you tiresome creature!

TRIGORIN (*To* SORIN): Howdy do, Peter Nikolaevich. How is it you are still indisposed? That's not so good. (*Pleased at seeing* MASHA) Masha Ilyinishna!

MASHA: You know me? (*Grasps his hand.*)

TRIGORIN: Married?

MASHA: Long ago.

TRIGORIN: Are you happy? (*Bows to* DORIN *and* MEDVEDENKO, *then hesitatingly goes to* TREPLEFF) Irina Nikolaevna tells me you have forgotten the past and given up being angry.

(TREPLEFF *holds out his hand.*)

ARKADINA (*To her son*): Look, Boris Alexeevich has brought you the magazine with your last story.

TREPLEFF (*Taking the magazine. To* TRIGORIN): Thank you. You're very kind.

(*They sit down.*)

TRIGORIN: Your admirers send their respects to you. In Petersburg and in Moscow, everywhere, there's a great deal of interest in your work, and they all ask me about you. They ask: what is he like, what age is he, is he dark or fair? For some reason they all think you are no longer young. And nobody knows your real name, since you always publish under a pseudonym. You're a mystery, like the Man in the Iron Mask.

TREPLEFF: Will you be with us long?

TRIGORIN: No, tomorrow I think I'll go to Moscow. I must. I'm in a hurry to finish a story, and besides I've promised to write something for an annual. In a word it's the same old thing.

(MADAME ARKADINA *and* PAULINE *have set up a card table.* SHAMREYEFF *lights candles, arranges chairs, gets box of lotto from a cupboard.*)

TRIGORIN: The weather's given me a poor welcome. The wind is ferocious. Tomorrow morning if it dies down I'm going out to the lake to fish. And I want to look around the garden and the place where . . . do you remember? . . . your play was done. The idea for a story is all worked out in my mind, I want only to refresh my memory of the place where it's laid.

MASHA: Papa, let my husband have a horse! He must get home.

SHAMREYEFF (*Mimics*): A horse . . . home. (*Sternly*) See for yourself: they are just back from the station.

They'll not go out again.

MASHA: They're not the only horses. . . . (*Seeing that he says nothing, she makes an impatient gesture*) Nobody can do anything with you . . .

MEDVEDENKO: I can walk, Masha. Truly . . .

PAULINE (*Sighs*): Walk, in such weather! (*Sits down at card table*) Sit down, friends.

MEDVEDENKO: It's only four miles. . . . Good-by. (*Kisses wife's hand*) Good-by, Mama. (*His mother-in-law put out her hand reluctantly*) I should not have troubled anybody, but the little baby. . . . (*Bowing to them*) Good-by. (*He goes out as if apologizing.*)

SHAMREYEFF: He'll make it. He's not a general.

PAULINE (*Taps on table*): Sit down, friends. Let's not lose time, they'll be calling us to supper soon.

(SHAMREYEFF, MASHA *and* DORN *sit at the card table.*)

ARKADINA (*To* TRIGORIN): When these long autumn evenings draw on we pass the time out here with lotto. And look: the old lotto set we had when my mother used to play with us children. Don't you want to take a hand with us till suppertime? (*She and* TRIGORIN *sit down at the table*) It's a tiresome game, but it does well enough when you're used to it. (*She deals three cards to each one.*)

TREPLEFF (*Turns magazine pages*): He's read his own story, but mine he hasn't even cut. (*He lays the magazine on the desk; on his way out, as he passes his mother, he kisses her on the head.*)

ARKADINA: But you, Kostya?

TREPLEFF: Sorry, I don't care to. I'm going for a walk. (*Goes out.*)

ARKADINA: Stake . . . ten kopecks. Put it down for me, Doctor.

DORN: Command me.

MASHA: Has everybody bet? I'll begin. Twenty-two.

ARKADINA: I have it.

MASHA: Three.

DORN: Here you are.

MASHA: Did you put down three? Eight! Eighty-one! Ten!

SHAMREYEFF: Not so fast.

ARKADINA: What a reception they gave me at Kharkoff! Can you believe it, my head's spinning yet.

MASHA: Thirty-four.

(*A sad waltz is heard.*)

ARKADINA: The students gave me an ovation, three baskets of flowers, two wreaths and look . . . (*She takes off a brooch and puts it on the table.*)

SHAMREYEFF: Yes, that's the real . . .

MASHA: Fifty!

DORN: Fifty, you say?

ARKADINA: I had a superb costume. Say what you like, but really when it comes to dressing myself I am no fool.

PAULINE: Kostya is playing. The poor boy's sad.

SHAMREYEFF: In the papers they often abuse him.

MASHA: Seventy-seven.

ARKADINA: Who cares what they say?

TRIGORIN: He hasn't any luck. He still can't discover how to write a style of his own. There is something strange, vague, at times even like delirious raving. Not a single character that is alive.

MASHA: Eleven!

ARKADINA (*Glancing at* SORIN) Petrusha, are you bored? (*A pause*) He's asleep.

DORN: He's asleep, the State Counselor.

MASHA: Seven! Ninety!

TRIGORIN: Do you think if I lived in such a place as this and by this lake, I would write? I should overcome such a passion and devote my life to fishing.

MASHA: Twenty-eight!

TRIGORIN: To catch a perch or a bass . . . that's something like happiness!

DORN: Well, I believe in Konstantine Gavrilovich. He has something! He has something! He thinks in images, his stories are bright and full of color, I always feel them strongly. It's only a pity that he's got no definite purpose. He creates impressions, never more than that, but on mere impressions you don't go far. Irina Nikolaevna, are you glad your son is a writer?

ARKADINA: Imagine, I have not read him yet. There's never time.

MASHA: Twenty-six!

(TREPLEFF *enters without saying anything, sits at his desk.*)

SHAMREYEFF: And, Boris Alexeevich, we've still got something of yours here.

TRIGORIN: What's that?

SHAMREYEFF: Somehow or other Konstantine Gavrilovich shot a sea gull, and you asked me to have it stuffed for you.

TRIGORIN: I don't remember. (*Reflecting*) I don't remember.

MASHA: Sixty-six! One!

TREPLEFF (*Throwing open the window, stands listen-*

ing): How dark! I don't know why I feel so uneasy.

ARKADINA: Kostya, shut the window, there's a draught.
(TREPLEFF *shuts window*.)

MASHA: Ninety-eight.

TRIGORIN: I've made a game.

ARKADINA (*Gaily*): Bravo! Bravo!

SHAMREYEFF: Bravo!

ARKADINA: This man's lucky in everything, always.
(*Rises*) And now let's go have a bite of something.
Our celebrated author didn't have any dinner today.
After supper we'll go on. Kostya, leave your manu-
script, come have something to eat.

TREPLEFF: I don't want to, Mother, I've had enough.

ARKADINA: As you please. (*Wakes* SORIN) Petrusha, supper! (*Takes* SHAMREYEFF's *arm*) I'll tell you how they
received me in Kharkoff.

> (PAULINE *blows out candles on table. She and* DORN
> *wheel* SORIN's *chair out of the room. All but* TREP-
> LEFF *go out. He gets ready to write. Runs his eye
> over what's already written*.)

TREPLEFF: I've talked so much about new forms, but
now I feel that little by little I am slipping into mere
routine myself. (*Reads*) "The placards on the wall
proclaimed" . . . "pale face in a frame of dark hair"
. . . frame . . . that's flat. (*Scratches out what he's
written*) I'll begin again where the hero is awakened
by the rain, and throw out all the rest. This descrip-
tion of a moonlight night is too long and too precious.
Trigorin has worked out his own method, it's easy
for him. With him a broken bottleneck lying on the
dam glitters in the moonlight and the mill wheel casts
a black shadow . . . and there before you is the

moonlight night; but with me it's the shimmering light, and the silent twinkling of the stars, and the faroff sound of a piano dying away in the still, sweet-scented air. It's painful. (*A pause*) Yes, I'm coming more and more to the conclusion that it's a matter not of old forms and not of new forms, but that a man writes, not thinking at all of what form to choose, writes because it comes pouring out from his soul. (*A tap at the window nearest the desk*) What's that? (*Looks out*) I don't see anything. (*Opens the door and peers into the garden*) Someone ran down the steps. (*Calls*) Who's there? (*Goes out. The sound of his steps along the veranda. A moment later returns with* NINA) Nina! Nina! (*She lays her head on his breast, with restrained sobbing.*)

TREPLEFF (*Moved*): Nina! Nina! It's you . . . you. I had a presentiment, all day my soul was tormented. (*Takes off her hat and cape*) Oh, my sweet, my darling, she has come! Let's not cry, let's not.

NINA: There's someone here.

TREPLEFF: No one.

NINA: Lock the doors. Someone might come in.

TREPLEFF: Nobody's coming in.

NINA: I know Irina Nikolaevna is here. Lock the doors.

TREPLEFF (*Locks door on right. Goes to door on left*): This one doesn't lock. I'll put a chair against it. (*Puts chair against door*) Don't be afraid, nobody's coming in.

NINA (*As if studying his face*): Let me look at you. (*Glancing around her*) It's warm, cozy. . . . This used to be the drawing room. Am I very much changed?

TREPLEFF: Yes . . . you are thinner and your eyes are

bigger. Nina, how strange it is I'm seeing you. Why wouldn't you let me come to see you? Why didn't you come sooner? I know you've been here now for nearly a week. I have been every day there where you were, I stood under your window like a beggar.

NINA: I was afraid you might hate me. I dream every night that you look at me and don't recognize me. If you only knew! Ever since I came I've been here walking about . . . by the lake. I've been near your house often, and couldn't make up my mind to come in. Let's sit down. (*They sit*) Let's sit down and let's talk, talk. It's pleasant here, warm, cozy. . . . You hear . . . the wind? There's a place in Turgenev: "Happy is he who on such a night is under his own roof, who has a warm corner." I . . . a sea gull . . . no, that's not it. (*Rubs her forehead*) What was I saying? Yes . . . Turgenev. "And may the Lord help all homeless wanderers." It's nothing. (*Sobs.*)

TREPLEFF: Nina, again . . . Nina!

NINA: It's nothing. It will make me feel better. I've not cried for two years. Last night I came to the garden to see whether our theatre was still there, and it's there still. I cried for the first time in two years, and my heart grew lighter and my soul was clearer. Look, I'm not crying now. (*Takes his hand*) You are an author, I . . . an actress. We have both been drawn into the whirlpool. I used to be as happy as a child. I used to wake up in the morning singing. I loved you and dreamed of being famous, and now? Tomorrow early I must go to Yelets in the third class . . . with peasants, and at Yelets the cultured merchants will plague me with attentions. Life's brutal!

TREPLEFF: Why Yelets?

NINA: I've taken an engagement there for the winter. It's time I was going.

TREPLEFF: Nina, I cursed you and hated you. I tore up all your letters, tore up your photograph, and yet I knew every minute that my heart was bound to yours forever. It's not in my power to stop loving you, Nina. Ever since I lost you and began to get my work published, my life has been unbearable . . . I'm miserable. . . . All of a sudden my youth was snatched from me, and now I feel as if I'd been living in the world for ninety years. I call out to you, I kiss the ground you walk on, I see your face wherever I look, the tender smile that shone on me those best years of my life.

NINA (*In despair*): Why does he talk like that? Why does he talk like that?

TREPLEFF: I'm alone, not warmed by anybody's affection. I'm all chilled . . . it's cold like living in a cave. And no matter what I write it's dry, gloomy and harsh. Stay here, Nina, if you only would! And if you won't, then take me with you.

(NINA *quickly puts on her hat and cape.*)

TREPLEFF: Nina, why? For God's sake, Nina. (*He is looking at her as she puts her things on. A pause.*)

NINA: My horses are just out there. Don't see me off. I'll manage by myself. (*Sobbing*) Give me some water.

(*He gives her a glass of water.*)

TREPLEFF: Where are you going now?

NINA: To town. (*A pause*) Is Irina Nikolaevna here?

TREPLEFF: Yes, Thursday my uncle was not well, we telegraphed her to come.

NINA: Why do you say you kiss the ground I walk on?
I ought to be killed. (*Bends over desk*) I'm so tired.
If I could rest . . . rest. I'm a sea gull. No, that's not
it. I'm an actress. Well, no matter. . . . (*Hears* ARKA-
DINA *and* TRIGORIN *laughing in the dining room. She
listens, runs to the door on the left and peeps through
the keyhole*) And he's here too. (*Goes to* TREPLEFF)
Well, no matter. He didn't believe in the theatre, all
my dreams he'd laugh at, and little by little I quit
believing in it myself, and lost heart. And there was
the strain of love, jealousy, constant anxiety about
my little baby. I got to be small and trashy, and
played without thinking. I didn't know what to do
with my hands, couldn't stand properly on the stage,
couldn't control my voice. You can't imagine the
feeling when you are acting and know it's dull. I'm
a sea gull. No, that's not it. Do you remember, you
shot a sea gull? A man comes by chance, sees it, and
out of nothing else to do, destroys it. That's not it.
. . . (*Puts her hand to her forehead*) What was
I . . . I was talking about the stage. Now I'm not
like that. I'm a real actress, I act with delight, with
rapture, I'm drunk when I'm on the stage, and feel
that I am beautiful. And now, ever since I've been
here, I've kept walking about, kept walking and
thinking, thinking and believing my soul grows
stronger every day. Now I know, I understand,
Kostya, that in our work . . . acting or writing . . .
what matters is not fame, not glory, not what I used
to dream about, it's how to endure, to bear my cross,
and have faith. I have faith and it all doesn't hurt
me so much, and when I think of my calling I'm
not afraid of life.

TREPLEFF (*Sadly*): You've found your way, you know where you are going, but I still move in a chaos of images and dreams, not knowing why or who it's for. I have no faith, and I don't know where my calling lies.

NINA (*Listening*): Ssh . . . I'm going. Good-by. When I'm a great actress, come and look at me. You promise? But now. . . . (*Takes his hand*) It's late. I can hardly stand on my feet, I feel faint. I'd like something to eat.

TREPLEFF: Stay, I'll bring you some supper here.

NINA: No, no . . . I can manage by myself. The horses are just out there. So, she brought him along with her? But that's all one. When you see Trigorin . . . don't ever tell him anything. I love him. I love him even more than before. "An idea for a short story"— I love, I love passionately, I love to desperation. How nice it used to be, Kostya! You remember? How gay and warm and pure our life was; what things we felt, tender, delicate like flowers . . . Do you remember? . . . (*Recites*) "Men and beasts, lions, eagles and partridges, antlered deer, mute fishes dwelling in the water, starfish and small creatures invisible to the eye . . . these and all life have run their sad course and are no more. Thousands of creatures have come and gone since there was life on the earth. Vainly now the pallid moon doth light her lamp. In the meadows the cranes wake and cry no longer; and the beetles' hum is silent in the linden groves . . . (*Impulsively embraces* TREPLEFF, *and runs out by the terrace door. A pause.*)

TREPLEFF: Too bad if any one meets her in the garden and tells Mother. That might upset Mother. (*He stands for two minutes tearing up all his manuscripts and throwing them under the desk, then unlocks door on right, and goes out.*)

DORN (*Trying to open the door on the left*): That's funny. This door seems to be locked. (*Enters and puts chair back in its place*) A regular hurdle race . . .

> (*Enter* MADAME ARKADINA *and* PAULINE, *behind them* YAKOV *with a tray and bottles;* MASHA, *then* SHAMREYEFF *and* TRIGORIN.)

ARKADINA: Put the claret and the beer for Boris Alexeevich here on the table. We'll play and drink. Let's sit down, friends.

PAULINE (*To* YAKOV): Bring the tea now, too. (*Lights the candles and sits down.*)

SHAMREYEFF (*Leading* TRIGORIN *to the cupboard*): Here's the thing I was telling you about just now. By your order.

TRIGORIN (*Looking at the sea gull*): I don't remember. (*Reflecting*) I don't remember.

> (*Sound of a shot offstage right. Everybody jumps.*)

ARKADINA (*Alarmed*): What's that?

DORN: Nothing. It must be . . . in my medicine case . . . something blew up. Don't you worry. (*He goes out right, in a moment returns*) So it was. A bottle of ether blew up. (*Sings*) Again I stand before thee! Enchanted. . . .

ARKADINA (*Sitting down at the table*): Phew, I was frightened! It reminded me of how . . . (*Puts her hands over her face*) Everything's black before my eyes.

DORN (*Turning through the magazine, to* TRIGORIN): About two months ago in this magazine there was an article . . . a letter from America, and I wanted to ask you among other things . . . (*Puts his arm around* TRIGORIN's *waist and leads him toward the front of the stage*) since I'm very much interested in this question . . . (*Dropping his voice*) Get Irina Nikolaevna somewhere away from here. The fact is Konstantine Gavrilovich has shot himself . . .

Curtain

Uncle Vanya

CHARACTERS

SEREBRIAKOFF, ALEXANDER VLADIMIROVICH,
a retired professor.

ELENA ANDREEVNA, *his wife, twenty-seven years old.*

SOFIA ALEXANDROVNA (SONIA), *his daughter by a first
marriage.*

VOINITSKAYA, MARIA VASILIEVNA, *widow of a privy
councillor, mother of the first wife of the professor.*

VOINITSKY, IVAN PETROVICH, *her son* (UNCLE VANYA).

ASTROFF, MIKHAIL LVOVICH, *a doctor.*

TELEGIN, ILYA ILYICH, *an impoverished landowner.*

MARINA, *an old nurse.*

A WORKMAN

The action takes place on the estate of Serebriakoff

ACT ONE

*A garden. A part of the house, and its terrace, can be
seen. Under an old poplar in the alley a table is set for
tea. There are benches and chairs; a guitar lies on one of
the benches. Not far from the table, there is a swing. It
is past two in the afternoon of a cloudy day.*

MARINA, *a plain, small old woman, sits near the samovar
without moving, and knits on a stocking.* ASTROFF *walks
to and fro near her.*

MARINA (*Pouring a glass*): Drink some tea, son, please.

ASTROFF (*Accepts the glass unwillingly*): Somehow I
don't feel like it.

MARINA: Maybe you'll drink a little vodka?

ASTROFF: No. I don't drink vodka every day. Besides, it's
very sultry today. (*A pause*) Nurse, how long have
we known each other?

MARINA (*Thinking it over*): How long? May God help
me to remember. . . . You came here to these parts
. . . When? . . . Vera Petrovna was still alive, little
Sonia's mother. In her time you were here for two
winters . . . so it comes to about eleven years in all.
(*Pausing to think*) And maybe even more. . . .

ASTROFF: Have I changed much since then?

MARINA: Much. Then you were young and handsome.

and now you have aged. And your good looks now
are not what they were. And what's more, might we
say . . . you drink a little vodka.

ASTROFF: Yes. . . . In ten years I have become a different man. And what is the reason? I am overworked,
nurse. From morning till night, always on your feet,
don't know what rest is, and at night you lie under a
blanket and are afraid you might be dragged off to
see some sick man. During all the time we have
known each other I have not had one free day. How
can anybody not grow old? And life itself is boring,
stupid, dirty . . . it strangles you, this life. Around
you only odd people, without exception, odd people;
and having lived with them two or three years, little
by little you get to be odd yourself. It's unavoidable
fate. (*Twirling his long mustache*) Look how I've
grown this enormous mustache . . . it's a silly mustache. I've grown odd. Nurse . . . I haven't grown
stupider; my brains, thank God, are in the right place,
but my feelings somehow have grown numb. There's
nothing I want, nothing I need, nobody I love. . . .
Maybe it's only you that I love. (*Kissing her head*)
When I was little I had a nurse like you.

MARINA: Maybe you'd like something to eat.

ASTROFF: No. The third week of Lent I went to Malit-
skoye to an epidemic . . . typhus. . . . The huts were
stacked full of people. Filth, stench, smoke, calves running around the floor among the sick . . . and pigs
too. . . . I was hard at it all day, never sat down,
didn't have a bite to eat and when I came home, they
wouldn't let me rest—they brought in a railroad
switchman; I put him on the table to perform an op-
eration, and he ups and dies on me under the chloro-

form. And just when I didn't need any feelings, my feelings woke up, my conscience was stricken, as if I had killed him deliberately. . . . I sat down, closed my eyes—like this—and I thought: those who will live one or two hundred years after us, and those we blaze the trail for now, will they remember us with a kind word? But they won't, Nurse.

MARINA: People won't remember but God will remember.

ASTROFF: Thank you very much. That was well said.

(VOINITSKY *comes out of the house; he has had a nap after lunch and looks rumpled. He sits down on the bench as he arranges his stylish necktie.*)

VOINITSKY: Yes. . . . (*A pause*) Yes. . . .

ASTROFF: Had enough sleep?

VOINITSKY: Yes . . . Very much so. (*Yawns*) Since the Professor and his spouse came to live here, life is off the track . . . I sleep at odd hours, for lunch and dinner I eat a lot of highly-spiced dishes, drink wine . . . all that is not good for your health. We never used to have a free minute, Sonia and I worked—I can tell you that—and now it's only Sonia who works, and I sleep, eat, drink. . . . There's no good in it.

MARINA (*Shaking her head*): No order to anything around here. The Professor gets up at twelve o'clock, but the samovar has been boiling since early morning, waiting for him. Without them here we used to have dinner right after noon as people do everywhere, and with them here it is nearly seven. At night the Professor reads and writes, and suddenly when it's after one at night there's a ring. . . . What is it, sir? Tea! Wake up people for him, start the samovar. (*Scornfully*) What order!

ASTROFF: And will they stay here long?

VOINITSKY: A hundred years. The Professor has decided to settle down here.

MARINA: There now. You see. The samovar has already been two hours on the table, and they are gone walking.

VOINITSKY: Here they are, here they are. . . . Don't get upset.

(*Voices are heard; from the depths of the garden, returning from a walk, come* SEREBRIAKOFF, ELENA ANDREEVNA, SONIA *and* TELEGIN.)

SEREBRIAKOFF: Wonderful, wonderful. . . . Wonderful views!

TELEGIN: Remarkable, your Excellency.

SONIA: We'll go into the woods tomorrow, Papa. Would you like to?

VOINITSKY: Ladies and gentlemen, tea!

SEREBRIAKOFF: Send my tea into my study, be so kind, my friends. I have something more that I must do today.

SONIA: And you will surely like the woods.

(ELENA ANDREEVNA, SEREBRIAKOFF, *and* SONIA *go into the house;* TELEGIN *goes to the table and sits down near* MARINA.)

VOINITSKY: It's hot, stifling really, but our great scientist has an overcoat on, rubbers, an umbrella and gloves.

ASTROFF: That means he is preserving his health.

VOINITSKY: But how beautiful she is! How beautiful! In all my life I have never seen a lovelier woman.

TELEGIN (*His speech is high-pitched and pretentious*): Whether I ride in the field, Marina Timofeevna, walk in the shady garden, or look at this table, I experience inexplicable delight! The weather is charming, the lit-

tle birds sing, we all live in this world in harmony—
what more could we have! (*Accepting a glass of tea*)
I am deeply grateful to you!

VOINITSKY (*Dreamily*): What eyes. . . . Wonderful
woman!

ASTROFF: Talk about something, Ivan Petrovich.

VOINITSKY (*Listlessly*): What shall I talk about?

ASTROFF: Isn't there anything new?

VOINITSKY: Nothing. Everything is an old story. I am
the same as I always was, grown worse very likely,
since I'm getting lazy; I do nothing and only make a
fuss like any old grumbler. My old magpie *Maman*
is still babbling about the emancipation of women;
with one eye she looks into the grave and with the
other she rummages through her learned books for
the dawn of a new life.

ASTROFF: And the Professor?

VOINITSKY: And the Professor as usual sits from morning till late at night in his study and writes. As the
poet says, "Straining our brain, knitting our brow, we
keep writing, writing odes, but neither we nor they
hear any praise anywhere." Poor paper! It would be
better if he wrote his autobiography. What a capital
subject that would be! A retired professor, you understand, an old crust, a learned old dried mackerel.
Gout, rheumatism, migraine, and his liver swollen
with jealousy and envy. . . . So this mackerel lives
on the estate of his first wife, lives there against his
will because he cannot afford to live in town. Forever
complains of his misfortunes, though as a matter of
fact, he is unusually lucky. (*Nervously*) You just
think what luck! He was the son of a humble sacris-
tan, he was a simple theological student, and attained

to a university degree and a professor's chair, became his Excellency, the son-in-law of a Senator, *et cetera, et cetera*. All that is unimportant, however; this is the point: a man for exactly twenty-five years reads and writes about art, and understands exactly nothing about art. Twenty-five years he chews over some other man's thoughts about realism, naturalism, and all the other nonsense; twenty-five years reads and writes about what intelligent people already know and stupid people are not interested in—which means that for twenty-five years he pours from empty to empty. And along with it what conceit! What pretense! He retired, and he is not known to a single living soul, he is absolutely unknown; which just means that for those twenty-five years he was occupying somebody else's place. But, mind you, he strides about like a demigod!

ASTROFF: Well, it seems you are envious.

VOINITSKY: Yes, I am envious! Look at his success with women! No Don Juan ever knew such complete success as he's had. His first wife, my sister—she was a beautiful, gentle creature, pure as this blue sky, noble, generous, who had more admirers than he had students—she loved him as only pure angels might love those who are as pure and beautiful as they are. His mother-in-law, my mother, still adores him, and he still inspires her with holy awe. His second wife, a beauty, clever—you just saw her—married him when he was already old, gave him her youth, beauty, freedom, brilliance. For what? Why?

ASTROFF: Is she faithful to the professor?

VOINITSKY: Unfortunately, yes.

ASTROFF: And why unfortunately?

VOINITSKY: Faithfulness like this is false from beginning to end; it has a fine sound but no logic. To be unfaithful to an old husband you cannot bear—is immoral; but to try to silence within yourself your poor youth and your live feelings—that is quite moral.

TELEGIN (*In a tearful voice*): Vanya, I don't like it when you say that. Really, now . . . anybody who is unfaithful to wife or to husband, is, it means so to me, an unfaithful person, who can even be unfaithful to his country!

VOINITSKY (*Annoyed*): Oh, turn off your tap, Waffles!

TELEGIN: Allow me, Vanya—my wife ran off with her lover the day after our wedding (*Pompously*) because of my unattractive appearance. After that I have not shirked my duty. I still, up till now, love her and am faithful to her, help her with what I can, and gave up my property to educate the little children she begot with her lover. Happiness I am robbed of, but I still have pride. And she? Her youth is gone, her beauty, under the influence of the laws of nature, is faded, her lover has passed away. . . . What has she left?

(*Enter* SONIA *and* ELENA ANDREEVNA; *a little later enter* MARIA VASILIEVNA *with a book; she sits down and reads; she is served tea and she drinks it without looking up.*)

SONIA (*Rapidly, to nurse*): There, Nurse, the peasants have come. Go talk to them, and I'll pour the tea. (*Pours tea*) (*The nurse leaves,* ELENA *takes her cup and drinks, sitting in the swing.*)

ASTROFF (*To* ELENA): I really came to see your husband. You wrote that he is very sick, rheumatism and something else, but apparently he is quite well.

ELENA: Yesterday evening he was down in the dumps,

complained of pains in his legs, and today he is quite fit.

ASTROFF: And with me, breaking my neck, galloping thirty versts. Well, it's all right, and it's not the first time. Just for that I'll stay with you till tomorrow and, at least, will sleep *quantum satis*.

SONIA: Wonderful! You so very seldom spend the night with us. Very likely you haven't had any dinner?

ASTROFF: No, I have not.

SONIA: So then you shall have dinner as well. We now dine after six o'clock. (*Drinking*) The tea's cold!

TELEGIN: In the samovar the temperature has already lowered considerably.

ELENA: Very well, Ivan Ivanovich, we will drink it cold.

TELEGIN: Excuse me . . . Not Ivan Ivanovich, but Ilya Ilyich . . . Ilya Ilyich Telegin, or, as some people call me with my pock-marked face, Waffles. Once upon a time it was I who christened Sonia, and his Excellency, your spouse, knows me very well. I live with you now on this estate. . . . If you have deigned to notice, I have dinner with you every day.

SONIA: Ilya Ilyich is our helper, our right hand. (*Tenderly*) Let me pour you some more, Godfather.

MARIA VOINITSKAYA: Oh!

SONIA: What is it, Grandmother?

MARIA VOINITSKAYA: I forgot to tell Alexander . . . I forgot something. . . . I received a letter today from Kharkoff from Pavel Alexeevich. . . . He sent his new pamphlet.

ASTROFF: Is it interesting?

MARIA VOINITSKAYA: Interesting, but it's strange somehow. He disapproves of what seven years ago he himself defended. It's terrible!

VOINITSKY: There is nothing terrible in that. Drink, Mama, drink your tea.

MARIA VOINITSKAYA: But I want to talk!

VOINITSKY: But for fifty years now we talk and talk, and read pamphlets. It's high time to stop.

MARIA VOINITSKAYA: You seem to find it hard to listen when I talk. Forgive me, Jean, but during the last year you have changed so that I absolutely do not recognize you. . . . You used to be a man of strong convictions, a bright personality.

VOINITSKY: Oh, yes! I used to be a bright personality that didn't give light to anybody. (*A pause*) I used to be a bright personality! . . . That couldn't be more venomous! I am forty-seven years old. Up to last year, I deliberately tried just as you do to blind my eyes with this pedantry of yours and not to see real life— and I thought I was doing well. And now, if you only knew! I don't sleep nights because of disappointment, and anger that I so stupidly let time slip by, when now I could have had everything that my old age denies me!

SONIA: Uncle Vanya, that's boring.

MARIA VOINITSKAYA (*To her son*): It looks as if you are challenging your former convictions. . . . But they are not guilty, it's you are guilty. You keep forgetting that conviction in itself is nothing, it's a dead letter. . . . You should have been doing something.

VOINITSKY: Doing something? Not everybody is capable of being a *perpetuum mobile* writing, like your *Herr* professor.

MARIA VOINITSKAYA: What do you mean by that?

SONIA (*Imploringly*): Grandmother! Uncle Vanya! I beg you!

VOINITSKY: I am silent. Silent and apologizing. (*A pause.*)

ELENA: And fine weather today . . . Not hot. . . . (*A pause.*)

VOINITSKY: It's fine weather to hang yourself. . . .

    (TELEGIN *tunes the guitar.* MARINA *walks near the house and calls the chickens.*)

MARINA: Here, Chick, Chick, Chick. . . .

SONIA: Nurse, why have the peasants come? . . .

MARINA: Still the same old thing, still about the waste plot of land. Here, Chick, Chick, Chick. . . .

SONIA: Which one are you calling?

MARINA: Spotty! She's gone off with her chicks. . . . The crows might get them. (*Goes out.*)

    (TELEGIN *plays a polka; everyone listens silently;* A WORKMAN *enters.*)

WORKMAN: Master Doctor here? (*To* ASTROFF) Please, Mikhail Lvovich, we came to get you.

ASTROFF: From where?

WORKMAN: From the factory.

ASTROFF (*Annoyed*): I thank you humbly. Then, I must go. (*Looks around for his cap*) Bother, the devil take it. . . . Where is that cap?

SONIA: How tiresome it is, really . . . to come from the factory to dinner!

ASTROFF: No. It will be too late. Where . . . Where to . . . (*To the* WORKMAN) Here's what, slip me a glass of vodka, my good fellow, anyhow. (WORKMAN *goes out*) Where . . . where to. . . . (*Finds his cap*) Ostroffsky in some play of his has a man with a big mustache and small abilities. . . . That's me. Well, I have the honor to bid you good-by, ladies and gentlemen. (*To* ELENA) If you would look in on me some

time, you and Sonia here, I'd be very glad—truly. I
have a tiny little estate, in all about thirty acres, but, if
it interests you, a model garden and nursery, such as
you won't find around here in a thousand miles. Next
to me is the state forestry. . . . The forester there is
old, always sick, and the truth is I handle all the work
that's done.

ELENA: They have told me that you love the woods
very much. Of course, one can be very useful, but
doesn't it interfere with your real calling? After all
you are a doctor.

ASTROFF: God only knows what is our real calling.

ELENA: And is it interesting?

ASTROFF: Yes, it's an interesting business.

VOINITSKY (Ironically): Very!

ELENA (To ASTROFF): You are still a young man, you
look . . . well thirty-six or -seven years old . . . and
it must not be quite so interesting as you say, with always the trees and the trees and the trees. I think it's
monotonous.

SONIA: No, it is extremely interesting. Every year Mikhail Lvovich plants new wood plots and they have already sent him a bronze medal and a diploma. He
petitioned not to have the old ones destroyed. If you
would only hear him out you would agree with him
completely. He says that forests adorn the earth, that
they teach a man to understand the beautiful and in-
spire him to lofty moods. Forests soften a severe climate. In countries where the climate is mild, you
spend less effort in the struggle with nature, and so
man there is gentler and tenderer; people are beautiful there, lively, easily excited, their speech is exquisite, their movements are graceful. Their sciences and

arts blossom, their philosophy is not gloomy, their relation to a woman is full of exquisite nobility . . .

VOINITSKY (*Laughing*): Bravo, bravo! . . . All this is
darling, but not convincing, and so (*To* ASTROFF)
allow me, my friend, to go on heating stoves with
wood and building barns out of wood.

ASTROFF: You can heat stoves with peat moss, and build
barns with stones. Well, I admit you may cut woods
out of some need, but why destroy them? Russian
woods are creaking under the ax, milliards of trees
perish, dwellings of beasts and birds are emptied, rivers go shallow and dry, wonderful landscapes vanish,
never to be brought back again, and all because lazy
man hasn't sense enough to bend down and pick up
fuel from the ground. (*To* ELENA) Isn't that the truth,
my lady? He must be a reckless barbarian to burn
this beauty in his stove, destroy what we cannot create again. Man is endowed with intellect and creative
powers so that he may multiply what is given to him,
but up to now he has not created, he has destroyed.
Forests are fewer and fewer, rivers dry up, game becomes extinct, the climate is ruined, and every day the
earth gets poorer and uglier. (*To* VOINITSKY) Here you
are with that mocking look in your eyes, and all I
say seems to you not very serious and . . . and, indeed
it may be foolishness; but, when I pass the peasants'
woods that I have saved from being chopped down,
or when I hear the sound of my young wood rustling,
the stand I planted with my own hands, I realize that
climate too is a little in my power, and that a thousand years from now if man should be happy, why,
then I'll be a small part of that too. When I plant a
birch and see it later on burst into green and wave

in the wind, my soul fills with pride, and I . . .
(*Seeing the* WORKMAN, *who has brought a tray with a
glass of vodka*) However . . . (*Drinks*) it's time.
The whole thing very likely is only foolishness after
all. I have the honor to bid you good-by. (*Going toward the house.*)

SONIA (*Taking his arm and going along with him*):
When will you come to see us?

ASTROFF: I don't know.

SONIA: Again after a month?

　　　(ASTROFF *and* SONIA *go into the house;* MARIA VASILI-
　　　EVNA *and* TELEGIN *remain near the table;* ELENA *and*
　　　VOINITSKY *go toward the terrace.*)

ELENA: And you, Ivan Petrovich, you behaved yourself
impossibly again. Did you have to annoy Maria Vasilievna, talking of *perpetuum mobile!* And today at
lunch you argued with Alexander again. How small
of you that is!

VOINITSKY: But what if I detest him!

ELENA: There is nothing to detest Alexander for, he is
the same as you all are. Not any worse than you are.

VOINITSKY: If you could see your face, your movements.
. . . How lazy your life is! Oh, how lazy!

ELENA: Oh, both lazy and bored! Everybody blames my
husband, everybody looks at me with pity: miserable
creature, she has an old husband! This concern over
me—oh, how I understand it! Just as Astroff said:
you all go on ruining our woods recklessly and soon
there will be nothing left on earth. In the same way
you ruin man recklessly and soon, thanks to you,
soon there will be no faithfulness, no purity, no capacity for sacrifice left on earth. Why can't you look at
a woman with indifference if she is not yours? Be-

cause—the doctor was right—in all of you sits the demon of destruction. You have no pity either for woods or birds, or women, or for each other.

VOINITSKY: I don't like this philosophy.

(*A pause.*)

ELENA: This doctor has a tired, nervous face. An interesting face. It's obvious Sonia likes him, she is in love with him, and I understand her. While I have been here he has been here three times already, but I am shy and have not really talked to him once even, and haven't been kind to him. He thought I had a grudge against him. It's quite possible that the reason you and I are such friends, Ivan, is that both of us are tiresome, boring people! Tiresome! Don't look at me that way, I don't like it.

VOINITSKY: How can I look at you differently if I love you? You are my joy, my life, my youth! I know my chance of any return is just about nil, but I don't want anything, just let me look at you, hear your voice. . . .

ELENA: Hush they might hear you!

(*They go toward the house.*)

VOINITSKY (*Following her*): Don't drive me away, let me talk about my love, and just that will be the greatest happiness for me.

ELENA: This is painful. (*Both enter the house.*)

(TELEGIN *strums some chords and plays a polka;* MARIA VASILIEVNA *is jotting something down on the margins of the pamphlet.*)

Curtain

ACT TWO

Dining room in SEREBRIAKOFF's *house. It is night; you can hear the watchman tapping in the garden.* SEREBRIAKOFF *is sitting in an easy chair in front of an open window, dozing.* ELENA ANDREEVNA *sits near him and is also dozing.*

SEREBRIAKOFF (*Awaking suddenly*): Who is there? Sonia, you?

ELENA: This is me.

SEREBRIAKOFF: You, Lenotchka. . . . This unbearable pain!

ELENA: Your robe has fallen on the floor (*Bundles up his legs*) I'll shut the window, Alexander.

SEREBRIAKOFF: No, not for me, to me it's stuffy. I just now dozed off and dreamed that my left leg did not belong to me. An excruciating pain woke me up. No, this is not the gout, it's rheumatism, more likely. What time is it now?

ELENA: Twenty minutes past midnight. (*A pause.*)

SEREBRIAKOFF: In the morning look in the library for Batyushkov. It seems to me we have him.

ELENA: What?

SEREBRIAKOFF: Look for Batyushkov in the morning. I seem to remember we had him. But why is it so hard for me to breathe?

ELENA: You are tired. Not sleeping a second night.

SEREBRIAKOFF: They say that Turgenev developed angina from gout. I am afraid it might be that way with me. This damned, disgusting old age, the devil take it! When I got old I began to be revolting to myself. And you all, I dare say, find it revolting to look at me.

ELENA: You speak of your old age as if we were all guilty of your being old.

SEREBRIAKOFF: And you are the first one to be revolted. (ELENA *moves away and sits down farther away from him*) Of course, you are right. I am not stupid and I understand. You are young, healthy, beautiful, you want to live, and I am an old man, almost a corpse. So? As if I didn't understand? And, of course, it's stupid of me to be still alive. But wait a little, soon I'll set you all free. It won't be much longer now that I shall have to drag myself around.

ELENA: I can't bear it. . . . For God's sake, be quiet.

SEREBRIAKOFF: It looks as if nobody can bear it, thanks to me; everyone is bored, everyone is ruining their youth, I am the only one. I'm the only one who's enjoying life and is content. Yes, of course!

ELENA (*In tears*): Be quiet! You have me all worn out.

SEREBRIAKOFF: I am torturing everybody. Of course.

ELENA (*Through her tears*): It's unbearable! Tell me, what do you want from me?

SEREBRIAKOFF: Nothing.

ELENA: Well, then, be quiet. I beg you.

SEREBRIAKOFF: It's a strange thing, Ivan Petrovich begins to talk or that old idiot, Maria Vasilievna—and it's quite all right with everybody listening; but if I say just one word, look how everybody begins to be miserable. Even my voice is revolting. Well, let us suppose I am revolting, I am an egoist, I am a despot —but don't I really, even in my old age, have some right to egotism? As if I have not earned it? As if, is what I'm asking you, I have no right to a quiet old age, to some attention from people?

ELENA: Nobody is disputing your rights. (*A window is banging in the wind*) A wind has come up, I'll close the window. (*Closing it*) It will rain soon. Nobody is disputing your rights.

(*A pause; the watchman in the garden is tapping and singing a song.*)

SEREBRIAKOFF: To work all your life for learning, grow used to your desk, to your auditorium, to your esteemed colleagues—and suddenly, for no reason, to find yourself in this morgue, to see here every day stupid people, to listen to flat conversations. . . . I want to live, I love success, I love fame, applause— and then here—here I am like an exile. To grieve over your past every minute, to watch the success of the others, to fear death . . . I can't! I haven't the strength for it! And here they are, they won't even forgive me for being old.

ELENA: Wait, do have patience: in five or six years I'll be old too.

(*Enter* SONIA.)

SONIA: Papa, you yourself gave orders to fetch Doctor Astroff, and when he got here you refused to see him. That is not very nice. We have just bothered a man for nothing.

SEREBRIAKOFF: What do I need your Astroff for? He understands just about as much of medicine as I understand of astronomy.

SONIA: We can't with your gout summon the entire medical faculty.

SEREBRIAKOFF: I wouldn't even talk to that imbecile.

SONIA: As you like. (*Sitting down*) It's all the same to me.

SEREBRIAKOFF: What time is it now?

ELENA: Past midnight.

SEREBRIAKOFF: I'm suffocating—Sonia, fetch me the drops from the table!

SONIA: Certainly, at once. (*She hands him the drops.*)

SEREBRIAKOFF (*With annoyance*): Ach, not those! You can't even ask—you can't even ask for anything!

SONIA: I beg you, don't be capricious. It might please some people, but not me; kindly leave me out of it. I don't like it. Besides I have no time to waste. I have to get up early tomorrow, I've got hay to cut. (*Enter* VOINITSKY *in a dressing gown, with a candle.*)

VOINITSKY: A storm is gathering outside. (*Lightning*) There, now! Elena and Sonia, go to sleep, I have come to take your place.

SEREBRIAKOFF (*Alarmed*): No, no! Don't leave me with him! No. He'll talk my head off.

VOINITSKY: But we must give them some rest! It is the second night now they have not had any sleep.

SEREBRIAKOFF: Let them go to sleep, but you go away too. Thank you. I implore you. For the sake of our former friendship, don't protest. We'll talk later.

VOINITSKY (*Smiling ironically*): Our former friendship . . . former . . . !

SONIA: Be quiet, Uncle Vanya.

SEREBRIAKOFF (*To his wife*): My dear, don't leave me with him! He'll talk my head off.

VOINITSKY: Really, this is just getting to be laughable.

(*Enter* MARINA *with a candle.*)

SONIA: You ought to lie down, Nurse. It's already late.

MARINA: The samovar hasn't been cleared from the table yet. How can you very well lie down?

SEREBRIAKOFF: Everybody doesn't sleep, everybody can't bear it, only I, I alone am blissfully happy.

MARINA (*Comes to* SEREBRIAKOFF, *tenderly*): What is it, dear sir? Does it hurt? My legs throb too, how they throb! (*Arranging the robe*) This is your old ailment. Vera Petrovna, Sonia's dear mother, used to spend sleepless nights, killing herself, pitying you. She loved you so. (*A pause*) Old ones like young ones want somebody to feel sorry for them, but nobody feels sorry for the old. (*Kisses* SEREBRIAKOFF *on his shoulder*) Dear sir, let's go to bed. . . . Let's go, my dear. . . . I will give you some linden tea to drink, it will warm up your feet. . . . I'll pray to God for you.

SEREBRIAKOFF (*Very much touched*): Let us go, Marina.

MARINA: My legs throb so, throb so! (*She and* SONIA *are leading him*) Your Vera Petrovna, Sonia's mother, was always killing herself with pity, always crying. . . . You were still small and foolish, Sonia, then. Come, come, dear sir.

(SEREBRIAKOFF, SONIA *and* MARINA *go out.*)

ELENA: I am worn out with him. I can hardly stand up.

VOINITSKY: You with him, I with myself. It's the third night now I have not slept.

ELENA: Things are not going very well in this house. Your mother hates everything except her pamphlets and the Professor; the Professor is cross, he won't trust me, and is afraid of you; Sonia is angry at her father, she is angry at me and hasn't spoken to me for two weeks now; you hate my husband and openly scorn your mother; I am irritable and twenty times today have been ready to cry. . . . Things are not going very well in this house.

VOINITSKY: Let's leave philosophy out of it!

ELENA: Ivan, you are educated and intelligent and you must understand that the world is going to ruin not from robbing, not from fires, but from hate, enmity, from all this petty squabbling. . . . Your business should not be to grumble, but to make peace among us all.

VOINITSKY: First of all you make me make peace with myself! My darling . . . (*Seizing her hand.*)

ELENA: Stop it! (*Takes away her hand*) Go away!

VOINITSKY: The rain will be over now and everything in nature will be fresh and breathing. Only I will not be refreshed by the storm. Day and night like a fiend at my throat is the thought that my life is hopelessly lost. No past, it was stupidly spent on trifles, and the present with all its absurdity is frightful. Here they are: my life and my love: where shall I put them, what shall I do with them? This feeling of mine is dying in vain, like a ray of sunlight that has strayed into a pit, and I myself am dying.

ELENA: When you talk to me of your love, I get numb somehow and don't know what to say. Forgive me, there is really nothing I can say to you. (*She wants to go*) Good night.

VOINITSKY (*Barring her way*): And if only you knew how I suffer from the thought that next to me in the same house another life is dying—yours! Your life.

What are you waiting for? What curst philosophy is
it in your way? Do understand, understand . . .

ELENA (*Looking at him closely*): Ivan Petrovich, are
you drunk?

VOINITSKY: Perhaps, perhaps . . .

ELENA: Where is the doctor?

VOINITSKY: He is there spending the night with me.
Perhaps, perhaps. . . . Anything is possible!

ELENA: And today you were drinking? Why is that?

VOINITSKY: Because it is like living. Somehow—like living. Don't stand in my way, Elena!

ELENA: You never used to drink and never used to talk
so much. Go to bed! I am bored with you.

VOINITSKY (*Seizing her hand*): My darling . . . My
beautiful!

ELENA (*Annoyed*): Let me alone. After all, it is revolting. (*Goes out.*)

VOINITSKY (*Alone*): She is gone. (*A pause*) Ten years
ago I used to meet her at my dear sister's. She was
seventeen then and I was thirty-seven years old. Why
didn't I fall in love with her then and propose to her?
It was so possible. And by now she would have been
my wife . . . Yes . . . Now we both would have
been awakened by the storm; she would have been
frightened by the thunder and I would have held her
in my arms and whispered: "Don't be afraid, I am
here." Oh, beautiful thoughts, how wonderful, I am
even smiling . . . but, my God, thoughts are getting
tangled up in my head. . . . Why am I old? Why
doesn't she understand me? Her rhetoric, her idle
moralizing, her foolish, idle thoughts about the end
of the world—all that is hateful to me. (*A pause*) Oh,

how I was deceived! I adored that Professor, that pitiful, gouty creature, I worked for him like an ox!
Sonia and I squeezed out of this estate its last drop of
juice; like thrifty peasants we sold vegetable oil,
beans, cottage cheese, went hungry ourselves so that
out of pennies and half-pennies we might pile up
thousands and send them to him. I used to be proud
of him and his learning, I lived and breathed it! All
he wrote and uttered seemed to me genius. . . . God,
and now here he is retired, and you can see now the
whole sum of his life. After he is gone there won't be
a single page of his work left behind; he is absolutely
unknown, he is nothing! A soap bubble! And I've
been fooled . . . I can see . . . stupid . . . fooled . . .

    (*Enter* ASTROFF *in a Prince Albert coat without a
waistcoat and without a necktie; he is a bit tipsy;
after him* TELEGIN *with a guitar.*)

ASTROFF: Play!

    (TELEGIN *strums softly.*)

ASTROFF (*To* VOINITSKY): Are you alone here? No ladies?

    (*Hands on hips, sings softly.*)

"Go away hut, go away stove,
The master has no room to lie down . . ." And I was
awakened by the storm. A downright, soaking rain it
was. What time is it now?

VOINITSKY: Ah, the devil only knows.

ASTROFF: It seems to me I heard the voice of Elena
Andreevna.

VOINITSKY: She was just here.

ASTROFF: Superb woman! (*Looking at the medicine
bottles on the table*) Medicines. Every sort of pre-
scription. From Kharkov, and Moscow, and Tula.

. . . All the towns in Russia have had enough of his gout. Is he ill or is he pretending to be?

VOINITSKY: Ill. He's ill.

(*A pause.*)

ASTROFF: Why are you so sad today? Is it the Professor you are sorry for, perhaps?

VOINITSKY: Leave me alone.

ASTROFF: And in love with the Professor's wife per haps?

VOINITSKY: She is my friend.

ASTROFF: Already?

VOINITSKY: What does that mean—"already"?

ASTROFF: A woman can be a man's friend only in some such sequence as this: first, a companion, then a mis-tress, and then after that a friend.

VOINITSKY: That's a vulgar philosophy.

ASTROFF: So that's it. Yes . . . I must confess I'm get-ting to be a vulgarian. You can see too I'm drunk. Usually I get drunk only once a month. When I'm like that I get very brazen and impertinent to the very limit. Then anything goes. I undertake the most diffi-cult operations and do them beautifully; I paint the broadest plans for the future; at such times I don't look like a fool to myself any more, and believe that I am bringing an enormous boon to humanity . . . enormous! . . . At such times I have my own system of philosophy, and all of you, my little brothers, seem to me such very small insects . . . microbes. (*To* TELEGIN) Waffles, play!

TELEGIN: My good friend, with all my soul, I should be glad to, but do understand—they are asleep in the house!

ASTROFF: Play!

(TELEGIN *strums softly.*)

ASTROFF: I need a drink. Come on, we still seem to have
some cognac left. And as soon as it begins to grow
light we will go to my place. All rightie? I have a
medical orderly who never says "all right" but "all
rightie." A terrible rascal. So, all rightie? (*Seeing*
SONIA *enter*) Pardon me, I am without a necktie.

(*Goes out quickly;* TELEGIN *goes out after him.*)

SONIA: And you, Uncle Vanya, you got drunk again
with the doctor. Struck up a friendship, you bright
hawks. That one is always like this, but why you? At
your age, it's not becoming.

VOINITSKY: Age has nothing to do with it. When one
has no real life, one lives in illusions. After all, that's
better than nothing.

SONIA: All our hay is mowed, it rains every day, everything is rotting and you occupy yourself with illusions. You have neglected the farming completely—
I'm the only one that works, and I have no strength
left. (*Alarmed*) Uncle, you have tears in your eyes!

VOINITSKY: What tears? There's nothing . . . nonsense
. . . You looked at me just now as your dead mother
used to. My dear . . . (*Kissing her hands and her
face*) My sister . . . my dear sister . . . Where is she
now? If she knew! Ah, if she knew!

SONIA: What? Uncle, knew what?

VOINITSKY: It's very hard, I'm not well . . . Nothing
. . . Later . . . It's nothing. I will go. . . .

(*Goes out.*)

SONIA (*Knocking at the door*): Mikhail Lvovich! Aren't
you asleep? Just one minute!

ASTROFF (*From behind the door*): Right away! (*A little*

later, he comes in; he is already in his vest and neck-tie) What is your command?

SONIA: You go ahead and drink if it is not revolting to you, but I implore you, don't let Uncle drink. It is bad for him.

ASTROFF: Very well. We shall not drink any more. (*A pause*) I will go home now. Resolved and signed. By the time they hitch up my team it will be dawn.

SONIA: It's raining. Wait till morning.

ASTROFF: The storm is passing by, only a fringe will hit us. I'm going. And, please, don't ask me any more to see your father. I say to him—gout, and he says rheumatism; I tell him to lie down, he sits up. And today he wouldn't even talk to me.

SONIA: He is spoiled. (*Going to the sideboard*) Would you like a little bite of something?

ASTROFF: Well, I think I will.

SONIA: I like to have a bite at night, and it seems there's something on the sideboard. In his time, they say, he had great success with women, and the ladies spoiled him. Here take some cheese.

(*Both stand by the sideboard and eat.*)

ASTROFF: I haven't eaten anything today, I only drank. Your father has a difficult character. (*Getting a bottle out of the sideboard*) May I? (*He drinks a glass*) Nobody is here and one can speak out straight. You know, it seems to me you know I could not live through a month in your house, I'd suffocate in this air . . . Your father, who is all absorbed in his gout and books, Uncle Vanya with his hypochondria, your grandmother, and, to top it all, your stepmother. . . .

SONIA: What about my stepmother?

ASTROFF: In a human being everything ought to be

beautiful: face and clothes, and soul and thoughts. She is beautiful, no disputing that, but she merely eats and sleeps and walks and charms us all with her beauty—and nothing more. She has no responsibilities whatever, other people work for her . . . isn't it so? An idle life can't be right. (*A pause*) However, perhaps I'm too hard on her. I am not satisfied by life, just as your Uncle Vanya is not, and we both are getting to be nothing but grumblers.

SONIA: And you are not content with your life?

ASTROFF: On the whole, I like life, but our rural Russian, average man's life, I can't bear it, with all the strength in my soul I have a contempt for it, and as far as my own personal life goes, there is, so help me God, absolutely nothing good in it. You know how it is when you are walking in the woods on a dark night and see far off a little light burning. You don't mind either the fatigue, or the darkness or the branches scratching you in the face. I work—as you know very well—as nobody else does in the district, fate never lets up her blow on me, at times what I go through is unbearable, but for me there is no little light in the distance. For myself I am not expecting anything any more, I don't like people. . . . It's a long time since I loved anyone.

SONIA: No one?

ASTROFF: No one. Only toward your nurse I feel a certain tenderness for old memories' sake. Peasants are all alike, monotonous, primitive, living in dirt. And it is hard to get on with the intelligentsia. They tire one. They all, all our good friends, will have shallow thoughts, shallow feelings and will not see farther than their noses—the simple fact is they are stupid

And those that are cleverer and more important, are
hysterical, absorbed with analyzing themselves—they
whine, they despise everything, they slander people
cruelly, they approach a man sideways, look at him
out of the corner of an eye and decide: "Oh, he is a
psychopath!" or: "He is a phrase-maker!" And when
they don't know which label to stick on to my forehead, they say: "He's an odd one, odd!" I love the
woods, that is odd; I don't eat meat—that's odd
too. There is no longer any spontaneous, pure, free
kinship to nature or to people. . . . No and no!

(*He is about to drink.*)

SONIA (*Stopping him*): No, I beg you, I implore you,
don't drink any more.

ASTROFF: Why?

SONIA: It is so unbecoming to you! You are refined, you
have such a gentle voice. . . . More than that you are
like nobody among the people I know, like nobody
else—you are beautiful. Then why do you want to
look like ordinary people who drink and play cards?
Oh, don't do that, I implore you! You always say that
people don't create but merely destroy that that's
given to them from above. Then why, why, are you
destroying yourself? Don't, don't, I entreat you, I implore you!

ASTROFF (*Holding out his hand to her*): I won't drink
any more.

SONIA: Give me your word.

ASTROFF: Word of honor.

SONIA (*Shaking his hand vigorously*): Thank you!

ASTROFF: Basta! I have sobered up. See, I am already
completely sober and will stay like this to the end of
my days. (*Looking at his watch*) And so, let's go on.

I say: my time has already passed, it's too late for me
. . . I am aged, overworked, I've become common, all
my feelings have become blunted and I never seem
able to attach myself to anyone. I don't love anybody
and . . . I'm already past loving anybody. What still
enthralls me is beauty. I am not indifferent to it. It
seems to me that if Elena Andreevna only wanted to,
in one day she could set my head in a whirl. . . .
But that is not love, it's not belonging to someone—
not—

(*Covering his eyes with his hand and shuddering.*)

SONIA: What is the matter with you?

ASTROFF: Well. . . . During Lent my patient died under
chloroform.

SONIA: It is time to forget about that. (*A pause*) Tell
me, Mikhail Lvovich. . . . If I had a friend, or a
younger sister, and if you learned that she . . . well,
let us say, loved you, just what way would you take
it?

ASTROFF (*Shrugging his shoulders*): I don't know. Very
likely no way. I would let her understand that I cannot fall in love with her. . . . Besides, I have other
things on my mind. Be that as it may, it's already
time for me to leave. Good-by, my dear, or else we
won't sleep till morning. (*Shaking her hand*) I'll go
through the living room, if you will let me—I am
afraid your uncle might get hold of me. (*Leaves.*)

SONIA (*Alone*): He didn't say anything to me. . . . His
soul and heart are still hidden from me; but why do I
feel so happy? (*Laughing from happiness*) I said to
him: You are refined, noble, you have such a gentle
voice. . . . Was it the wrong moment for just that?
His voice trembles, caresses you— Here I feel him in

the air. And when I told him about a younger sister, he didn't understand. . . . (*Wringing her hands*) Oh, how terrible it is that I am not pretty! How terrible! And I know I am not pretty, I know, I know. . . . Last Sunday as we were leaving church, I heard them talking about me and one woman said: "She is kind, generous, but it's a pity she is not pretty." . . . not pretty.

(*Enter* ELENA.)

ELENA (*Opening the windows*): The storm has passed. What fine air! (*A pause*) Where is the doctor?

SONIA: Gone. (*A pause.*)

ELENA: Sofia!

SONIA: What?

ELENA: How long will you be cross with me? We haven't done each other any wrong. Why then should we be enemies? Enough is enough.

SONIA: I myself wanted to . . . (*Embracing her*) Yes, enough of our being angry.

ELENA: Excellent. (*Both are excited.*)

SONIA: Papa is lying down?

ELENA: No, he is sitting in the living room. . . . We don't speak to each other for whole weeks, you and I. God knows why. (*Seeing that the sideboard is open*) What is that?

SONIA: Mikhail Lvovich had supper.

ELENA: And there is some wine. . . . Let us drink *bruderschaft*.

SONIA: Let's.

ELENA: Out of one glass . . . (*Pours*) That's better. (*They drink and kiss.*)

SONIA: It's a long time I wanted to make peace, but somehow I felt embarrassed . . . (*Crying.*)

ELENA: Why are you crying?

SONIA: Nothing, no special reason.

ELENA: Well, there—there—(*Crying*) You foolish creature, and I am crying too. . . . (*A pause*) You resent
me because it looks as if I married your father cal-
culatingly. . . . Then, if you believe in oaths, I swear
to you—I married him for love. I was infatuated with
him as a learned and famous man. My love was not
real; my love was artificial, but it seemed real to me
then. I am not guilty. And you from the very day of
the wedding have never stopped accusing me with
your intelligent, suspecting eyes.

SONIA: Well, peace, peace! Let us forget.

ELENA: Don't look at it like that—'tisn't like you . . .
One must have faith in everybody, otherwise life is
impossible.

(*A pause.*)

SONIA: Tell me in all honesty, as a friend . . . are you
happy?

ELENA: No.

SONIA: I knew it. Here's one more question. Tell me
frankly—would you have liked to have a young husband?

ELENA: What a child you still are. Of course I should
have. (*Laughing*) Now, ask me something else, ask
me . . .

SONIA: Do you like the doctor?

ELENA: Yes, very much.

SONIA (*Laughing*): I have a silly face . . . haven't I?
Here he is, gone, and I keep hearing his voice and his
steps, and when I look at a dark window I see his face
there. Let me try to say what I mean—but I can't talk
so loud, I am ashamed. Let's go to my room, there

we'll talk. Do I seem silly to you? Confess . . . tell
me something about him. . . .

ELENA: But what?

SONIA: He is clever. . . . He can do anything, is able to
do anything. . . . He heals the sick and he plants
woodlands.

ELENA: It isn't a matter of woods and medicine. . . .
My dear, understand, it's the genius! And do you
know what genius means? Bravery, a free mind, a
broad sweep. When he plants a little tree, he is already
imagining what it will be like in a thousand years, he
is already dreaming of the happiness of mankind.
Such people are rare, one must love them. . . . He
drinks, he is sometimes rude—but what harm is there
in that! A genius in Russia can't be too much of a
saint. Think yourself what a life that doctor has! Im-
passable mud on the roads, frost, blinding snow,
enormous distances, people crude and wild, poverty
all around, diseases. In such a setting it is hard for
anyone who works and struggles day after day to
keep himself steady and sober at forty. . . . (*Kisses
her*) From the bottom of my soul I wish you—you
deserve happiness. . . . (*Getting up*)—I am a tedi-
ous, passing face—in music, and in my husband's
house, in all the novels—the truth is, everywhere I
was merely a passing face. The truth is, Sonia, when
you stop and think of it, I am very, very unhappy!
(*Walking on the stage excitedly*) There's no happiness for me in this world. No! Why are you laughing?

SONIA (*Laughing, covering her face*): I am so happy
. . . so happy!

ELENA: I feel like playing . . . I would like to play something now.

SONIA: Do play. (*Embraces her*) I cannot sleep. . . . Do play!

ELENA: Right away. Your father is not asleep. When he is ill music irritates him. Go ask. If he is quite well then I'll play. Go on.

SONIA: Right away. (*Goes out.*)

(*The watchman is tapping in the garden.*)

ELENA: It is a long time since I've played. I shall play and cry—cry like a fool. (*Through the window*) Is it you tapping, Efim?

THE VOICE OF THE WATCHMAN: Me!

ELENA: Don't tap, the master is not well.

THE VOICE OF THE WATCHMAN: I'll go right away! (*Whistles*) Hey, you, Nicky! Boris! Nicky! (*Another whistle*) (*A pause.*)

SONIA (*Returning*): No, you cannot!

Curtain

ACT THREE

Living room in the house of SEREBRIAKOFF. *Three doors: to the right, to the left, and in the middle. Daytime.*

VOINITSKY, SONIA *are sitting down, and* ELENA ANDREEVNA *is walking around the room, busy with her thoughts.*

VOINITSKY: Herr Professor deigned to express a wish, that we all gather today in this living room by one o'clock. (*Looks at the clock*) Quarter to one. He wished to disclose something to the world.

ELENA: Perhaps some kind of business.

VOINITSKY: He hasn't got any business. He writes nonsense, grumbles, and is jealous, and nothing else.

SONIA (*Reproachfully*): Uncle!

VOINITSKY: Well, well, sorry. (*Pointing to* ELENA) Do admire: she walks around and sways a bit from laziness. Very sweet! Very!

ELENA: All day long you buzz, always buzzing—aren't you tired of it. (*With anguish*) I am dying of boredom, I don't know what to do.

SONIA (*Shrugging her shoulders*): Isn't there enough to do? If you wanted to.

ELENA: For example?

SONIA: Occupy yourself with running the house, teaching the children, caring for the sick. Is that so little? When you and Papa were not here, Uncle Vanya and I went to the market ourselves to sell the flour.

ELENA: I don't know how. Besides it is not interesting. It is only in sociological novels they teach and cure sick peasants, and how can I suddenly for no reason go to curing and teaching them?

SONIA: And in the same way I don't understand how not to go and not to teach. Wait, and you will get used to it. (*Embracing her*) Don't be bored, darling. (*Laughing*) You are bored, you can't find a place for yourself, and boredom and idleness are infectious. Look how Uncle Vanya does nothing but walk behind you, like a shadow. I dropped my work and ran here to talk with you. I am getting lazy, I can't do anything. Doctor Mikhail Lvovich used to come to us very seldom, once a month, it was hard to coax him and now he drives here every day, he has forsaken both his woods and his medicine. You must be a witch.

VOINITSKY: Why are you wilting away? (*With animation*) Now, my darling, my magnificent one, be a good girl! In your veins flows the blood of a water nymph, so be it a water nymph! Let yourself go if only for once in your life, hurry and fall in love with some River God up to your ears—and plunge head foremost into a whirlpool, so that Herr Professor and all of us hold up our hands we are so astonished.

ELENA (*Angrily*): Leave me alone! How cruel it is! (*She wants to go.*)

VOINITSKY (*Preventing her*): Now, now, my joy, forgive me . . . I apologize. (*Kissing her hand*) Be patient.

ELENA: An angel wouldn't have the patience—you must agree . . .

VOINITSKY: As a token of peace and harmony, I'll bring a bouquet of roses, now; I made it for you this morning. . . . Autumn roses—charming, sad roses . . . (*Goes out.*)

SONIA: Autumn roses—charming, sad roses. (*Both of them look out of the window.*)

ELENA: And September is already with us. How will we live through the winter here! (*A pause*) Where's the doctor?

SONIA: In Uncle Vanya's room. Writing something. I am glad Uncle Vanya went out, I must talk to you.

ELENA: About what?

SONIA: About what? (*Puts her head on* ELENA's *breast.*)

ELENA: Well, there, there . . . (*Stroking her hair*) Enough.

SONIA: I am not pretty.

ELENA: You have beautiful hair.

SONIA: No! (*Looking back to glance at herself in the mirror*) No! When a woman is not pretty they tell her: "You have beautiful eyes, you have beautiful hair." I have loved him now for six years, loved him more than my own mother; every minute I hear his voice, feel the touch of his hand; and I watch the door, waiting; it always seems to me that he will be coming in. And here, you see I keep looking for you, to talk about him. He is here every day now but does not look at me, doesn't see me. . . . It's such agony! I haven't any hope, no, no! (*In despair*) Oh, God, grant me strength. . . . I prayed all night. . . . I often come to him, start talking to him myself, look into his eyes. . . . I have no more pride, I've no power to control myself. . . . I could not contain myself and yesterday I confessed to Uncle Vanya, that I am in love . . . and all the servants know I love him. Everybody knows.

ELENA: And he?

SONIA: No. He never notices me.

ELENA (*Meditating*): A strange man he is . . . Do you know what? Let me, I'll talk to him . . . Carefully, by hinting. . . . (*A pause*) Really, how long can you be in some uncertain state! Do let me! (SONIA *nods her head to agree*) That's wonderful. He loves you or he doesn't love you—that won't be hard to find out. Don't be embarrassed, my little dove, don't worry— I'll question him carefully, he won't even know. All we want is to find out: Yes or No? (*A pause*) If no, then let him stop coming here. Isn't that so? (SONIA *nods her head to agree*) Easier when you don't see

him. We won't file it away in a box; we'll question
him right now. He intended to show me some
sketches. . . . Go tell him I want to see him.

SONIA (*In great excitement*): You will tell me the
whole truth?

ELENA: Yes, of course. It seems to me the truth, whatever it is, is not so frightful as uncertainty after all.
You may count on me, little dove.

SONIA: Yes, yes . . . I'll tell him that you want to see
his charts—(*Going, she stops near the door*) No, uncertainty is better . . . After all, there is hope—

ELENA: What is it?

SONIA: Nothing. (*Goes out.*)

ELENA (*Alone*): There is nothing worse than when
you know someone's secret and are no help. (*Meditating*) He is not in love with her—that is clear, but
why doesn't he marry her? She is not pretty but for a
country doctor, at his age she would be a fine wife.
Intelligent, so kind, true. . . . No, it isn't that, not
that. . . . (*A pause*) I understand this poor girl. She
lives in the midst of uninterrupted boredom. Instead
of people she has some sort of gray shadows, wandering around her, what they say is trifling, all they
know is that they eat and they drink, and they sleep.
And then sometimes he comes, not like the others,
handsome, interesting, charming, as if in the twilight
rises a bright moon. . . . Oh, to give in to the charm
of such a man, to forget yourself. . . . It looks as if I
were a little carried away myself. Yes, I am bored
without him; here I am smiling, when I think of him.
. . . Uncle Vanya says that in my veins perhaps flows
the blood of a water nymph. "Let yourself go at least
once in your life. . . ." What then? Perhaps, it must

be so . . . To fly away like a free bird, away from you all, from your sleepy faces, from your conversations, to forget that you exist in the world . . . But I am cowardly, I'm shy . . . I'll be tortured by my conscience . . . You see. He comes here every day, I can guess why he is here and I already feel myself guilty, I'm ready to fall on my knees before Sonia and ask her forgiveness, and to cry . . .

ASTROFF (*Enters with a chart*): Good morning. (*Shaking her hand*) You'd like to see my . . .

ELENA: You promised yesterday to show me your work . . . are you free?

ASTROFF: Oh, of course. (*Spreads the chart on the card table and fastens it with thumb tacks*) Where were you born?

ELENA (*Helping him with the chart*): In Petersburg.

ASTROFF: And received your education?

ELENA: In the conservatory.

ASTROFF: This may not interest you.

ELENA: Why? It's true I don't know the country, but I read a great deal.

ASTROFF: Here in the house I have my own table . . . In Ivan's room. When I'm utterly tired out, and in a complete torpor, I drop everything and run to this house, and amuse myself with this thing here an hour or so . . . Ivan and Sonia do the accounts and I sit near them at my own table dabbling, and I feel warm, at peace, and the cricket chirps. But this pleasure I don't allow myself often, not often, once a month. . . . (*Pointing it out on the chart*) Now look here at this. The picture of our district as it was fifty years ago. The dark green and light green colors are forests; half of the whole area is forests. The red crosslines on the green show where elks and goats used to be—I am showing here both *flora* and *fauna*. On this lake used to live swans, geese, ducks and, as the old men say, a powerful lot of all kinds of birds; you saw nothing but birds. They floated like a cloud. Besides the villages and small towns, you see various settlements were scattered, farms, monasteries, water-mills. . . . There were a great many cattle and horses; you can tell by the blue color. For example, in this district the blue is thick; whole herds were there, and each farm owned three horses. (*A pause*) Now we'll look lower down. What there was twenty-five years ago. Only a third of the whole area is woodland. There are no longer any goats, but there are elks. The green and the blue colors are already paler. And so on, and so forth. Now here's the third part: a picture of the district today. The green comes here and there, but not solid, only in spots; the elks have disappeared, the swans, and the grouse. . . . Of the villages, settlements, monasteries, mills, there is not even a trace. On the whole a picture of gradual, plain degeneration, which apparently needs only some ten or fifteen years more to be complete. You will say that there are cultural influences at work here, that the old life must naturally have yielded place to the new. Yes, I understand that if in place of these destroyed forests, roads were laid out, railroads, if there were mills, factories, schools—people would become healthier, richer, more intelligent; but there is nothing of the kind! In the district the same swamps, mosquitoes, the same absence of roads, poverty, typhus, diphtheria, fires. . . . We have here a case of degeneration that results from a struggle that's beyond men's strength for existence; degeneration caused by sloth, by ignorance, by the complete absence of any conscience, when a cold, hungry, sick man to save what life he has left, for his children, instinctively, subconsciously grabs at everything that might satisfy his hunger, or warm him, destroys everything, without a thought of tomorrow. Nearly everything is already destroyed and in its place there is nothing created. (*Coldly*) I can see by your face that this is not interesting to you.

ELENA: But I understand so little of that. . . .

ASTROFF: There is nothing to understand, it's simply uninteresting.

ELENA: To be frank, my mind is not on that. Forgive me. I must do a little cross-questioning and I am embarrassed and don't know how to begin.

ASTROFF: A cross-examination?

ELENA: Yes, a cross-examination, but . . . rather innocent. Let's sit down! (*They sit down*) The matter concerns one young person. We shall talk like honest people, as friends, without beating about the bush. We shall talk and then forget what the talk was about. Yes?

ASTROFF: Yes.

ELENA: The matter concerns my stepdaughter Sonia. Do you like her?

ASTROFF: Yes, I respect her.

ELENA: Do you like her as a woman?

ASTROFF (*Not at once*): No.

ELENA: Two or three words more—and that's the end of it. Have you noticed nothing?

ASTROFF: Nothing.

ELENA (*Taking his hand*): You don't love her, I see it
in your eyes . . . she's suffering—understand it and
. . . stop coming here.

ASTROFF (*Getting up*): My season has already passed.
. . . Besides, I have no time. . . . (*Shrugging his
shoulders*) When can I find it. (*He is embarrassed.*)

ELENA: Pooh, what a disagreeable conversation! I am as
upset as if I were dragging twenty tons. Well, thank
God, we have finished. Let us forget, as if we had not
talked at all, and . . . and you ride away. You are an
intelligent man, you will understand. . . . (*A pause*)
I am blushing red all over.

ASTROFF: If you had told me a month or two ago, then I
possibly would have considered it, but now. . . .
(*Shrugs his shoulders*) And, if she is suffering, then,
of course. . . . There is only one thing I do not understand: Why did you have to have this cross-examination? (*Looks into her eyes and moves a finger
from side to side*) You are sly!

ELENA: What does that mean?

ASTROFF (*Laughing*): Sly! Let us suppose, Sonia is suffering. I readily admit it, but why this cross-examination of yours? (*With much animation, not letting her
talk*) Permit me, don't make an astonished face, you
know very well why I come here every day . . . Why
and for whose sake I come, that you know very well.
You darling bird of prey, don't look at me like that, I
am a wise old sparrow. . . .

ELENA (*Incredulous*): Bird of prey? I don't understand
a bit of it.

ASTROFF: A beautiful, fluffy little thing . . . you must
have victims! Here I am already a whole month not
doing anything, I have dropped everything, I look

greedily for you—and this you like hugely. Well, then? I am conquered, you knew it even without the questioning. (*Folds his arms and bows his head*) I give up. Here, eat me!

ELENA: Have you lost your mind?

ASTROFF (*Laughing through his teeth*): You are sly.

ELENA: Oh, I am better and more superior than you think! I swear to you! (*Wants to go.*)

ASTROFF (*barring her way*): I will leave today, I will not be here again, but . . . (*Taking her hand, looking around*) Where are we going to see each other? Tell me quickly: Where? Someone might come in here, tell me quickly . . . (*Passionately*) What a wonderful, luscious . . . One kiss . . . For me just to kiss your fragrant hair . . .

ELENA: I swear to you . . .

ASTROFF (*Not letting her talk*): Why swear? Mustn't swear. No use for needless words . . . Oh, how beautiful! What hands! (*Kisses her hands.*)

ELENA: But that's enough, after all . . . go away . . . (*Withdraws her hands*) You forget yourself.

ASTROFF: Tell me, tell me where will we see each other tomorrow? (*Holds her by the waist*) You can see, it can't be escaped, we've got to see each other.

　　(*He kisses her; at that point* VOINITSKY *enters with a bouquet of roses and stops at the door.*)

ELENA (*Not seeing* VOINITSKY): Have mercy . . . leave me alone. . . . (*Puts her head on* ASTROFF's *breast*) No! (*She moves to go.*)

ASTROFF (*Restraining her by the waist*): Come tomorrow to the wood . . . about two o'clock . . . Yes? Yes? You will come?

ELENA (*Noticing* VOINITSKY): Let me go! (*In great*

embarrassment moves to the window) This is terrible.

VOINITSKY (*Puts the bouquet on the chair; excitedly wipes his face and behind his collar with a handkerchief*): So? . . . Yes . . . So?

ASTROFF (*With false nonchalance*): Today, much esteemed Ivan Petrovich, the weather is not bad. In the morning it was cloudy, as if it would rain, and now the sun's shining. Honestly speaking, autumn turned out beautiful . . . and the winter crop not bad. (*Folds the chart into a cylinder*) Except for one thing: the days are getting short. . . . (*Goes out.*)

ELENA (*Quickly goes to* VOINITSKY): You will try, you will use all your influence, so that my husband and I can go away from here today even! Do you hear me? Today!

VOINITSKY (*Wiping his face*): Ah? Well, yes . . . very well. Elena, I saw everything, everything . . .

ELENA (*Nervously*): Do you hear me? I must leave here this very day!

(*Enter* SEREBRIAKOFF, SONIA, TELEGIN, *and* MARINA.)

TELEGIN: I myself somehow your excellency, am not entirely well. It is two days now I have been ailing. My head somehow . . .

SEREBRIAKOFF: But where are the others? I don't like this house. A sort of labyrinth. Twenty-six enormous rooms, everybody scatters and can never find anybody. (*Rings*) Ask Maria Vasilievna and Elena Andreevna here.

ELENA: I am here.

SEREBRIAKOFF: I beg you, ladies and gentlemen, sit down.

SONIA (*Approaching* ELENA, *impatiently*): What did he say?

ELENA: Later.

SONIA: You are trembling. You are upset. (*Peering in-quisitively into her face*) I understand . . . He said, that he will not be here any more . . . yes? (*A pause*) Say it: Yes?

(ELENA *nods her head.*)

SEREBRIAKOFF (*To* TELEGIN): One can still make peace with illness, no matter what, but what I cannot digest is this regime of country life. I have a feeling as if I had fallen from the earth on to some foreign planet. Sit down, ladies and gentlemen, I beg you. Sonia! (SONIA *does not hear him, she stands with her head down, sadly*) Sonia! (*A pause*) She doesn't hear. (*To* MARINA) And you, Nurse, sit down. (NURSE *sits down and knits on a stocking*) I beg you, ladies and gentle-men. Hang your ears, so to speak, on a peg of atten-tion. (*He laughs.*)

VOINITSKY (*Excitedly*): Maybe I'm not needed. Shall I leave?

SEREBRIAKOFF: No, you are needed here more than any-body.

VOINITSKY: What do you want from me?

SEREBRIAKOFF: You . . . But why are you angry? (*A pause*) If I am guilty in your eyes of anything, then pardon me please.

VOINITSKY: Drop that tone. Let's proceed with busi-ness . . . What do you need?

(*Enter* MARIA VASILIEVNA.)

SEREBRIAKOFF: Here is Mama. I'll begin, ladies and gentlemen. (*A pause*) I invited you, ladies and gentlemen, so that I might explain that the Inspector General is on his way. However, jokes aside. It is a serious matter. I, ladies and gentlemen, gathered you together, to ask you for help and advice, and, knowing your undying courtesy, I hope I will get it. I am a learned man, a bookworm, and have always been a stranger to practical life. Do without directions of well-informed people, I cannot, and I beg you, Ivan Petrovich, and you here, Ilya Ilyich, and you, *Maman.* . . . The fact is *manet omnes una nox,* that is: we are all mortal; I am old, sick, and therefore find it timely to regulate my property terms in so far as that concerns my family. My life is already finished, I am not thinking of myself, but I have a young wife, a maiden-daughter. (*A pause*) To go on living in the country is impossible for me. We are not made for country life. Yet to live in town on the income we get from this estate, is impossible. If we sell, let's say, a wood, that would be an unusual measure which we cannot do every year. One must find such measures as would guarantee us a permanent, more or less definite figure of income. I have thought of one such measure and have the honor to propose it for your discussion. Aside from details, I will state it along general lines. Our estate gives an average of not more than two percent. I propose to sell it. If the proceeds we convert into interest-bearing paper, then we will receive from four to five percent, and I think there will even be a surplus of several thousand, which will allow us to buy a small villa in Finland.

VOINITSKY: Wait . . . my ears must be deceiving me. Repeat what you said.

SEREBRIAKOFF: To convert money into interest-bearing

paper, and with the surplus, what is left, buy a villa in Finland.

VOINITSKY: Not Finland . . . You said something else.

SEREBRIAKOFF: I propose to sell the estate.

VOINITSKY: That's it. You will sell the estate, excellent, a fine idea . . . and where would you order me to go with my old mother and with Sonia here?

SEREBRIAKOFF: All this we will discuss in good time. Not everything at once.

VOINITSKY: Wait. Apparently, up to now I have had not a drop of common sense. Up to now I was so stupid as to think that this estate belongs to Sonia. My late father bought this estate as a dowry for my sister. Up to now I have been naïve, have understood that this was not a Turkish law but Russian; I thought that the estate passed from my sister to Sonia.

SEREBRIAKOFF: Yes. The estate belongs to Sonia. Who is arguing that? Without Sonia's consent I would not decide to sell. Besides what I propose to do is for Sonia's benefit.

VOINITSKY: This is incomprehensible, incomprehensible! Either I have lost my mind, or . . . or . . .

MARIA VASILIEVNA: Jean, don't contradict Alexander. You must believe he knows better than we do what is good and what is bad.

VOINITSKY: No, let me have some water. (*Drinking the water*) Say whatever you want to, whatever you want to!

SEREBRIAKOFF: I don't understand why you excite yourself. I don't say that my project is ideal. If everybody finds it unsuitable then I will not insist.

(*A pause.*)

TELEGIN (*Confusedly*): Your Excellency, I nourish to-

ward learning not only reverence, but feelings of kinship as well. My brother, Gregory Ilyich's wife's
brother, perhaps you know him, Konstantine Tro-
fimovich Lakedemonov, was a magistrate . . .

VOINITSKY: Hold on there, Waffles, we are talking about
business. . . . Wait, later on . . .

(*To* SEREBRIAKOFF)

Here, you ask him. This estate was bought from his
uncle.

SEREBRIAKOFF: Ah, and why should I ask? What for?

VOINITSKY: This estate was bought with things as they
were at that time for ninety-five thousand. Father
paid down only seventy and there was a debt left of
twenty-five thousand. Now listen . . . This estate
would not have been bought had I not given up my
inheritance in favor of my sister, whom I loved
deeply. As if that were not enough, for ten years I
worked like an ox, and paid off the entire debt . . .

SEREBRIAKOFF: I regret that I began this conversation.

VOINITSKY: The estate is clear of debts and intact only
because of my personal efforts. And here when I have
grown old, they want to throw me out on my neck!

SEREBRIAKOFF: I don't understand what you are driving at.

VOINITSKY: For twenty-five years I have managed this
estate, worked, sent you money, like a most conscien-
tious clerk, and during all that time you not once
thanked me. All the time—both in my youth and now
—you paid me five hundred roubles a year for wages
—fit for a beggar—and you never once thought of in-
creasing it by even one rouble!

SEREBRIAKOFF: Ivan Petrovich, how could I know? I

am not a practical man and understand nothing. You could have yourself increased it as much as you wanted to . . .

VOINITSKY: Why didn't I steal? Why don't you all hold me in contempt for not having stolen? It would have been just and now I would not be a beggar!

MARIA VASILIEVNA (*Sternly*): Jean!

TELEGIN (*Excitedly*): Vanya, my friend, don't, don't. . . . I am trembling. . . . Why spoil good relations? (*Kissing him*) Don't!

VOINITSKY: For twenty-five years with this mother here I sat like a mole inside these four walls. All our thoughts and feelings belonged to you alone. In the daytime we talked of you, of your works, felt proud of you, pronounced your name with reverence; the nights we wasted reading magazines and books, which I now despise from the depths.

TELEGIN: Don't, Vanya, don't . . . I cannot . . .

SEREBRIAKOFF (*Indignantly*): I don't understand, what do you want?

VOINITSKY: You were to us a creature of the highest order and your articles we knew by heart . . . But now my eyes are open! I see everything! You write about art, but you understand nothing of art! All your works, that I used to love, are not worth a brass penny! You fooled us!

SEREBRIAKOFF: Ladies and gentlemen! Do make him stop, after all! I shall go!

ELENA ANDREEVNA: Ivan Petrovich, I demand that you stop talking! Do you hear?

VOINITSKY: I will not stop talking! (*Barring* SEREBRIAKOFF's *way*) Wait, I haven't finished! You have ruined my life! I have not lived, have not lived!

Thanks to you I destroyed, swept away, the best years of my life! You are my worst enemy!

TELEGIN: I cannot . . . cannot . . . I'll go . . . (*Leaves in great agitation.*)

SEREBRIAKOFF: What do you want from me? And what right have you to talk to me in such a tone? Imbecile! If the estate is yours, then take it, I don't need it.

ELENA: This very minute I'm going away from this hell! (*Shouting*) I can't bear it any longer.

VOINITSKY: My life is lost to me! I am talented, intelligent, brave . . . Had I lived a normal life, there might have come out of me a Schopenhauer, a Dostoevski . . . I am through with keeping accounts, making reports. I am losing my mind. . . . Mother, I am in despair! Mother!

MARIA VASILIEVNA (*Sternly*): Listen to Alexander!

SONIA (*Kneels down before the nurse and huddles close to her*): Nurse, darling! Nurse, darling!

VOINITSKY: Mother! What am I to do? Don't, don't I know myself what I should do! (*To* SEREBRIAKOFF) You will remember me! (*Goes out through the middle door.*)

(MARIA VASILIEVNA *goes after him.*)

SEREBRIAKOFF: Ladies and gentlemen, but what is it, after all? Take this madman away from me! I cannot live with him under the same roof! He lives there (*Pointing to the middle door*) almost next to me . . . Let him move to the village, into some cottage, or I will move away from here, but remain with him in the same house I cannot.

ELENA (*To her husband*): We will go away from here today! We must make arrangements at once.

SEREBRIAKOFF: Contemptible you are!

SONIA (*Kneeling, turns to her father; nervously, through her tears*): One must be merciful, Papa! Uncle Vanya and I are so miserable! (*Controlling her despair*) One must be merciful! Try to remember when you were younger, Uncle Vanya and Grandmother translated books for you at night, copied your papers . . . every night, every night! Uncle Vanya and I worked without any rest, we were afraid to spend a penny on ourselves and sent everything to you . . . We did not eat our bread free. I am not saying the right thing, not the right thing I am saying, but you have to understand us, Papa. One must be merciful!

ELENA (*Excited, to her husband*): Alexander, for God's sake, have it out with him . . . I implore you.

SEREBRIAKOFF: Very well, I shall have it out with him. I am not accusing him of anything, I am not angry, but, please agree with me, his conduct is at least strange. As you wish, I will go to him.
(*Goes out through the middle door.*)

ELENA: Be gentler with him, quiet him. . . .
(*Goes out after him.*)

SONIA (*Nestling against* MARINA): Nurse! Nurse!

MARINA: It's all right, my child. The geese will cackle —and then stop . . . cackle—and stop.

SONIA: Nurse!

MARINA (*Patting her head*): You are shivering, as if it were frost! Well, well, my little orphan, God is merciful. Some linden tea or some raspberry, and it will pass, you'll forget it. Don't be sad, my little orphan . . . (*Looking at the middle door, fiercely*) There, you geese—
(*Offstage there is a shot; one hears* ELENA *scream;* SONIA *shudders.*)

MARINA: Oh, you!

SEREBRIAKOFF (*Runs in, swaying with fright*): Hold him! Hold him! He has lost his mind.

(ELENA *and* VOINITSKY *struggle in the doorway.*)

ELENA (*Trying to grab the revolver from him*): Give it to me! Give it to me, I tell you!

VOINITSKY: Let me go, Elena! Let me go! (*Freeing himself, runs in and looks around for* SEREBRIAKOFF) Where is he? Ah, there he is! (*Shoots at him*) Bang! (*A pause*) Didn't hit? Missed again? (*Angrily*) Ah, the devil, devil . . . devil take you. . . .

(*Beating the revolver on the floor and sitting down exhausted in a chair.* SEREBRIAKOFF *is stunned;* ELENA *leaning against the wall is fainting.*)

ELENA: Take me away from here! Take me away, kill me, but . . . I cannot stay here, cannot!

VOINITSKY (*In despair*): Oh, what am I doing! What am I doing.

SONIA (*Softly*): Nurse, darling! Nurse, darling!

Curtain

ACT FOUR

IVAN PETROVICH's *room. It is his bedroom, and also is the office of the estate. Near the window a large table with books for cash accounts, and papers of all kinds, a desk, bookcases, scales. A smaller table for* ASTROFF; *on this table there are paints and drawing instruments; next to them a portfolio. There is a bird cage with a starling. On*

*the wall a map of Africa, which apparently is of no use
to anyone here. There's an enormous sofa, upholstered
in oilcloth. To the left—a door leading into bedrooms; to
the right—a door leading into a passage; at the door to
the right a mat is spread so that the peasants won't
muddy up the floor.*

It is an autumn evening; all is tranquil. TELEGIN *and*
MARINA *sit facing each other and wind wool for stockings.*

TELEGIN: You be faster, Marina Timofeevna, because
they will be calling us right away to say good-by.
They've already ordered the horses brought.

MARINIA (*Trying to wind faster*): There is not much
left.

TELEGIN: To Kharkov they are going. And there they
will live.

MARINA: And it is better so.

TELEGIN: Got scared . . . Elena, she says, "I do not wish
to live here one hour," she says . . . "let us go, and
let us go . . . Let's live," she says, "in Kharkov, we'll
look around and then we will send for our things,"
she says. Going away light, no goods to carry. It
means, Marina Timofeevna, that it's not their fate to
live here. Not their fate . . . (*Somewhat pompously*)
A fatal predestination.

MARINA: And it is better so. Just a while ago they raised
a racket firing, what a shame!

TELEGIN: Yes, it's a subject worthy of the brush of
Aivazovski.

MARINA: I'd hope my eyes could not see it. (*A pause*)
We'll live again, the way it used to be in the old days.
In the morning shortly after seven the tea, shortly

after noon the dinner, in the evening sit down to supper; everything in its proper order, the way people have them, Christian-like. (*With a sigh*) It is a long time since I, sinner that I am, have eaten noodle soup.

TELEGIN: Yes, for a long time they have not made noodle soup here. (*A pause*) A long time. . . . This morning, Marina Timofeevna, I walked through the village, and the storekeeper shouted after me: "Hey, you sponger!" And very bitter I began to feel!

MARINA: And don't you pay attention, friend. All of us are spongers on God. Like you, like Sonia, like Ivan —nobody sits doing nothing, we are all working! Everybody. . . . Where is Sonia?

TELEGIN: In the garden. Keeps walking with the doctor, looking for Ivan. They are afraid he might lay hands on himself.

MARINA: And where is his pistol?

TELEGIN (*Whispering*): I hid it in the cellar!

MARINA (*With a smile*): Oh, our sins!

(*Enter from outside* VOINITSKY *and* ASTROFF.)

VOINITSKY: Leave me alone. (*To* MARINA *and* TELEGIN) Go away from here, leave me alone if only for one hour! I cannot stand being treated like someone's ward. I don't need a guardian.

TELEGIN: Right off, Vanya.

(*Goes out on tiptoes.*)

MARINA: You geese—goo—goo—

(*Gathers up the wool and goes out.*)

VOINITSKY: Leave me alone!

ASTROFF: With much pleasure, I should have left here a long time ago, but, I repeat, I am not leaving till you return what you took from me.

VOINITSKY: I did not take anything from you.

ASTROFF: Seriously—I mean it—don't detain me. I
  should have left a long time ago.
VOINITSKY: I took nothing from you.
    (*Both sit down.*)
ASTROFF: Yes? Well then, I shall wait a little, and then,
  excuse me, I'll have to use force. We will tie you up
  and search you. I am saying this seriously, absolutely.
VOINITSKY: As you wish. (*A pause*) To play such a
  fool: to fire twice and not to hit even once! That I'll
  never forgive myself for!
ASTROFF: Well, if you feel like shooting, why not fire at
  your own forehead?
VOINITSKY (*Shrugging his shoulders*): Strange. I attempted a murder, and they don't arrest me, don't
  prosecute me. That means they consider me insane.
  (*He gives an angry laugh*) I—insane, and they are
  not insane. They are not insane who under the guise
  of a professor, a learned wizard, hide their lack of
  talent and their stupidity and crying heartlessness
  They are not insane who marry old men and then in
  front of everybody's eyes deceive them. I saw, saw.
  how you embraced her!
ASTROFF: Yes-s, embraced her—and this for you.
    (*Thumbs his nose.*)
VOINITSKY (*Looking at the door*): No, it's the earth
  is insane that still holds you.
ASTROFF: And that is silly.
VOINITSKY: Why not—I am insane, irresponsible, I have
  the right to say silly things.
ASTROFF: That's an old story. You are not insane, you
  are simply odd. A little clown. There was a time
  when I too regarded every person who was odd as
  sick, abnormal, and now I am of the opinion that the

normal state of man is to be odd. You are entirely normal.

VOINITSKY (*Covering his face with his hands*): I'm ashamed! If you knew how ashamed I am! This sharp feeling of shame is not like just pain. It's unbearable! (*Bending down on the table*) What am I to do? What am I to do?

ASTROFF: Nothing.

VOINITSKY: Give me something! Oh, my God . . . I am forty-seven years old; if—suppose I'll live till sixty— if so I still have thirteen years left. That long! How shall I live through these thirteen years? What will I do, what will I fill them with? Oh, do you understand. . . . (*Convulsively pressing* ASTROFF's *hand*) Do you understand, if I could only live through what is left of life somehow differently. To wake up on a clear, quiet morning and to feel that you have begun to live anew, that all the past is forgotten, faded away, like smoke. (*Crying*) To begin a new life . . . teach me how to begin . . . from what to begin . . .

ASTROFF (*Annoyed, sharply*): Eh, you! What new life is there? Our situation, yours and mine, is hopeless.

VOINITSKY: Yes?

ASTROFF: I am convinced of that.

VOINITSKY: Give me something . . . (*Pointing to his heart*) Here inside me it burns.

ASTROFF (*Angrily*): Stop it! (*Relenting*) Those who will live a hundred, two hundred years after us and who will despise us because we have lived our lives so stupidly and so without any taste—those, perhaps, will find the way how to be happy. And there's but one hope for you and me. The hope that when we'll be sleeping in our coffins, we might be visited by

dreams, perhaps even pleasant ones. (*Sighing*) Yes,
brother. In the whole district there were only two
decent, cultured men: you and I. But in some ten
years, narrow-minded life, despised life, has strangled
us with its rotten fumes. It has poisoned our blood
and we have become just as much vulgarians as the
rest of them. (*In a lively voice*) But, however, you
stop trying to talk the toothache away. Give me back,
you, what you took from me.

VOINITSKY: I did not take anything from you.

ASTROFF: You took from my traveling medicine chest a
jar of morphine. (*A pause*) Listen, if you, no matter
what, want to commit suicide, then go into the woods
and shoot yourself there. The morphine, however,
give it back to me, or there will be talk, guesses, they
will think I gave it to you. As for me, it is enough
that I will have to cut you open. Do you think that
would be interesting?

  (*Enter* SONIA.)

VOINITSKY: Leave me alone.

ASTROFF (*To* SONIA): Sonia, your uncle stole a jar of
morphine from my medicine chest and won't give it
back. Tell him that after all that's not very intelligent
of him. Besides I haven't time for it, it's time for me
to go.

SONIA: Uncle Vanya, did you take the morphine?

  (*A pause.*)

ASTROFF: He took it. I am certain of that.

SONIA: Give it back. Why do you want to frighten us?
(*Tenderly*) Give it back, Uncle Vanya! I am just as
unhappy as you are, maybe, but I don't despair. I bear
it and I will bear it till the end of my life. Then you
bear it too. (*A pause*) Give it back! (*Kisses his hand*)

My dear, nice Uncle, darling, give it back! (*Crying*) You are kind, you will take pity on us and give it back. You bear it too, Uncle! Bear it!—

VOINITSKY (*Gets the jar from the table and gives it to* ASTROFF): Here, take it! (*To* SONIA) But we must get to work quickly, quickly do something, or else I cannot . . . cannot . . .

SONIA: Yes, yes, to work. As soon as we see them off, we will sit down to work. . . . (*Nervously handling the papers on the desk*) We have let everything go.

ASTROFF (*Putting the jar into his medicine chest and fastening the straps*): Now I can start off.

ELENA (*Entering*): Ivan, are you here? We are leaving now. Go to Alexander, he wants to tell you something.

SONIA: Go on, Uncle Vanya. (*Taking* VOINITSKY *by the arm*) Let's go. Papa and you must make peace. You really must.

(SONIA *and* VOINITSKY *go out.*)

ELENA: I am leaving. (*Proffers her hand to* ASTROFF.)

ASTROFF: Already?

ELENA: They have already brought the horses.

ASTROFF: Good-by.

ELENA: Today you promised me that you would go away from here.

ASTROFF: I remember. I am leaving now. (*A pause*) Were you frightened? (*Takes her hand*) Is it really so alarming?

ELENA: Yes.

ASTROFF: And maybe you would stay! Would you? Tomorrow at the forester's. . . .

ELENA: No. . . . I've already decided . . . and that is why I look at you so bravely, because our departure is

already decided. . . . I ask you one thing: think better of me. I want you to respect me.

ASTROFF: Ah! (*With a gesture of impatience*) Stay here,
I beg you. Confess that you have nothing to do in this
world, you have no aim whatsoever, you have nothing to occupy your attention with, and sooner or later
anyhow you'll give up to your feelings—you can't escape it. So it is better not in Kharkov and not somewhere in Kursk but here in nature's bosom—at least
it is poetic, very beautiful even. . . . Here at the forester's there are houses that are half in ruins, quite to
Turgenev's taste.

ELENA: How funny you are . . . I am angry with you,
but yet. . . . I'll be thinking of you with pleasure.
You are an interesting, original man. We shall never
see each other again, and so why hide it? I was even
carried away a little by you. So let us shake each other's hand and part as friends. Don't think evil of me.

ASTROFF (*Shaking her hand*): Yes, go away from here
. . . (*Meditating*) It seems you are a good, sincere
person, but it seems also there is something strange in
your whole nature. You came here with your husband, and everyone who worked here, bustling about
or building something, had to drop work and for
the entire summer they occupied themselves with
your husband's gout and you. Both of you, he and you
—infected us with your idleness. I was carried away,
I have not done anything for a whole month, and
during that time people were ailing, and the peasants
were grazing their cattle in my woods, so that no
matter where you and your husband went, you
brought destruction everywhere. I am joking, of
course, yet . . . it's strange how I am convinced that

if you should stay on, there would be an enormous devastation. And I would perish, and you too would not survive. Well, go away. *Finita la commedia.*

ELENA (*Takes a pencil from his desk and hides it quickly*): I am taking this pencil to remember you by.

ASTROFF: It's odd somehow. . . . We have known each other, and suddenly for some reason—we will never see each other again. And that's how it is in this world . . . While no one is here, until Uncle Vanya comes in with a bouquet, let me . . . kiss you . . . for good-by . . . Yes? (*Kissing her cheek*) So there . . . it's all beautiful.

ELENA: I wish you the best of everything. (*Glancing around quickly*) No matter what, once in a lifetime! (*Embracing him impetuously. They both back away from each other*) I must go.

ASTROFF: Go away quickly. If the horses are ready, then start right off.

ELENA: They seem to be coming.

(*They stand there listening.*)

ASTROFF: *Finita!*

(*Enter* SEREBRIAKOFF, VOINITSKY, MARIA VASILIEVNA *with a book,* TELEGIN *and* SONIA.)

SEREBRIAKOFF (*To* VOINITSKY): He who remembers the past should have his eye plucked out. After what happened, in those few hours I have lived through so much and have thought so much that it seems to me I could write an entire treatise for the edification of posterity on how one should live. I accept your apologies willingly and beg you myself to forgive me. Good-by!

(*Exchanges kisses with* VOINITSKY *three times.*)

VOINITSKY: You will receive what you used to receive accurately. Everything will be as always.

(ELENA *embraces* SONIA.)

SEREBRIAKOFF (*Kissing* MARIA VASILIEVNA'S *hand*): Mama . . .

MARIA VASILIEVNA (*kissing him*): Alexander, have another picture taken and send it to me. You know, how dear you are to me.

TELEGIN: Good-by, Your Excellency! Don't forget us!

SEREBRIAKOFF (*Having kissed his daughter*): Good-by . . . Everybody good-by! (*Offering his hand to* ASTROFF) Thank you for the pleasant company. . . . I respect your trend of thought, your fascinations, your impulses, but allow an old man to add to his farewell salutations just one remark: One must, ladies and gentlemen, do something. One must do something! (*Bowing to all in general*) The best of everything to you.

(*Goes out;* MARIA VASILIEVNA *and* SONIA *follow him.*)

VOINITSKY (*Kissing* ELENA'S *hand fervently*): Good-by. . . . Forgive me. . . . Never, we'll never meet again.

ELENA (*Touched*): Good-by, my dear.

(*She kisses his head and goes out.*)

ASTROFF (*To* TELEGIN): Tell them, Waffles, to bring my horses too at the same time.

TELEGIN: At your service, my friend.

(*Goes out. Only* ASTROFF *and* VOINITSKY *remain.*)

ASTROFF (*Taking his paints from the table and putting them into his suitcase*): Why aren't you going to see them off?

VOINITSKY: Let them go, and I . . . I can't. I feel very low, I must busy myself quickly with something . . .

Work, work! (*He fumbles with the papers on the desk.*)

    (*A pause. Bells are heard.*)

ASTROFF: They are gone. The Professor is glad to go. Nothing could tempt him back here.

MARINA (*Entering*): They are gone.

    (*Sitting down in an armchair and knitting on a stocking.*)

SONIA (*Enters*): They are gone. (*Wiping her eyes*) God grant everything will be well with them. Well, Uncle Vanya, let's do something.

VOINITSKY: To work, to work. . . .

SONIA: It's a long, long time now we haven't sat together at this table. (*Lighting a lamp on the table*) There seems to be no ink. . . . (*She takes the inkwell, goes to the cupboard, and pours out some ink*) And I feel sad that they are gone.

MARIA VASILIEVNA (*Entering slowly*): They are gone! (*She sits down and buries herself in her reading.*)

SONIA (*Sitting down at the table and turning the pages of an account book*): Up the bills first of all, Uncle Vanya. In our hands that's been terribly neglected. They sent again today for a bill. Write. You write one bill, I'll write another.

VOINITSKY (*Writing*): "The bill . . . to Mr. . . ."

    (*Both write silently.*)

MARINA (*Yawning*): I'm getting sleepy. . . .

ASTROFF: It is quiet. Pens are scratching, crickets are chirping. It's warm and cozy . . . I don't feel like leaving here. (*There is the sound of bells*) There, they are bringing the horses. . . . That means that all there is left is for me to tell you good-by, my dear friends, and say good-by to my table and—be off!

(*Puts the charts into the portfolio.*)

MARINA: And why are you fidgeting? You could sit down.

ASTROFF: I can't.

VOINITSKY (*Writing*): "And of the old debt there remains two seventy-five . . ."

(*Enter* A WORKMAN.)

THE WORKMAN: Mikhail Lvovich, the horses are ready.

ASTROFF: I heard it. (*Giving him the traveling medicine chest, the suitcase, and the portfolio*) Here, take this. See that you don't crumple the portfolio.

THE WORKMAN: I'll see to it.

(*He goes out.*)

ASTROFF: Well . . . (*He starts saying good-by.*)

SONIA: When will we see each other?

ASTROFF: Not before summer very likely. I doubt during the winter. . . . Obviously, if anything should happen, then let me know—I will come. (*Shaking hands*) Thanks for bread, for salt, for kindness . . . in a word, for everything. (*Goes to the nurse and kisses her on the head*) Good-by, good-by, old one.

MARINA: And so you will leave without tea?

ASTROFF: I don't want any, Nurse.

MARINA: Maybe you will drink a little vodka?

ASTROFF (*Undecided*): Well, maybe . . .

(MARINA *goes out.*)

ASTROFF (*After a pause*): My side horse is lame for some reason. I noticed it even yesterday when Peter led him to water.

VOINITSKY: Must change his shoe.

ASTROFF: I will have to stop by at the blacksmith's in Rojhdestvenoy. There's no dodging it. (*He goes to the map of Africa and looks at it*) And it must be burning hot in this very Africa—that's something hellish.

VOINITSKY: Yes, very likely.

MARINA (*Returning with a tray on which there is a glass of vodka and a piece of bread*): Drink please. (ASTROFF *drinks the vodka.*)

MARINA: To your health, Son. (*Bowing low*) And why not a bite of bread.

ASTROFF: No, just that . . . And now, the best of everything. (*To* MARINA) Don't see me off, Nurse. Don't.

(*He goes out;* SONIA *follows him with a candle, to light the way;* MARINA *sits down in her armchair.*)

VOINITSKY (*Writing*): "Second of February, vegetable oil twenty pounds . . . sixteenth of February again vegetable oil twenty pounds . . . Buckwheat . . ."

(*A pause. There is the sound of bells.*)

MARINA: He is gone.

(*A pause.*)

SONIA (*Returning and putting the candle on the table*): He is gone . . .

VOINITSKY (*Adding on the abacus and writing down the sum*): That makes . . . fifteen . . . twenty-five . . . (SONIA *sits down and begins writing.*)

MARINA (*Yawning*): A-ah, our sins . . .

(TELEGIN *enters on tiptoes, sits down near the door and quietly tunes the guitar.*)

VOINITSKY (*To* SONIA, *stroking her hair with his hand*): My child, how heavy this is on me. Oh, if you knew how heavy it is!

SONIA: What can we do, we must live! (*A pause*) We shall live, Uncle Vanya. We'll live through a long,

long line of days, endless evenings; we'll bear patiently the trials fate sends us; we'll work for others now and in our old age without ever knowing any rest, and when our hour comes, we'll die humbly and there beside the coffin we'll say that we suffered, that we cried, that we felt bitter, and God will take pity on us, and you and I, Uncle, darling Uncle, shall see life bright, beautiful, fine, we shall be happy and will look back tenderly with a smile on these mis-fortunes we have now—and we shall rest. I have faith, I believe warmly, passionately . . . (*Kneeling before him and putting her head on his hands; in a tired voice*) We shall rest!

(TELEGIN *plays the guitar quietly.*)

SONIA: We shall rest! We shall hear the angels, we shall see the whole sky all diamonds, we shall see how all earthly evil, all our sufferings, are drowned in the mercy that will fill the whole world. And our life will grow peaceful, tender, sweet as a caress. I believe, I do believe . . . (*Wipes away his tears with a handkerchief*) Poor, dear Uncle Vanya, you are crying . . . (*Through her tears*) In your life you haven't known what joy was; but wait, Uncle Vanya, wait. . . . We shall rest. . . . (*Embraces him*) We shall rest! (*The night watchman taps.* TELEGIN *is strumming quietly;* MARIA VASILIEVNA *is writing on the margins of a pamphlet;* MARINA *is knitting on a stocking.*)

SONIA: We shall rest!

The curtain falls slowly.

The Three Sisters

CHARACTERS

PROZOROFF, ANDREI SERGEEVICH.

NATALIA IVANOVNA, *his fiancée, later his wife.*

OLGA
MASHA } *his sisters*
IRINA

KULYGIN, FYODOR ILYICH, *a high-school teacher, husband of Masha.*

VERSHININ, ALEXANDER IGNATIEVICH, *Lieutenant Colonel, a battery Commander.*

TUSENBACH, NIKOLAI LVOVICH, *Baron, Lieutenant.*

SOLYONY, VASILI VASILIEVICH, *Staff Captain.*

TCHEBUTYKIN, IVAN ROMANOVICH, *an Army Doctor.*

FEDOTIK, ALEXEI PETROVICH, *Second Lieutenant.*

RODAY, VLADIMIR KARLOVICH, *Second Lieutenant.*

FERAPONT, *porter of the District Board, an old man.*

ANFISA, *the nurse, an old woman of eighty.*

The action takes place in a provincial town in Russia

window) The weather is beautiful today. I don't know why my heart's so light! This morning I remembered it was my saint's day and suddenly felt happy, and remembered when I was a child and Mother was still alive. And such wonderful thoughts thrilled me; such thoughts!

OLGA: You look radiant today, lovelier than ever. And Masha is lovely too. Andrei would be good-looking if he hadn't got so heavy, it's not becoming to him. And I've grown older, a lot thinner; it must be because I get cross with the girls. Now that I'm free today and am here at home and my head's not aching, I feel younger than yesterday. I'm only twenty-eight. . . . It's all good, all God's will, but it seems to me if I had married and stayed at home the whole day long, it would have been better. (*A pause*) I'd have loved my husband.

TUSENBACH (*To* SOLYONY): You talk such nonsense that I'm tired of listening to you. (*Entering the drawing room*) Forgot to tell you. Today you'll receive a call from our new Battery Commander Vershinin. (*Sitting down at the piano.*)

OLGA: Well, I'll be very glad of it.

IRINA: Is he old?

TUSENBACH: No, not very. Forty or forty-five at most. (*Playing softly*) He seems a nice chap. Not stupid, that's certain. Except that he talks a lot.

IRINA: Is he an interesting person?

TUSENBACH: Yes, quite, only there is a wife, a mother-in-law and two girls. What's more he's married for the second time. He pays calls and says everywhere that he has a wife and two girls. And he'll say so here. The wife is sort of half-crazy, wears long girlish braids, speaks only of lofty matters, philosophizes, and often tries to commit suicide, obviously to plague the husband. I'd have left such a woman long ago myself, but he puts up with her and merely complains.

SOLYONY (*Entering the drawing room from the dining room with* TCHEBUTYKIN): With one hand I can lift only fifty pounds, but with both, one hundred eighty, or even two hundred pounds. From this I conclude that two men are not twice as strong as one, but three times, even more. . . .

TCHEBUTYKIN (*Reading a newspaper as he comes in*): For falling hair . . . two ounces of naphthalene to half a bottle of spirits. . . . Dissolve and use daily. . . . (*Writing it down in his notebook*) Let's write it down! (To SOLYONY) And so, I tell you, a little cork is put in a bottle and through the cork there's a glass tube. . . . Then you take a pinch of plain ordinary alum . . .

IRINA: Ivan Romanovich, dear Ivan Romanovich!

TCHEBUTYKIN: What is it, my child, my sweet?

IRINA: Tell me, why am I so happy today? It's just as if I were going full sail, with the wide blue sky above me and great white birds floating there. Why is that? Why?

TCHEBUTYKIN (*Kissing both her hands tenderly*): My white bird . . .

IRINA: This morning when I awoke and got up and bathed, it seemed all at once that everything in this world was clear to me and I knew how one must live. Dear Ivan Romanovich, I know everything. A man must do something, he must toil by the sweat of his brow, no matter who he is; and all the meaning and aim of his life, his happiness, his ecstasies must lie in this only. How good it is to be a workman who gets up at dawn and breaks stones in the street, or a shepherd, or a schoolmaster who teaches children, or an engineer on a railroad. My God! Next to being a man, it's better to be an ox, it's better to be a common horse, if only you do some work, than be a young woman who wakes up at twelve o'clock, has coffee in bed, and then dresses for two hours. . . . Oh, but that's dreadful! Just as on hot days one may have a craving for water, I have a craving for work. And if I don't get up early and go to work, give me up as a friend, Ivan Romanovich.

TCHEBUTYKIN (*Tenderly*): I'll give you up, I'll give you up—

OLGA: Father trained us to get up at seven. Now Irina wakes at seven and lies there till at least nine thinking. And looking so serious! (*Laughing.*)

IRINA: You are used to thinking of me as a little girl, so it seems strange to you when I look serious. I'm twenty years old.

TUSENBACH: Longing for work. Oh my God, how I understand that! I have never worked in my life. I was born in Petersburg, cold, idle Petersburg, in a family that never knew any sort of work or worry. I remember when I came home from military school the footman pulled off my boots while I fidgeted and my mother looked adoringly at me, and was surprised when the others didn't look at me the same way. I was shielded from work. Though I doubt if they succeeded in shielding me, I doubt it! The time has come, something tremendous is hovering over us all, a vast, healing storm is gathering; it's coming, it's near already, and will soon clear our society of the laziness, the indifference, the prejudice against work, the rotten boredom. I'll work and in another twenty-five or thirty years, every man will be working. Every one!

TCHEBUTYKIN: I shan't work.

TUSENBACH: You don't count.

SOLONY: Twenty-five years from now you won't even be on earth, thank God! In two or three years you'll die of distemper, or I'll forget myself and put a bullet in your forehead, my angel. (*Taking a phial of perfume from his pocket and sprinkling his chest and hands.*)

TCHEBUTYKIN (*Laughing*): And I really never did anything. Since I left the University, I haven't lifted a finger, I've not read a single book even, but just read the newspapers. . . . (*Taking another newspaper out of his pocket*) Listen—I know from the newspapers that there was, let's say, a Dobrolyubov, but what he wrote about I don't know. God only knows. (*A knock is heard on the floor from the floor below*) Listen. . . . They are calling me from downstairs, somebody has come to see me. I'll be back right away. . . . Wait. . . . (*He leaves hurriedly, combing out his beard as he goes.*)

IRINA: He's up to something.

TUSENBACH: Yes. He left with a triumphant face, obviously he will now bring you a present.

IRINA: That's too bad.

OLGA: Yes, it's awful. He always does something childish.

MASHA: By the curved seashore a green oak, a golden chain upon that oak . . . a golden chain upon that oak. (*Getting up and singing softly.*)

OLGA: You are not very merry today, Masha.

(MASHA *sings as she puts on her hat.*)

OLGA: Where to?

MASHA: Home.

IRINA: That's strange. . . .

TUSENBACH: To leave a saint's day party!

MASHA: It's all the same. . . . I'll come this evening. Good-by, my pretty . . . (*Kissing* IRINA) I wish you once again good health and happiness. When father was alive, thirty or forty officers used to come to our birthday parties, it was good and noisy; but nowadays there's only a man and a half, and it's quiet as the desert. . . . I'm going. . . . I've got the blues today, I feel depressed, so don't listen to me. (*Laughing through her tears*) We'll talk later on, so good-by now, my dear, I'll go somewhere or other.

IRINA (*Vexed*): Oh, you are such a . . .

OLGA (*Tearfully*): I understand you, Masha.

SOLYONY: If a man philosophizes, it will be philosophy or sophistry; but if a woman philosophizes, or two women, it will be—like cracking your fingers.

MASHA: What are you trying to say, you terribly dreadful man?

SOLYONY: Nothing. Quick as a flash, the bear made a dash. . . . (*A pause.*)

MASHA (*To* OLGA, *crossly*): Don't howl.

    (ANFISA *enters, and after her,* FERAPONT *with a cake.*)

ANFISA: Here, little Father. Come in, your feet are clean. (*To* IRINA) From the District Board, from Mikhail Ivanovich Protopopov . . . a cake.

IRINA: Thank you. Thank him for me. (*Taking the cake.*)

FERAPONT: How's that?

IRINA (*Louder*): Thank him for me.

OLGA: Nursey, give him some pie. Go on, Ferapont. They'll give you some pie.

FERAPONT: How's that?

ANFISA: Come on, little Father, Ferapont Spiridonich. Come on. . . . (*Goes out with* FERAPONT.)

MASHA: I don't like Protopopov, that Mikhail Potopich or Ivanovich. He should not be invited.

IRINA: I didn't do the inviting.

MASHA: That's fine!

> (TCHEBUTYKIN *enters, behind him an* ORDERLY *with a silver samovar; there is a hum of astonishment and displeasure.*)

OLGA (*Covering her face with her hands*): A samovar! This is terrible. (*Going to the table in the dining room.*)

IRINA: Darling Ivan Romanovich, what are you doing?

TUSENBACH (*Laughing*): I told you so.

MASHA: Ivan Romanovich, you're simply shameless.

TCHEBUTYKIN: My darlings, my good little ones, you are all I have, to me you are everything that's most precious in the world. I'll soon be sixty, I'm an old man, a lonely worthless old man. . . . There is nothing good about me but this love for you, and if it weren't for you I'd long ago have stopped living in this world. . . . (To IRINA) My dear, my little child, I have known you since the day you were born. . . . I carried you in my arms. . . . I loved your dear mother. . . .

IRINA: But why such expensive presents!

TCHEBUTYKIN (*Through his tears, angrily*): Expensive presents! . . . Why, you're completely . . . (To *the* ORDERLY) Carry the samovar in there. . . . (*Mimicking*) Expensive presents . . .

(*The* ORDERLY *carries the samovar into the dining room.*)

ANFISA (*Passing through the drawing room*): My dears, there's a colonel, a stranger. He's already taken off his overcoat, children, and is coming in here. Irinushka, now be a nice, polite girl. (*As she goes out*) And it was time for lunch long ago. . . . Lord have mercy! . . .

TUSENBACH: It must be Vershinin.

(VERSHININ *enters.*)

TUSENBACH: Lieutenant Colonel Vershinin!

VERSHININ (*To* MASHA *and* IRINA): I have the honor to introduce myself: Vershinin. I'm very, very glad that at last I am in your house. How you've grown! Ay! Ay!

IRINA: Please sit down. We are delighted.

VERSHININ (*Gaily*): How glad I am! How glad I am! But you are three sisters. I remember—three girls. Your faces I don't remember now, but your father, Colonel Prozoroff, had three little girls, I remember that perfectly, I saw them with my own eyes. How time does pass! Oh, oh, how time does pass!

TUSENBUCH: Alexander Ignatievich is from Moscow.

IRINA: From Moscow. You are from Moscow?

VERSHININ: Yes, from there. Your father was a battery commander there, and I was an officer in the same brigade. (*To* MASHA) It seems to me now I do remember your face rather.

MASHA: And you I—No!

IRINA: Olya! Olya! (*Calling into the dining room*) Olya! Come here. (OLGA *comes in from the dining room*) Lieutenant Colonel Vershinin, it turns out, is from Moscow.

VERSHININ: You must be Olga Sergeevna, the eldest. . . .
And you Maria. . . . And you Irina—the young-
est. . . .

OLGA: You are from Moscow?

VERSHININ: Yes. I was at school in Moscow and began my
service in Moscow, served there a long time, was finally
assigned a battery here—moved here, as you see. I don't
remember you, as a matter of fact, but only that you
were three sisters. Your father is fresh in my memory; I
can close my eyes now and see him as plain as life. I
used to pay you calls in Moscow. . . .

OLGA: I thought I remembered everybody, and look, all
of a sudden . . .

VERSHININ: My name is Alexander Ignatievich.

IRINA: Alexander Ignatievich, you are from Moscow.
What a surprise!

OLGA: We are going to move there, you know.

IRINA: We think by autumn we'll be there. It's our native
town, we were born there. . . . In Old Basmanny
Street.

　　　(*They both laugh delightedly.*)

MASHA: Unexpectedly we see a fellow countryman.
(*Vivaciously*) Now I remember! Do you remember,
Olya, at our house they used to say, "The lovesick
major." You were a lieutenant then and in love with
someone, and they all teased you for some reason as
the lovesick major.

VERSHININ (*Laughing*): That's right! That's right! The
lovesick major. That was it!

MASHA: But you had only a mustache then. . . . Oh,
how much older you look! (*Tearfully*) How much
older you look!

VERSHININ: Yes, when they called me the lovesick major, I was still young, I was in love. Not so now.

OLGA: But you still haven't a single gray hair. You look older, but you are still not old.

VERSHININ: For all that, I'm in my forty-third year. Is it long since you left Moscow?

IRINA: Eleven years. But why are you crying, Masha, you little fool? (*Through her tears*) I'm starting to cry, too. . . .

MASHA: I'm all right. And in what street did you live?

VERSHININ: In Old Basmanny.

OLGA: And we lived there, too. . . .

VERSHININ: At one time I lived in Nemetzky Street. I used to walk from Nemetzky Street to the Red Barracks. There's a sullen-looking bridge on the way, and under the bridge you hear the water roaring. A lonely man feels sick at heart there. (*A pause*) But here, what a broad, what a superb river! A wonderful river!

OLGA: Yes, except that it's cold. It's cold here and there are mosquitoes. . . .

VERSHININ: How can you! You have such a fine, healthy Russian climate here. Woods, river . . . and birches too. Sweet, modest birches, of all trees I love them best. It's good to live here. And yet, strangely enough, the railway station is thirteen miles away. . . . And nobody knows why that is.

SOLYONY: But I know why it is. (*Everyone looks at him*) Because if the station were right here then 'twere not off there, and if it is off there, then it's not right here. (*An awkward silence.*)

TUSENBACH: You're a joker, Vasili Vasilievich.

OLGA: Now I remember you too. I remember.

VERSHININ: I knew your mother.

TCHEBUTYKIN: She was a lovely woman . . . bless her soul!

IRINA: Mother is buried in Moscow.

OLGA: In the Novo Devichy. . . .

MASHA: Imagine, I'm already beginning to forget her face. Just as we won't be remembered either. They'll forget us.

VERSHININ: Yes. They'll forget us. Such is our fate, it can't be helped. What seems to us serious, significant, highly important—the time will come when it will be forgotten or seem unimportant. (*A pause*) And it's an interesting thing, we can't possibly tell now just what will be considered great, or important, and what pitiful, ridiculous. Didn't the discoveries of Copernicus or, let's say, Columbus, seem at first unnecessary, ridiculous, and some shallow nonsense written by a fool seem to be the truth? And it may be that our present life, to which we are so reconciled, will seem very strange some day, uncomfortable, stupid, not pure enough, perhaps even sinful. . . .

TUSENBACH: Who knows? Perhaps our life will be called superior and remembered with respect. Nowadays there are no tortures, no executions, no invasions, though, for all that, there's so much unhappiness!

SOLYONY (*In a high-pitched voice*): Chick, chick, chick. . . . Don't feed the Baron grain, just let him philosophize.

TUSENBACH: Vasili Vasilievich, I beg you leave me alone. (*Sits at another place*) After all, it's tiresome.

SOLYONY (*In a high-pitched voice*): Chick, chick, chick . . .

TUSENBACH (*To* VERSHININ): The unhappiness we see

now, however, though there is still so much of it even now—bespeaks a certain moral regeneration that has already reached society. . . .

VERSHININ: Yes, yes, of course.

TCHEBUTYKIN: You just said, Baron, that they will call our present life superior; but, all the same, people are small. . . . (*Standing up*) Look how small I am. It would only be to console me if anybody called my life a superior, understandable thing.

(*Behind the scenes a violin plays.*)

MASHA: It's Andrei playing, our brother.

IRINA: He is the learned member of the family. It looks as if he'd be a professor. Father was a military man, but his son chose for himself a learned career.

MASHA: According to Father's wish.

OLGA: Today we teased him to death. It seems he's a bit in love.

IRINA: With a local girl. She'll be with us today, there's every chance of it.

MASHA: Oh, how she dresses! Not merely ugly and out of style but simply pitiful. Some sort of strange, loud, yellowish skirt with a vulgar fringe and a red blouse. And her cheeks are so scrubbed, scrubbed! Andrei isn't in love—I won't admit it, after all he has taste, he's simply teasing us, he's fooling. I heard yesterday that she is marrying Protopopov, the Chairman of the Board. And that's fine—(*At the side door*) Andrei, come here! Darling, just for a minute!

(ANDREI *enters.*)

OLGA: This is my brother, Andrei Sergeevich.

VERSHININ: Vershinin.

ANDREI: Prozoroff. (*He wipes his perspiring face*) You are our new Battery Commander?

OLGA: Can you imagine, Alexander Ignatievich is from Moscow.

ANDREI: Yes? Well, I congratulate you, now my little sisters won't give you any peace.

VERSHININ: I have already had time to tire your sisters out.

IRINA. Look at the frame Andrei gave me today! (*Showing the frame*) He made it himself.

VERSHININ (*Looking at the frame and not knowing what to say*): Yes. . . . A thing . . .

IRINA: And the frame that's over the piano there, he made that, too.

> (ANDREI *waves his hand as if disparagingly and moves away.*)

OLGA: He is not only our learned one, he also plays the violin and he saws various things out of wood. In sum he has a hand for anything. Andrei, don't go away! That's the way he does—he's always leaving us. Come here!

> (MASHA *and* IRINA, *laughing, take him by the arms and lead him back.*)

MASHA: Come! Come!

ANDREI: Let me alone, please.

MASHA: How funny he is! Alexander Ignatievich used to be called the lovesick major and he didn't get a bit angry.

VERSHININ: Not a bit.

MASHA: And I want to call you the lovesick violinist!

IRINA: Or the lovesick professor! . . .

OLGA: He's in love! Andrusha's in love!

IRINA (*Applauding*): Bravo, bravo! *Bis!* Andrushka is in love!

TCHEBUTYKIN (*Comes up behind* ANDREI *and puts both*

arms around his waist): For love alone did Nature put us in this world. (*Laughing. All the while he is holding a newspaper.*)

ANDREI: Well, that's enough, that's enough. . . . (*Wiping his face*) I haven't slept all night and now I'm not myself, as they say. Till four o'clock I read, then lay down, but nothing happened. I thought of this and of that, and then, of course, at the crack of dawn here the sun swarms into my bedroom. During the summer while I am here, I want to translate a certain book from English.

VERSHININ: And do you read English?

ANDREI: Yes. Our father—bless his soul!—loaded us down with education. It's ridiculous and stupid, but all the same I must admit that in a year after his death, I began to fill out and get fat like this, as if my body were freed from the load. Thanks to Father, my sisters and I know the French, German and English languages and Irina knows Italian too. But at what a cost!

MASHA: In this town, to know three languages is an unnecessary luxury. It isn't even a luxury, it's a sort of unnecessary appendage like a sixth finger. We know a lot that's useless.

VERSHININ: There we have it! (*Laughing*) You know a lot that is useless! It seems to me there's not and can't be a town so boring and dull that a clever, educated person would be unnecessary in it. Let's suppose that among the hundred thousand inhabitants of this town, which evidently is backward and crude, there are only three such people as you. It is obvious that you cannot triumph over the dark masses that surround you; in the course of your life you'll have to yield little by little and be lost in the crowd of a hundred thousand; life will stifle you, but just the same you'll still be there and not without influence; your kind, after you, will begin to appear, six, perhaps, then twelve, and so on, until finally your kind will get to be the majority. After two or three hundred years, life on earth will be unimaginably beautiful, wonderful. Man needs such a life, and if it is not here yet, he must anticipate it, wait, dream of it, be prepared for it, for it he must see and know more than his grandfather and father saw and knew. (*Laughing*) And you complain of knowing a lot that's useless.

MASHA (*Taking off her hat*): I am staying for lunch.

IRINA (*With a sigh*): Really all that should be written down. . . .

(ANDREI *is not to be seen, he has gone out unobserved.*)

TUSENBACH: After many years, you say, life on earth will be beautiful, wonderful. That's true. But to share it now, even from afar, we must prepare ourselves for it, must be doing something. . . .

VERSHININ (*Getting up*): Yes. How many flowers you have! (*Looking around*) And a beautiful apartment. I envy you! And all my life I have hung around little apartments with two chairs, a sofa and a stove that always smokes. In my life I have lacked just such flowers . . . (*Rubbing his hands*) Well, nothing can be done about it!

TUSENBACH: Yes, one must work. You probably think the German is getting sentimental. But on my word of honor, I am Russian and don't even speak German, My father was Orthodox. . . .

(*A pause.*)

VERSHININ (*Walking about the stage*): I often think: what might happen if we began life anew, and did it consciously? If one life, already lived through, had been, as it were the first draft, the other, the final copy! Then each of us, I think, would try above all things not to repeat himself, at least he would create for himself a different setting for his life, would arrange for himself an apartment such as this, with flowers, with a flood of light. . . . I have a wife and two girls; and, at that, the wife is a delicate lady, and so forth and so on, well, and if I were to begin life anew, I would never marry. . . . No, no!

(KULYGIN *enters, in a schoolteacher's uniform.*)

KULYGIN (*Going up to* IRINA): My dear sister, allow me to congratulate you on your saint's day and wish you sincerely, from my heart, health and all that could be wished for a girl of your age. And then to present this book to you as a gift. (*Giving her the book*) A history of our high school covering fifty years, written by me. A trifle of a book, written out of nothing else to do, but all the same you must read it. Good morning, gentlemen! (*To* VERSHININ) Kulygin, teacher in the local high school, County Councilor. (*To* IRINA) In this book you will find a list of all the graduates of our high school for the last fifty years. *Feci, quod potui, faciant meliora potentes.* (*He kisses* MASHA.)

IRINA: But you've already given me a book like that at Easter.

KULYGIN (*Laughing*): It couldn't be! In that case give it back, or better still, give it to the Colonel. Take it,

Colonel. Read it sometime when you are bored.

VERSHININ: Thank you. (*He is about to leave*) I am extremely glad I made your acquaintance. . . .

OLGA: You are leaving? No, no!

IRINA: Stay and lunch with us. Please.

OLGA: I beg you!

VERSHININ (*Bowing*): It seems I've stumbled on to a saint's day party. Forgive me, I didn't know, didn't congratulate you. (*Goes with* OLGA *to the dining room.*)

KULYGIN: Today is Sunday, gentlemen, a day of rest, let us rest, let us be gay, each one according to his age and position. The rugs should be taken up for the summer and stored till winter. . . . Persian powder or naphthalene. . . . The Romans were healthy because they knew how to work, knew how to rest, they had *mens sana in corpore sano.* Their life flowed on according to fixed forms. Our director says: the principal thing in every life is its form. . . . That which loses its form ends itself—and it's the same with our everyday existence. (*Takes* MASHA *by the waist, laughing*) Masha loves me. My wife loves me. And the window curtains, too, together with the rugs. . . . Today, I am gay, in a splendid mood. Masha, at four o'clock today we are to be at the director's. There's a walk being arranged for the teachers and their families.

MASHA: I am not going.

KULYGIN (*Aggrieved*): Dear Masha, why?

MASHA: Later on about that. . . . (*Angrily*) Oh, very well, I'll go, but just leave me alone, please. . . . (*Walks away.*)

KULYGIN: And then we'll spend the evening at the director's. In spite of his sickly state of health, this man tries above all else to be sociable. A superior, bright personality. A magnificent man. Yesterday, after the teacher's conference, he says to me: "I am tired, Fyodor Ilyich: I am tired!" (*Looks at the clock on the wall, then at his watch*) Your clock is seven minutes fast. Yes, he says, I am tired!

(*Behind the scene a violin is playing.*)

OLGA: Ladies and gentlemen, come to lunch, please! There's a meat-pie.

KULYGIN: Ah, my dear Olga, my dear! Yesterday, I worked from early morning till eleven o'clock in the evening, got tired and today I feel happy. (*Goes into the dining room and up to the table.*)

TCHEBUTYKIN (*Puts the newspaper in his pocket, combs his beard*): A meat-pie? Splendid!

MASHA (*To* TCHEBUTYKIN, *sternly*): Only, look out: nothing to drink today. Do you hear? Drinking's bad for you.

TCHEBUTYKIN: Oh, go on! I'm past all that. It is two years I've not been on a drunk. (*Impatiently*) Ah, old girl, isn't it all the same?

MASHA: All the same, don't you dare drink. Don't you dare. (*Angrily, but so that her husband doesn't hear*) The Devil take it, to be bored again all evening long at the director's.

TUSENBACH: I wouldn't go if I were in your place. It's very simple.

TCHEBUTYKIN: Don't go, dearie.

MASHA: Yes, don't go. . . . This curst, unbearable life . . . (*Going to the dining room.*)

TCHEBUTYKIN (*Going with her*): Now!

SOLYONY (*Going to the dining room*): Chick, chick, chick. . . .

TUSENBACH: That's enough, Vasili Vasilievich. Drop it!

SOLYONY: Chick, chick, chick. . . .

KULYGIN (*Gaily*): Your health, Colonel! I am a pedagogue and here in this house I'm one of the family, Masha's husband. . . . She is kind, very kind. . . .

VERSHININ: I'll have some of that dark vodka. . . . (*Drinking*) Your health! (*To* OLGA) I feel so good in your house! . . .

> (*In the drawing room only* IRINA *and* TUSENBACH *are left.*)

IRINA: Masha is in a bad humor today. She got married at eighteen, when he seemed to her the most intelligent of men. But now it's not the same. He's the kindest but not the most intelligent.

OLGA (*Impatiently*): Andrei, do come, after all!

ANDREI (*Behind the scenes*): This minute. (*Enters and goes to the table.*)

TUSENBACH: What are you thinking about?

IRINA: This: I dislike and I'm afraid of that Solyony of yours. He talks nothing but nonsense. . . .

TUSENBACH: He is a strange person. I am both sorry for him and annoyed, but more sorry. It seems to me he's shy. . . . When the two of us are alone, he's very clever and gentle sometimes; but in company he is a crude fellow, a bully. Don't go away, let them get settled at the table. Let me be near you awhile. What are you thinking about? (*A pause*) You are twenty, I am not yet thirty. How many years there are left for us ahead, a long, long row of days, full of my love for you. . . .

IRINA: Nikolai Lvovich, don't talk to me of love.

TUSENBACH (*Not listening*): I have a passionate thirst for life, struggle, work, and that thirst is mingled in my soul with love for you, Irina. And it's as though it were by some design that you are beautiful and life seems beautiful to me because of you. What are you thinking about?

IRINA: You say life is beautiful. Yes, but what if it only seems so! With us three sisters, life hasn't yet been beautiful, it has stifled us as weeds do grass. . . . I'm letting my tears fall. I shouldn't do that. . . . (*Quickly wiping her face, smiling*) We must do something, must work. That's why we are not happy and look at life so gloomily—we don't know anything about working. We come of people who despised work.

    (NATALIA IVANOVNA *enters; she has a pink dress with a green belt.*)

NATASHA: Look, they are already sitting down to lunch. . . . I'm late. . . . (*She steals a glance at herself in the mirror and tidies herself up*) My hair seems to be all right. . . . (*Seeing* IRINA) Dear Irina Sergeevna, I congratulate you! (*Kissing her vigorously and long*) You have lots of guests, I really feel shy. . . . How do you do, Baron!

OLGA (*Entering the living room*): Well, and here is Natalia Ivanovna. Good day, my dear. (*They kiss.*)

NATASHA: Congratulations on the saint's day. You have so much company, I feel awfully that . . .

OLGA: Never mind, it's just the family. (*In an undertone, alarmed*) You have on a green belt! My dear, that's not right!

NATASHA: Is it a sign of something?

OLGA: No, it just doesn't match . . . and somehow it looks odd—

NATASHA (*In a tearful voice*): Yes? But it's not really green, it's more of a neutral color. (*Follows* OLGA *into the dining room.*)

(*In the dining room they are sitting down to lunch; there is not a soul in the living room.*)

KULYGIN: I wish you, Irina, a good fiancé! It's time you married.

TCHEBUTYKIN: Natalia Ivanovna, I wish you a fiancé too.

KULYGIN: Natalia Ivanovna already has a fiancé.

MASHA (*Strikes her plate with her fork*): I'll take a little drink! What the . . . life is all roses, I'll risk it. . . .

KULYGIN: Your conduct gets C minus.

VERSHININ: And the liqueur tastes good. What's it made of?

SOLYONY: Cockroaches.

IRINA (*In a tearful voice*): Phew! How disgusting! . . .

OLGA: For supper there will be roast turkey and apple pie. Thank the Lord, I'll be at home all day, and in the evening—at home. . . . Everybody must come this evening. . . .

VERSHININ: Allow me, too, to come this evening!

IRINA: Please do.

NATASHA: They are very informal.

TCHEBUTYKIN: For love alone did Nature put us in this world. (*Laughing.*)

ANDREI (*Angrily*): Stop it, everybody! Aren't you tired of it?

(FEDOTIK *and* RODAY *enter with a big basket of flowers.*)

FEDOTIK: But say, they are already lunching.

RODAY (*Talking loud and affectedly*): Lunching? Yes, already lunching. . . .

FEDOTIK: Wait a minute! (*Taking a snapshot*) One! Wait, just one more. . . . (*Taking another snapshot*) Two! Now, ready! (*They pick up the basket and go to the dining room, where they are greeted noisily.*)

RODAY (*In a loud voice*): Congratulations, I wish you everything, everything! The weather today is charming, perfectly magnificent. Today, all morning long, I was walking with the high school boys. I teach gymnastics at the high school. . . .

FEDOTIK: You may move, Irina Sergeevna, you may! (*Taking a snapshot*) You look well today. (*Getting a top out of his pocket*) By the way, see this top. . . . It has an amazing sound. . . .

IRINA: How delightful!

MASHA: By the curved seashore a green oak, a golden chain upon that oak. . . . A golden chain upon that oak. . . . (*Tearfully*) Now, why do I say that? This phrase has stuck in my mind ever since morning. . . .

KULYGIN: Thirteen at the table!

RODAY (*In a loud voice*): Could it really be, ladies and gentlemen, that you attach importance to these superstitions?

  (*Laughing.*)

KULYGIN: Thirteen at the table shows that there are lovers here. It's not you, Ivan Romanovich by any chance? (*Laughter.*)

TCHEBUTYKIN: I am an old sinner, but why Natalia Ivanovna should be embarrassed I simply can't understand.

  (*Loud laughter; NATASHA runs out from the dining*

room into the living room, ANDREI *following her.*)

ANDREI: Come on, don't pay any attention to them! Wait. . . . Stop. . . . I beg you. . . .

NATASHA: I'm ashamed. . . . I don't know what it's all about and they are making fun of me. It was bad manners for me to leave the table just now, but I can't . . . I can't . . . (*Covers her face with her hands.*)

ANDREI: My dear, I beg you, I entreat you, don't be upset. I assure you they are only joking, they have kind hearts. My darling, my beautiful, they all are gentle, kind-hearted people and they love me and you. Come over here to the window, they can't see us here. . . .

(*He glances around.*)

NATASHA: I am so unused to being in society! . . .

ANDREI: Ah, youth, wonderful, beautiful youth! My dear, my darling, don't be so upset! . . . Believe me, believe . . . I feel so happy, my soul is full of love, ecstasy. . . . Oh, they can't see us! They can't see! Why, why I fell in love with you; when I fell in love. My dear, darling, pure one, be my wife! I love you, love . . . as nobody ever. . . . (*A kiss.*)

(*The* TWO OFFICERS *enter and seeing the pair kissing, stop in astonishment.*)

Curtain

ACT TWO

The setting is the same as in Act One. It is eight o'clock in the evening. Offstage faintly we hear an accordion, playing in the street. There are no lights.

NATALIA IVANOVNA *enters in a dressing gown, with a candle; she comes in and stops at the door that leads into* ANDREI'S *room.*

NATASHA: Andrusha, what are you doing? Reading? It's nothing, I just . . . (*Goes and opens another door and after looking in, closes it*) If there's a light . . .

ANDREI (*Enters with a book in his hand*): You what, Natasha?

NATASHA: Looking to see if there's a light. . . . Now it's Carnival week the servants are beside themselves, we have to look and look, so that nothing goes wrong. Last night at midnight, I passed through the dining room, and a candle was burning there. Who lighted it I couldn't find out. (*Putting down her candle*) What time is it?

ANDREI (*Looking at his watch*): It's a quarter past eight.

NATASHA: And Olga and Irina not in yet. They haven't come in. Always working, poor girls! Olga at the Teachers' Council, Irina at the telegraph office. . . . (*Sighing*) This morning I say to your sister: "Spare yourself, I say, Irina darling." But she won't listen. Quarter past eight, you say? I am anxious for fear, our Bobik is not at all well. Why is he so cold? Yesterday he had fever, and today he is cold all over. . . . I am so anxious!

ANDREI: It's nothing, Natasha. The boy is all right.

NATASHA: Still it's better to put him on a diet. I'm anxious. And tonight, around ten o'clock, they said, the maskers will be here, it would be better if they didn't come, Andrusha.

ANDREI: Really, I don't know. But they were invited.

NATASHA: This morning the little fellow wakes up and looks at me and all at once he smiles; so he knew me. "Bobik," I say, "good morning! Good morning, dear!" And he laughs. Children understand, they understand perfectly. So, Andrusha, I'll tell them not to let the maskers in.

ANDREI (*Indecisively*): But that's for my sisters to say, they are mistresses here.

NATASHA: And they too, I'll tell them. They are kind. . . . (*Going*) For supper I ordered some buttermilk. The doctor says, you're to have nothing but buttermilk or you'll never get any thinner. (*Stopping*) Bobik is cold. I'm afraid he may be cold in that room of his. We ought to—at least till warm weather comes —put him in a different room. For instance, Irina's room is just right for a child; it's dry and sunny too all day long. I must tell her that. For a while at least she could be in the same room with Olga. . . . She's not at home during the day anyhow, she only spends the night. . . . (*A pause*) Andrushanchik, why don't you say something?

ANDREI: I was just thinking— Besides there's nothing to talk about. . . .

NATASHA: Yes. . . . There's something I wanted to tell you. . . . Oh, yes. Ferapont has just come from the District Board, he's asking for you.

ANDREI (*Yawning*): Call him in.

(NATASHA *goes out.* ANDREI, *bending over to the candle, which she has forgotten to take along, reads his book.* FERAPONT *enters; he is in a shabby old coat, with the collar turned up, a scarf over his ears.*)

ANDREI: Good evening, my good soul. What have you got to say?

FERAPONT: The Chairman has sent you a book and a paper of some kind. Here. . . . (*He gives the book and an envelope to* ANDREI.)

ANDREI: Thanks. Good! But why did you come so late? It's after eight now?

FERAPONT: How's that?

ANDREI (*Louder*): I say you came late, it's now after eight.

FERAPONT: Exactly. I got here when it was still light, but they all wouldn't let me in. The master, they said, is busy. Well, it's like this. You're busy, very busy. I have nowhere to hurry to. (*Thinking that* ANDREI *is asking him something*) How's that?

ANDREI: Nothing. (*Examining the book*) Tomorrow is Friday, we haven't any school, but all the same I'll come, just to be doing something. It's tiresome at home. . . . (*A pause*) Dear Grandpa, how strangely it changes, how life deceives one! Today, out of boredom, out of nothing else to do, I picked up this book here—old university lectures, and I felt like laughing. . . . My God! I'm the secretary of the District Board, that board where Protopopov presides, I am the secretary and the very most I can hope for—is to be a member of the District Board! Me, a member of the local district board, I who dream every night that I'm a professor in Moscow University, a famous scholar whom this Russian land is proud of!

FERAPONT: I wouldn't know. Don't hear well. . . .

ANDREI: If you could hear well, I might not have talked to you. I must talk to somebody, but my wife doesn't understand me, and I am afraid of my sisters somehow, I'm afraid they will laugh at me, make me ashamed. . . . I don't drink, don't like bars; but with what pleasure I could be sitting right now in Moscow at Testoff's or in the Bolshoy Moscoffsky, my dear fellow.

FERAPONT: And in Moscow, so a contractor was saying the other day at the District Board, some merchants were eating bliny; one of them, it seems, ate forty blinies and died. It was either forty or fifty. I wouldn't remember.

ANDREI: You sit in Moscow in a huge room at a restaurant, you don't know anybody, and nobody knows you, but at the same time you don't feel like a stranger. . . . And here you know everybody and everybody knows you, but you are a stranger, a stranger. . . . A stranger and lonely.

FERAPONT: How's that? (*A pause*) And the same contractor was saying—maybe he was just lying—that a rope is stretched all the way across Moscow.

ANDREI: What for?

FERAPONT: I wouldn't know. The contractor said so.

ANDREI: Fiddlesticks. (*Reading*) Were you ever in Moscow?

FERAPONT (*After a pause*): Never was. God didn't grant me that. (*A pause*) Shall I go?

ANDREI: You may go. Good-by. (FERAPONT *goes out*) Good-by. (*Reading*) Come tomorrow morning and get these papers. . . . Go. . . . (*A pause*) He's gone. (*A bell rings*) Yes, it's a business— (*Stretching and going slowly into his room.*)

(*Behind the scenes a nurse is singing, rocking a child.* MASHA *and* VERSHININ *enter conversing. In the dining room one of the maids is lighting a lamp and the candles.*)

MASHA: I don't know. (*A pause*) I don't know. Of course habit means a lot. For example, after Father's death it took us a long time to get used to not having orderlies in the house. But even apart from habit, I think, common justice makes me say it—in other places it may not be so, but in our town the most decent, the most honorable and well-brought-up people —are the military.

VERSHININ: I'm thirsty. I'd drink some tea.

MASHA (*Glancing at the clock*): It will soon be here. They married me off when I was eighteen years old, and I was afraid of my husband because he was a teacher, and that was when I had barely finished my courses. He seemed to me terribly learned then, clever, and important. But now it's not the same, unfortunately.

VERSHININ: So—yes.

MASHA: I am not talking about my husband. I'm used to him, but among the civilians generally there are so many people who are crude and unfriendly and haven't any manners. Rudeness upsets me and offends me, I suffer when I see that a man is not fine enough, gentle enough, polite. When I happen to be among the teachers, my husband's colleagues, I'm simply miserable.

VERSHININ: Yes. . . . But it seems to me it's all the same whether they are civilian or military, they are equally uninteresting, at any rate in this town they are. It's all the same! If you listen to one of the local intelligentsia—civilian or military—what you hear is that he's worn out with his wife, worn out with his home, worn out with his estate, worn out with his horses. . . . A Russian is quite supremely given to lofty ways in thought, but will you tell me why it is that in life he strikes so low? Why?

MASHA: Why?

VERSHININ: Why is he worn out with his children, worn out with his wife? And why are the wife and the children worn out with him?

MASHA: You are not in a very good humor today.

VERSHININ: Perhaps. I haven't had any dinner today, nothing to eat since morning. One of my daughters is not very well, and when my girls are ailing, I am seized with anxiety, and my conscience torments me for their having such a mother. Oh, if you'd seen her today! What a miserable wretch! We began to quarrel at seven o'clock in the morning, and at nine I slammed the door and went out. (*A pause*) I never speak of it, and strangely enough I complain just to you. (*Kissing her hand*) Don't be angry with me. But for you alone, I'd not have anybody—nobody. . . .

>   (*A pause.*)

MASHA: What a noise in the stove! At home, just before Father died, it was howling in the chimney. There, just like that!

VERSHININ: Are you superstitious?

MASHA: Yes.

VERSHININ: That's strange. (*Kissing her hand*) You are a magnificent, wonderful woman. Magnificent, wonderful! It is dark here, but I see the sparkle of your eyes.

MASHA (*Moving to another chair*): It's lighter here.

VERSHININ: I love, love, love. . . . Love your eyes, your gestures, I see them in my dreams. . . . Magnificent, wonderful woman!

MASHA (*Laughing quietly*): When you talk to me like that, for some reason or other, I laugh, though I'm frightened. Don't do it again, I beg you. . . . (*In a low voice*) But talk, though, it's all the same to me. (*Covering her face with her hands*) It's all the same to me. They're coming here—talk about something else. . . .

> (IRINA *and* TUSENBACH *enter from the dining room.*)

TUSENBACH: I have a triple name. I am called Tusen-bach—Krone—Altschauer—but I am Russian, Ortho-dox, like you. There's very little German left in me, perhaps only this patience and stubbornness that I bore you with. I see you home every evening.

IRINA: I'm so tired!

TUSENBACH: And every day I'll come to the telegraph office and see you home, I'll do that for ten, twenty, years, for as long as you don't drive me away. . . . (*Seeing* MASHA *and* VERSHININ, *delightedly*) It's you? Good evening.

IRINA: Here I am home at last. (*To* MASHA) Just now a lady came, telegraphed her brother in Saratov that her son died today, and couldn't remember the address at all. So she sent it without the address, simply to Sara-tov. She was crying. And I was rude to her for no rea-son whatever. "I haven't got time," I said. 'Twas so silly! Are the maskers coming tonight?

MASHA: Yes.

IRINA (*She sits down in an armchair*): I must rest. I'm tired.

TUSENBACH (*Smiling*): When you come back from your office, you seem so young, unhappy. . . .
(*A pause.*)

IRINA: I'm tired. No, I don't like the telegraphing, I don't like it.

MASHA: You are thinner. . . . (*She begins to whistle*) And look younger and your face begins to look like a little boy's.

TUSENBACH: That's from her hair.

IRINA: I must try and find another position, this one is not for me. What I wanted so, what I dreamed of, that's exactly what's not there. Work without poetry, without thoughts. . . . (*A knock on the floor*) The doctor is knocking. . . . (*To* TUSENBACH) Knock back, dear. . . . I can't. . . . I'm tired. . . .
(TUSENBACH *knocks on the floor.*)

IRINA: He'll come this minute. Something or other will have to be done about it. The doctor and our Andrei were at the club yesterday and lost again. They say Andrei lost two hundred roubles.

MASHA (*Indifferently*): So what's there to do now?

IRINA: Two weeks ago he lost, in December he lost. If he'd lose everything soon, perhaps we'd go away from this town. Oh my Lord God, I dream of Moscow every night, I am like someone completely possessed. (*Laughing*) We are moving there in June and from now to June leaves still . . . February, March, April, May. . . . Almost half a year!

MASHA: The only thing is Natasha mustn't some way or other hear of his losses.

IRINA: It's all one to her, I imagine.
(TCHEBUTYKIN, *who has just got out of bed—he has been resting after dinner—enters the dining room*

put it? It seems to me everything on earth must change little by little and is already changing before our very eyes. In two or three hundred, eventually a thousand, years—it's not a matter of time—a new, happy life will come. We won't share in that life of course, but we are living for it now, working, well— suffering; we are creating it—and in that alone lies the purpose of our being and, if you like, our happiness.

(MASHA *laughs softly.*)

TUSENBACH: What are you laughing at?

MASHA: I don't know. All day today I've been laughing, ever since morning.

VERSHININ: I was graduated from the same school you were, but was not at the academy; I read a great deal, but don't know how to choose books, and read, perhaps, not at all what I should; and meanwhile the longer I live the more I want to know. My hair is turning gray, I'm almost an old man now, but I know very little, oh, how very little! And yet it does seem to me that what's most important and real I do know, know solidly. And I'd so like to prove to you that there's no happiness, there should not be, and there won't be, for us. . . . We should only work and work, and happiness—that's the lot of our remote descendants. (*A pause*) Not I, but at least the descendants of my descendants.

(FEDOTIK *and* RODAY *appear in the dining room; they sit down and sing softly, strumming a guitar.*)

TUSENBACH: According to you, we are not even to dream of happiness! But what if I'm happy?

VERSHININ: No.

combing his beard, then sits down at the table an
takes a newspaper from his pocket.)

MASHA: There he comes. . . . Has he paid anything or
his apartment?

IRINA (*Laughing*): No. Not a kopeck for eight months.
He's forgotten it evidently.

MASHA (*Laughing*): How importantly he sits!
(*Everybody laughs; a pause.*)

IRINA: Why are you so quiet, Alexander Ignatievich?

VERSHININ: I don't know. What I'd like is some tea.
Half my life for a glass of tea! I've eaten nothing
since morning. . . .

TCHEBUTYKIN: Irina Sergeevna!

IRINA: What do you want?

TCHEBUTYKIN: Please come here. *Venez ici!* (IRINA
goes and sits down at the table) I can't do without
you.
(IRINA *lays out the cards for patience.*)

VERSHININ: Well? If they are not giving us any tea, let's
at least philosophize.

TUSENBACH: Yes, let's. What about?

VERSHININ: What about? Let's dream . . . for example,
of the life that will come after us in two or three hundred years.

TUSENBACH: Well? After us they will fly in balloons,
the style of coats will change, they will discover the
sixth sense perhaps, and develop it; but life will remain quite the same, a difficult life, mysterious and
happy. And after a thousand years, man will be sighing the same: "Ah, how hard it is to live!" and meanwhile, exactly the same as now, he will be afraid of
death and not want to die.

VERSHININ (*After a moment's thought*): How shall 1

TUSENBACH (*Throwing up his hands and laughing*):
Obviously we don't understand each other. Well, how
can I convince you?

(MASHA *laughs softly.*)

TUSENBACH (*Holding up a finger to her*): Laugh! (*To*
VERSHININ) Not only in two or three hundred but in
a million years, even, life will be just the same as it
was; it doesn't change, it stays constant, following its
own laws, which are none of our affair, or which, at
least you will never know. Birds of passage, cranes,
for example, fly and fly, and no matter what thoughts,
great or small, stray through their heads, they will fly
just the same and not know why and where. They fly
and will fly, no matter what philosophers spring up
among them; and they may philosophize as much as
they like so long as they fly. . . .

MASHA: Just the same, has it meaning?

TUSENBACH: Meaning. . . . Look, it's snowing. What
meaning has that?

(*A pause.*)

MASHA: It seems to me a man must be a believer or
must seek some belief, otherwise his life is empty,
empty. . . . To live and not know why the cranes fly,
why children are born, why there are stars in the sky.
. . . Either he knows what he's living for, or it's all
nonsense, waste.

VERSHININ: Yet it's a shame youth is gone. . . .

MASHA: Gogol says: It is boring to live in this world,
gentlemen.

TUSENBACH: And I say: it is difficult to argue with you,
gentlemen! Why you completely. . . .

TCHEBUTYKIN (*Reading a newspaper*): Balzac was
married in Berdichev. (IRINA *sings softly*) Really I'll

put that in my book. (*Writing*) Balzac was married in Berdichev. (*Reading his newspaper.*)

IRINA (*As she lays out cards for patience, musing*): Balzac was married in Berdichev.

TUSENBACH: The die is cast. You know, Maria Sergeevna, I have tendered my resignation.

MASHA: So I heard. And I don't see anything good about that. I don't like civilians.

TUSENBACH: Just the same . . . (*Getting up*) I'm not handsome, what sort of military man am I? Well, well, but all the same, however. . . . I shall work. For just one day in my life, work so that I come home in the evening, drop exhausted into bed and fall asleep right off. (*Going into the dining room*) Workmen must sleep soundly!

FEDOTIK (*To* IRINA): I bought you some crayons on Moscoffsky Street, at Pyjokoff's, and this penknife.

IRINA: You are used to treating me as if I were little, but I'm grown up now. . . . (*She takes the crayons and the penknife, gaily*) How delightful!

FEDOTIK: And I bought a knife for myself. . . . Look here . . . a blade, and another blade, a third, this to pick the ears, these small scissors, this to clean the nails. . . .

RODAY (*Talking very loud*): Doctor, what's your age?

TCHEBUTYKIN: Me? Thirty-two.

(*Laughter.*)

FEDOTIK: I'll now show you another game of patience. . . . (*Laying out cards for patience.*)

(*The samovar is brought:* ANFISA *is at the samovar; a little later* NATASHA *also comes in and hovers near the table;* SOLONY *enters and after greetings, sits down at the table.*)

VERSHININ: But what a wind!

MASHA: Yes. I'm tired of winter. I've already forgotten what summer is like.

IRINA: It's coming out right, the patience, I see. We shall be in Moscow.

FEDOTIK: No, it's not coming out right. Look, the eight falls on the two of spades. (*Laughing*) So you will not be in Moscow.

TCHEBUTYKIN (*Reading his newspaper*): Tsitsikar. Smallpox is raging here.

ANFISA (*Approaching* MASHA): Masha, have some tea, little one. (*To* VERSHININ) If you please, Your Excellency. . . . Excuse me, dear sir, your name, your family name, I've forgotten. . . .

MASHA: Bring it here, Nurse. I'm not going there.

IRINA: Nurse!

ANFISA: I'm coming!

NATASHA (*To* SOLYONY): Bobik understands beautifully. "Good morning," I say, "Bobik. Good morning, dear!" He gave me a special look somehow. You think I'm only a mother talking, but no, no, I assure you! That's an unusual child.

SOLYONY: If this child were mine, I would have fried him in a skillet and eaten him. (*He goes with his glass into the living room and sits down in the corner.*)

NATASHA (*Covering her face with her hands*): Rude, ill-bred man!

MASHA: Happy is he who does not notice whether it's summer now or winter. If I were in Moscow, I think I should scorn the weather. . . .

VERSHININ: The other day I read the diary of a certain French Minister, written in prison. The Minister was convicted of fraud. With what rapture and delight, he mentions the birds he saw through the prison window and had never noticed before when he was a Minister. And now, of course, that he's released, it's the same as it was before, he doesn't notice the birds. Just as you won't notice Moscow when you live there. Happiness we have not and it does not exist, we only long for it.

TUSENBACH (*Taking a box from the table*): But where's the candy?

IRINA: Solyony ate it all.

TUSENBACH: All of it?

ANFISA (*Serving tea*): A letter for you, dear sir.

VERSHININ: For me? (*Taking the letter*) From my daughter. (*Reading*) Yes, of course. . . . Forgive me, Maria Sergeevna, I'll just slip out. Not any tea for me— (*Getting up very much disturbed*) These eternal messes. . . .

MASHA: What is it? Not a secret?

VERSHININ (*In a low voice*): The wife has taken poison again. Got to go. I'll slip out, won't be seen. Terribly unpleasant, all this. (*Kissing* MASHA's *hand*) My dear, kind, good woman. . . . I'll slip out of here quietly. . . . (*He goes out.*)

ANFISA: Where is he going now? And I have poured his tea. . . . Such a . . .

MASHA (*Losing her temper*): Let it be! Plaguing us around here, there's no rest from you. . . . (*Going to the table with her cup*) I am tired of you, old woman!

ANFISA: Why are you offended? Darling!

ANDREI'S VOICE: Anfisa!

ANFISA (*Mocking him*): Anfisa! Sitting there. . . . (*She goes out.*)

MASHA (*In the dining room at the table, angrily*): Do let me sit down! (*Musses up the cards on the table*) Lounging here with the cards. Drink your tea!

IRINA: You are spiteful, Masha.

MASHA· If I'm spiteful, don't talk to me. Don't touch me!

TCHEBUTYKIN (*Laughing*): Don't touch her, don't touch. . . .

MASHA: You are sixty years old, and you are like a little boy, always prattling the devil knows what.

NATASHA (*Sighing*): Dear Masha, why use such expressions in your conversation? With your beautiful looks you'd be, I'll tell you candidly, simply charming in a decent, well-bred society, if it weren't for these words of yours. *Je vous prie, pardonnez-moi, Marie, mais vous avez des manières un peu grossières.*

TUSENBACH (*Suppressing a laugh*): Give me. . . . Give me. . . . Seems there's some cognac.

NATASHA: *Il paraît que mon Bobik déjà ne dort pas,* he's waked up. He doesn't seem to me very well today. I'm going to him, excuse me. . . . (*She goes out.*)

IRINA: And where's Alexander Ignatievich gone?

MASHA: Home. There's something extraordinary the matter with his wife again.

TUSENBACH (*Going to* SOLYONY, *with a decanter of cognac*): You sit by yourself all the time, you are thinking of something—and there's no grasping what it is. Well, let's make peace. Let's drink some cognac. (*Drinking*) I'll have to play the piano all night to-night probably, play all kinds of trash. . . . Come what may!

SOLYONY: Why make peace? I have not quarreled with you.

TUSENBACH: You always give me a sort of feeling that something has happened between us. You are a strange character, we must admit.

SOLYONY (*Declaiming*): I am strange, who isn't strange! Don't be angry, Aleko!

TUSENBACH: But why this Aleko. . . .
     (*A pause.*)

SOLYONY: When I am alone with someone I'm all right, I am like everybody else, but in company I am gloomy, shy and . . . talk all kinds of rot. Nevertheless, I am more honest and nobler than many, many others are. And I can prove it.

TUSENBACH: I often get sore at you, you are forever plaguing me when we are in company, but just the same you attract me somehow. Come what may, I'll get drunk today. Let's drink!

SOLYONY: Let's do. (*Drinking*) I've never had anything against you, Baron. But I have the disposition of Lermontov. (*In a low voice*) I even resemble Lermontov a little. . . . So they say. . . . (*Getting a bottle of perfume out of his pocket and pouring some of it over his hands.*)

TUSENBACH: I am sending in my resignation. *Basta!* For five years I kept pondering it and finally decided. I'm going to work.

SOLYONY (*Declaiming*): Don't be angry, Aleko. . . . Forget, forget those dreams of yours. . . .
     (*While they are talking,* ANDREI *comes in quietly with a book and sits down near a candle.*)

TUSENBACH: I'm going to work.

TCHEBUTYKIN (*Going into the living room with* IRINA):

And the refreshments were real Caucasian too: onion soup, and for the roast—tchehartma, meat.

SOLYONY: Tcheremsha is not meat at all, but a plant something like our onion.

TCHEBUTYKIN: No, my angel . . . Tchehartma is not onion but a mutton roast.

SOLYONY: And I tell you, tcheremsha—onion.

TCHEBUTYKIN: And I tell you, tchehartma—mutton.

SOLYONY: And I tell you, tcheremsha—onion.

TCHEBUTYKIN: But why should I argue with you, you never were in the Caucasus, and never ate tchehartma.

SOLYONY: I haven't eaten it because I can't bear it. Tcheremsha smells exactly like garlic.

ANDREI (*Imploringly*): That's enough, gentlemen! I beg you!

TUSENBACH: When are the maskers coming?

IRINA: They promised toward nine; which means, this minute.

TUSENBACH (*Embracing* ANDREI. *Singing*): Oh, you porch, my porch, new porch of mine. . . .

ANDREI (*Dancing and singing*): New porch of maple. . . .

TCHEBUTYKIN (*Dancing*): Made of lattice!
    (*Laughter.*)

TUSENBACH (*Kissing* ANDREI): The Devil take it, let's have a drink! Andrusha, let us drink with you. And I'll go with you, Andrusha, to Moscow, to the university.

SOLYONY: To which one? In Moscow there are two universities.

ANDREI: In Moscow, there's one university.

SOLYONY: And I tell you—two.

ANDREI: Let there be three even. So much the better!

SOLYONY: In Moscow there are two universities! (*Disapproval and hisses*) In Moscow there are two universities: the old and the new. And if you don't want to listen, if my words irritate you, I can stop talking. I can even go to another room. . . . (*He goes out through one of the doors.*)

TUSENBACH: Bravo, bravo! (*Laughing*) Ladies and gentlemen, begin, I am sitting down to play! Funny this Solyony. . . . (*Sitting down at the piano and playing a waltz.*)

MASHA (*Waltzing by herself*): The Baron is drunk, the Baron is drunk, the Baron is drunk.

    (NATASHA *enters.*)

NATASHA (*To* TCHEBUTYKIN): Ivan Romanovich!

    (*She says something to* TCHEBUTYKIN, *then goes out quietly.* TCHEBUTYKIN *touches* TUSENBACH *on the shoulder and whispers something to him.*)

IRINA: What is it?

TCHEBUTYKIN: It's time for us to go.

TUSENBACH: Good night. It's time to go.

IRINA: But look here—what about the maskers?

ANDREI (*Embarrassed*): There won't be any maskers. Don't you see, my dear, Natasha says that Bobik isn't quite well, and therefore . . . In sum, I don't know, it's all the same to me, absolutely.

IRINA (*Shrugging her shoulders*): Bobik not well!

MASHA: What of it! If they run us out, we must go. (*To* IRINA) It is not Bobik that's sick, but she herself is. . . . Here! (*Tapping her forehead*) Common creature!

    (ANDREI *goes through the right door into his room.* TCHEBUTYKIN *follows him: in the dining room good-bys are being said.*)

FEDOTIK: What a pity! I counted on spending the evening, but if the child is sick, of course . . . Tomorrow I'll bring him some toys. . . .

RODAY (*In a loud voice*): I purposely took a nap after dinner today, thought I would dance all night. Why, it's only nine o'clock now.

MASHA: Let's go out in the street: we'll talk things over there. We'll decide what's what.

(*Sounds of:* "Good-by! . . . Farewell!" *You can hear* TUSENBACH's *gay laughter. Everyone is gone.* ANFISA *and a maid clear the table, put out the lights. A nurse can be heard singing.* ANDREI *in his coat and hat and* TCHEBUTYKIN *enter quietly.*)

TCHEBUTYKIN: I've had no time to marry because life has flashed by me like lightning, and also because I was madly in love with your mother, who was married. . . .

ANDREI: One shouldn't marry. One shouldn't, it's boring.

TCHEBUTYKIN: That may be so, but the loneliness! You may philosophize as much as you please, but loneliness is a frightful thing, my boy. . . . Though as a matter of fact . . . of course it's absolutely all the same.

ANDREI: Let's go quick.

TCHEBUTYKIN: Why hurry? We have time.

ANDREI: I am afraid the wife might stop us.

TCHEBUTYKIN: Ah!

ANDREI: Today I shan't play, but just sit. I don't feel well. . . . What shall I do, Ivan Romanovich, for shortness of breath?

TCHEBUTYKIN: Why ask me? Don't remember, my boy. Don't know.

ANDREI: Let's go through the kitchen.

> (*They go out. A ring, then another ring; voices are heard, laughter.* IRINA *enters.*)

IRINA: What is it?

ANFISA (*In a whisper*): The maskers!

> (*A ring.*)

IRINA: Tell them, Nursey, nobody's at home. They must excuse us.

> (ANFISA *goes out.* IRINA *paces the room, thinking things over, she is perturbed.* SOLYONY *enters.*)

SOLYONY (*In a quandary*): Nobody here. . . . But where are they all?

IRINA: Gone home.

SOLYONY: That's odd. Are you alone here?

IRINA: Alone (*A pause*) Good-by.

SOLYONY: I behaved without enough restraint just now, tactlessly. But you are not like the rest of them, you are superior and pure, you can see the truth. . . . Only you alone can understand me. I love you, deeply, love you without end. . . .

IRINA: Good-by! Go away.

SOLYONY: I can't live without you. (*Following her*) Oh, my delight! (*Through his tears*) Oh, happiness! Such glorious, wonderful, marvelous eyes as I have never seen in any other woman. . . .

IRINA (*Coldly*): Stop it, Vasili Vasilievich!

SOLYONY: I'm speaking of love to you for the first time and it's as if I were not on earth but on another planet. (*Rubbing his forehead*) Well, it's all the same. Love is not to be forced, certainly. . . . But lucky rivals I cannot have. . . . Cannot. . . . I swear to you by all that's holy, I'll kill any rival. . . . Oh, wonderful creature!

(NATASHA *passes by with a candle.*)

NATASHA (*Looks in at one door, then at another and passes by the door leading into her husband's room*): Andrei is there. Let him read. Excuse me, Vasili Vasilievich, I didn't know you were here. I'm in my dressing gown.

SOLYONY: It's all the same to me. Good-by! (*He goes out.*)

NATASHA: And you are tired, my dear, poor girl! (*Kissing* IRINA) You should go to bed a little earlier.

IRINA: Is Bobik asleep?

NATASHA: Asleep. But not sound asleep. By the way, dear, I wanted to tell you, but you are never here, or else I haven't time. . . . In the nursery Bobik has now, seems to me it's cold and damp. And your room is so good for a child. My dear, my own, move in with Olya for a while!

IRINA (*Not understanding*): Where?

(*A troika with bells is heard driving up to the house.*)

NATASHA: You and Olya will be in one room, for this little while, and your room will be for Bobik. He's such a darling, today I say to him: "Bobik, you are mine! Mine!" And he looks at me with his little eyes. (*A ring*) It must be Olga. How late she is!

(*A* MAID *comes and whispers in* NATASHA's *ear.*)

NATASHA: Protopopov? What a queer man! Protopopov has come, he's asking me to go for a ride with him in a troika. (*Laughing*) How strange these men are . . . ! (*A ring*) Somebody's come out there. I might go ride for a quarter of an hour. . . . (*To the* MAID) Tell him right away—(*A ring*) There's a ring. . . . Olga must be here. (*She goes out.*)

(*The* MAID *runs out;* IRINA *sits there thinking.*
KULYGIN, OLGA *enter, behind them* VERSHININ.)

KULYGIN: There you are! And they said there would be
a party.

VERSHININ: Strange, I went away a while ago, half an
hour ago, and they were expecting the maskers. . . .

IRINA: They have all gone.

KULYGIN: And Masha's gone? Where did she go? And
why is Protopopov downstairs waiting in the troika?
Who's he waiting for?

IRINA: Don't ask questions. . . . I'm tired.

KULYGIN: Well, Miss Caprice . . .

OLGA: The council has just finished. I'm exhausted. Our
headmistress is ill, and I'm taking her place. My head,
my head aches, my head . . . (*Sitting down*) Andrei
lost two hundred roubles yesterday at cards. . . . The
whole town is talking about it. . . .

KULYGIN: Yes, and I got tired at the council. (*He sits
down.*)

VERSHININ: My wife decided just now to scare me, she
almost poisoned herself. It all passed over and I'm
happy, I'm easy now. . . . The order is we must leave
here. So—let me wish you all well. Fyodor Ilyich, go
somewhere with me. I can't stay at home, absolutely
cannot. . . . Let's go!

KULYGIN: I'm tried. I'm not going. (*Rising*) I'm tired.
Has the wife come home?

IRINA: She must have.

KULYGIN (*Kissing* IRINA's *hand*) Good-by. Tomorrow
and the day after I'll rest all day long. I wish you well.
(*Going*) I'd like some tea very much. I counted on
spending the evening in pleasant company and—o,

fallacem hominum spem! Accusative case exclamatory. . . .

VERSHININ: Which means I'm going by myself. (*He goes out with* KULYGIN, *whistling.*)

OLGA: My head aches, my head . . . Andrei has lost . . . the whole town is talking. . . . I'll go lie down. . . . (*Starting out of the room*) Tomorrow I am free. . . . O Lord, how pleasant it is! Tomorrow is free, day after tomorrow is free. . . . My head aches, my head . . . (*She goes out.*)

IRINA (*Alone*): They've all gone. There's nobody here. (*In the street an accordion is heard, the* NURSE *sings a song.*)

NATASHA (*With a fur coat and cap, passes through the dining room; behind her a* MAID): I'll be home in half an hour. I'll take just a little ride. (*She goes out.*)

IRINA (*Left alone, dejected*): To Moscow! To Moscow! To Moscow!

Curtain

ACT THREE

OLGA'S *and* IRINA'S *room. To the left and to the right are beds, with screens around them. It is going on three o'clock in the morning. Offstage they are ringing the fire-bell for a fire that began a long time back. Plainly no one in the house has gone to bed yet.* MASHA *lies on the sofa, she wears, as usual, a black dress.* OLGA *and* ANFISA *enter.*

ANFISA: Sitting down there now under the staircase . . .
I say—"If you please, come upstairs, as if," I say,
"you could sit there like that!"—they are crying,
"Daddy," they say, "we don't know where Daddy is.
God forbid," they say, "he's burned!" They thought
that up! And in the courtyard there are some
people. . . . They are undressed too.

OLGA (*Taking some dresses out of the closet*): Here,
this gray one—take it. . . . And this one here. . . .
The blouse too . . . And take the skirt, Nursey. . . .
All Kirsanoffsky Street seems to be burned down.
. . . Take this. . . . Take this. . . . (*Throws the
dresses for her to catch*) The poor Vershinins were
frightened. . . . Their house nearly burned up. They
must spend the night here. . . . We can't let them go
home. . . . At poor Fedotik's everything got burned,
there's nothing left. . . .

ANFISA: You'll have to call Ferapont, Olyushka, or I
can't carry . . .

OLGA (*She rings*): Nobody answers. . . . (*Through the
door*) Come here, whoever it is! (*Through the open
door she sees a window glowing red with the fire; a
fire brigade is heard passing the house*) How frightful! And how sickening! (FERAPONT *enters*) Here, take
this and carry it downstairs. . . . Down there under
the staircase are the young Kolotilin girls. . . . Give it
to them. And give this. . . .

FERAPONT: Yes, miss. In the year '12, Moscow also
burned. Oh my Lord God! The French were astonished.

OLGA: Go on, step along. . . .

FERAPONT: Yes, miss. (*He goes out.*)

OLGA: Nursey, dear, give everything away. We don't

need anything. Give everything away! Nursey . . . I'm tired, I can barely stand on my feet. . . . The Vershinins shouldn't be allowed to go home. . . . The girls can sleep in the drawing room, and Alexander Ignatievich downstairs at the Baron's . . . Fedotik too at the Baron's, or let him stay with us in the dining room. . . . The doctor, as if he'd done it on purpose, is drunk, terribly drunk, and we mustn't send anyone to him. And Vershinin's wife too in the drawing room.

ANFISA (*Wearily*): Olyushka, dear, don't you drive me away! Don't drive me away!

OLGA: You are talking nonsense, Nurse. Nobody's driving you away.

ANFISA (*Laying her head on* OLGA's *breast*): My own, my treasure, I do try, I work. . . . I'll get feeble and everybody will say: get out! And where will I go? Eighty years old. My eighty-second year. . . .

OLGA: You sit down a while, Nursey. . . . You are tired, poor thing. . . . (*Making her sit down*) Rest, my dear good old Nurse. You look so pale!

(NATASHA *enters*.)

NATASHA: They are saying it around that we must form right off a relief society for those who have been burnt out. Why not! It's a fine idea. We must be quick to help poor people, that's the duty of the rich. Bobik and Sofotchka have just gone to sleep, they sleep as if nothing had happened. There are so many people everywhere here that anywhere you go the house is full. There's influenza in town now, I'm afraid the children may catch it.

OLGA (*Not listening to her*): In this room you don't see the fire, it's peaceful here. . . .

NATASHA: Yes. . . . I must be very much disheveled. (*In front of the mirror*) They say I have filled out. . . . And it isn't true! Not at all! And Masha's sleeping, exhausted . . . poor thing. . . . (*To* ANFISA, *coldly*) In my presence, don't you dare sit down! Get up! Get out of here! (ANFISA *goes out; a pause*) Why you keep this old woman I don't understand!

OLGA (*Taken aback*): Excuse me, I don't understand either. . . .

NATASHA: For no reason at all she's here. She is a peasant, she should live in the country. . . . What a lot of pampering! I like in a house to have order. Useless people shouldn't be in a house. (*Stroking* OLGA's *cheek*) Poor dear, you are tired! Our headmistress is tired. And when my Sofotchka grows up and enters high school, I shall be afraid of you.

OLGA: I shan't be the headmistress.

NATASHA: You will be elected, Olitchka, that's decided.

OLGA: I'll decline it. I can't, I've not the strength for it. (*Drinking some water*) You were so rude just now to Nurse. . . . Forgive me, I'm not in any condition to bear . . . It's getting all black before my eyes. . . .

NATASHA (*Disturbed*): Forgive me, Olya, forgive me. . . . I didn't mean to distress you.

(MASHA *gets up, takes a pillow and goes out, angrily.*)

OLGA: Understand, my dear . . . perhaps we were brought up strangely, but I can't bear it. That kind of attitude depresses me, I get sick. . . . I'm just sick at heart!

NATASHA: Forgive me, forgive me. . . . (*Kissing her*)

OLGA: Every rudeness, even the slightest, even a word indelicately spoken, upsets me. . . .

NATASHA: I often talk too much, it's true, but you must agree, my dear, she might very well have lived in the country.

OLGA: She's been these thirty years with us.

NATASHA: But now, though, she can't do anything. It's either that I don't understand or else you don't want to understand me. She is not up to doing any sort of work, she just sleeps and sits.

OLGA: But let her sit.

NATASHA (*Surprised*): How let her sit? She's a servant nevertheless. (*Tearfully*) I don't understand you, Olya. I have a nurse, have a wet nurse, we have a maid, a cook. . . . What do we have that old woman too for? What for?

(*Behind the scene the fire-alarm rings.*)

OLGA: I have aged ten years in this one night!

NATASHA: We must come to some sort of understanding, Olya. You are at high school, I'm at home; you have the teaching, I have the housekeeping. And if I say anything about the servants, I know what I'm saying. I know what I'm saying. . . . And by tomorrow there won't be this old thief here, this old hag. (*Stamping her foot*) This witch . . . Don't dare cross me! Don't you dare! (*Catching herself*) Really, if you don't move downstairs, we'll always be quarreling. It's terrible.

(KULYGIN *enters.*)

KULYGIN: Where is Masha? It's quite time to go home. The fire, they say, is subsiding. (*Stretching*) Burnt just one section of the town, in spite of the fact that there was a wind; at first it looked as if the whole town was on fire. (*Sitting down*) I'm tired out, Olitchka, my dear. . . . I often think if there hadn't been Masha, I'd have married you, Olitchka. You are so good. . . . I'm exhausted. (*Listening for something.*)

OLGA: What is it?

KULYGIN: As if on purpose, the doctor is drunk, he's terribly drunk. As if on purpose! (*Getting up*) There he is coming here, I imagine . . . Do you hear? Yes, coming . . . (*Laughing*) What a fellow, really . . . I'll hide. (*Going to the cupboard and standing in the corner*) Such a rascal!

OLGA: For two years he hasn't been drinking and here all of a sudden he's gone and got drunk. (*Following* NATASHA *to the back of the room.*)

(TCHEBUTYKIN *enters; without staggering, as if he were sober, he walks across the room, stops, looks around, then goes to the washstand and begins to wash his hands.*)

TCHEBUTYKIN (*Crossly*): The Devil take all of 'em, take —They think I'm a doctor, know how to cure any sickness, but I know absolutely nothing, I've forgotten everything I ever knew, remember nothing, absolutely nothing. (OLGA *and* NATASHA *go out, unnoticed by him*) The Devil take it! Last Wednesday, I treated a woman at Zasip—she died, and I'm to blame for her dying. Yes . . . I knew a little something twenty-five years ago, but now I don't remember anything. Nothing. Perhaps I'm not even a man, but only give the appearance here of having hands and legs and a head; perhaps I don't even exist, and it only seems to me that I walk and eat and sleep. (*Crying*) Oh, that I didn't exist! (*No longer crying, crossly*) The Devil knows . . . ! Three days ago there was a conversation at the club, they were talking about Shakespeare, Voltaire . . . I hadn't read them, hadn't read them at all, but I looked as if I had read them. And the others did too, just as I did. The banality of it! The meanness! And that woman I killed Wednesday came back to me . . . And everything came back to me, and it weighed on my soul, crooked, foul, disgusting . . . I went and got drunk. . . .

> (IRINA, VERSHININ and TUSENBACH enter; TUSENBACH wears civilian clothes, new and stylish.)

IRINA: Let's sit here. Nobody's coming here.

VERSHININ: If it were not for the soldiers, the whole town would be burnt up. Brave boys! (Rubbing his hands with pleasure) Salt of the earth! Ah, what brave boys!

KULYGIN: What's the time, gentlemen?

TUSENBACH: Going on four by now. It's getting light.

IRINA: Everybody is sitting in the dining room, nobody is going out. And that Solyony of yours is sitting . . . (To TCHEBUTYKIN) Doctor, you should have gone to sleep.

TCHEBUTYKIN: Not at all . . . Thank you . . . (Combing his beard.)

KULYGIN (Laughing): You got a little tispy, Ivan Romanovich! (Slapping him on the shoulder) Bravo! In vino veritas, said the ancients.

TUSENBACH: They keep asking me to arrange a concert for the benefit of the refugees.

IRINA: Well, who is there to . . . ?

TUSENBACH: It could be arranged if we wanted to do it. Maria Sergeevna, in my opinion, plays the piano wonderfully.

KULYGIN: She does play wonderfully!

IRINA: She has forgotten how by now. It's three years since she's played. . . . Or four.

TUSENBACH: Here in this town absolutely nobody understands music, not one soul; but I, I do understand it, and on my word of honor, I assure you that Maria Sergeevna plays magnificently, almost with genius.

KULYGIN: You are right, Baron. I love her very much, I love my Masha. She's sweet.

TUSENBACH: Think of being able to play so splendidly and at the same time know quite well that nobody, nobody, understands you!

KULYGIN (*Sighing*): Yes. . . . But is it proper for her to take part in a concert? (*A pause*) Really, gentlemen, I don't know anything about that. Perhaps it would be a good thing. I must admit our director is a fine man, in fact, very fine, of the brainiest; but he has such views that . . . Of course, it's not his affair, but just the same, if you like, I might talk with him. (TCHEBUTYKIN *is taking up a china clock in both hands and examining it.*)

VERSHININ: I got all covered with dirt at the fire—I'm not presentable. (*A pause*) Yesterday I heard in passing that they might transfer our brigade somewhere far away. Some say to the Kingdom of Poland, others—that it looks like Chita.

TUSENBACH: I heard that too. And so what? The town will be completely empty then.

IRINA: And we shall go away!

TUHEBUTYKIN (*He drops the clock, shattering it.*): All to pieces!

(*A pause; everyone is distressed and embarrassed.*)

KULYGIN (*Picks up the pieces*): To break such a precious thing— Oh, Ivan Romanovich, Ivan Romanovich! Minus zero to you for conduct.

IRINA: That clock was our dear mother's.

TCHEBUTYKIN: Perhaps . . . Mother's, then, mother's. Perhaps I didn't break it but only seemed to break it. Perhaps it only seems to us that we exist, and we don't really. I don't know anything, nobody knows anything. (*By the door*) What are you looking at? Natasha has an affair with Protopopov, and you don't see it. . . . There you sit and see nothing, and Natasha has an affair with Protopopov. . . . (*Singing*) How do you like swallowing that dose . . . ? (*He goes out.*)

VERSHININ: Yes. . . . (*Laughing*) How strange all this is at bottom! (*A pause*) When the fire began, I ran home fast; got there, looked . . . our house was unharmed and out of danger, but my two girls stood at the door in nothing but their underclothes, the mother wasn't there, people were scurrying about, horses running around, and dogs, and on my girls' faces was all that anxiety, terror, entreaty, who knows what; my heart was wrung when I saw those faces. My God, I thought, what more will these girls have to go through, in a long life! I grabbed them, ran and kept thinking one thing: What more will they have to live through in this world! (*Fire-alarm; a pause*) I came this way and the mother was here, shouting, angry.

(MASHA *enters with a pillow and sits down on the sofa.*)

VERSHININ: And while my girls were standing at the door in nothing but their underclothes and the street

was red with the fire, the noise was terrible, I reflected that something like that used to happen when
the enemy made a sudden raid, plundering and
burning as they went. Meanwhile what a difference
there is essentialy between what is and what was!
And a little more time will pass, some two or three
hundred years, and they will look on this life of ours
now with fear and derision, everything now will
seem then to be all angles and heavy and most in-
convenient and strange. Oh, what a life that will be,
what a life! (*Laughing*) Forgive me, I'm philoso-
phizing again. Allow me to continue, ladies and
gentlemen. I'd like awfully to philosophize, now that
I'm in such a mood for it. (*A pause*) It's as if everybody were asleep. And so I say: What a life it will
be! You can just imagine. . . . Here in town there
are only three of your kind now, but in coming
generations there will be more, always more and
more; a time will come when everything will veer to
you, they will live like you, and then, too, later on
you'll get antiquated, there'll be people springing up
who are better than you. . . . (*Laughing*) I am in a
most singular mood today. I want like the devil to
live. . . . (*Singing*) Unto love all ages bow, its pangs
are blest. . . .

MASHA: Tram-tum-tum. . . .

VERSHININ: Tum-tum. . .

MASHA: Tra-ra-ra?

VERSHININ: Tra-ta-ta. (*Laughing.*)

(FEDOTIK *enters.*)

FEDOTIK (*Dancing*): Burnt out, burnt out! Absolutely
everything!

(*Laughter.*)

IRINA: What sort of a joke is that? Is it all gone?

FEDOTIK (*Laughing*): Absolutely everything. There's nothing left. And the guitar burned, and the photography outfit burned, and all my letters. . . . And I wanted to present you with a notebook . . . it burned up too.

(SOLYONY *enters.*)

IRINA: No. Please go away, Vasili Vasilievich. You can't come in here.

SOLYONY: But why is it the Baron can and I can't?

VERSHININ: We must go, really. How's the fire?

SOLYONY: They say its's subsiding. No, it's decidedly strange to me, why is it the Baron can and I can't? (*Taking out the perfume bottle and sprinkling himself.*)

VERSHININ: Tram-tum-tum.

MASHA: Tram-tum.

VERSHININ (*Laughing, to* SOLYONY): Let's go to the dining room.

SOLYONY: Very well, I'll make a note of it so. This thought could be made more clear, but 'twould annoy the geese, I fear. . . . (*Looking at* TUSENBACH) Chick, chick, chick. . . . (*He goes out with* VERSHININ *and* FEDOTIK.)

IRINA: How that Solyony has smoked things up. (*With surprise*) The Baron is asleep! Baron! Baron!

TUSENBACH (*Waking up*): I'm tired, however. . . . The brickyard. . . . I'm not saying this in my sleep, for it's a fact that I'll soon be going to the brickyard to start work. . . . It's already been discussed. (*To* IRINA, *tenderly*) You are so pale, beautiful, bewitching. . . . It seems to me your paleness brightens the dark air like light. . . . You are sad, you are not satisfied with

life. . . . Oh, come along with me, let's go to work
together!

MASHA: Nikolai Lvovich, do go on out of here!

TUSENBACH (*Laughing*): You here? I didn't see you.
(*Kissing* IRINA's *hand*) Good-by, I'm going. . . . I'm
looking at you now and am reminded of how long
ago once on your saint's day you were all so gay and
happy, talking of the joy of work. . . . And what a
happy life I dreamed of then! Where is it? (*Kissing
her hand*) You have tears in your eyes. Go to bed.
. . . It's getting light now . . . morning has begun.
. . . If only it were granted me to give my life for
you!

MASHA: Nikolai Lvovich, go on! Why, really, what . . .

TUSENBACH: I'm going. . . . (*He goes out.*)

MASHA (*Lying down*): Are you asleep, Fyodor?

KULYGIN: Eh?

MASHA: You ought to go home.

KULYGIN: My darling Masha, my dear Masha. . . .

IRINA: She's tired. . . . You ought to let her rest, Fedya.

KULYGIN: I'm going right away. . . . My good wife,
darling . . . I love you, my one and only. . . .

MASHA (*Bored and cross*): *Amo, amas, amat, amamus,
amatis, amant.*

KULYGIN (*Laughing*): No, really, she's amazing. I've
been married to you for seven years; but it seems as
if we'd married only yesterday. Word of honor! No,
really, you are an amazing woman. I am content, I
am content, I am content!

MASHA: Bored, bored, bored. . . . (*She sits up, and
speaks sitting*) It just won't go out of my head. . . .
It's simply shocking. It's there like a nail in my head.
I can't stay silent. I mean about Andrei. . . . He's

mortgaged this house to the bank and his wife
grabbed all the money, but the house belongs not just
to him, but to the four of us! He ought to know that
if he's a decent man.

KULYGIN: What do you care, Masha! Why should you?
Andrusha is in debt all round, well, God reward him!

MASHA: Anyhow it's shocking. (*She lies back down.*)

KULYGIN: You and I are not poor. I work, I go to the
high school, and then give private lessons. . . . I'm an
honest man. Simple. . . . *Omnia mea mecum porto,*
as they say.

MASHA: I don't need anything. But injustice makes me
furious. (*A pause*) Go on, Fyodor!

KULYGIN (*Kissing her*): You are tired, rest about half
an hour, and I'll sit and wait out there. Sleep. . . .
(*Going*) I am content, I am content, I am content.
(*He goes out.*)

IRINA: How small our Andrei has grown, how he has
dried up and aged beside that woman! There was a
time when he was preparing for a professorship, and
yesterday he was bragging that at last he could become
a member of the District Board. He a member of the
board and Protopopov chairman. . . . The whole
town's talking, is laughing, and he's the only one
who knows nothing and sees nothing. And now, everybody has rushed off to the fire, but he sits there in
his room and pays not the least attention to it. He
just plays the violin. (*Nervously*) Oh, it's awful, awful, awful! (*Crying*) I can't, I can't bear any more!
. . . I can't—I can't!

(OLGA *enters. She tidies up her dressing table.*)

IRINA (*Sobbing aloud*): Cast me out, cast me out, I
can't stand any more! . . .

OLGA (*Alarmed*): What is it, what is it? Darling!

IRINA (*Sobbing*): Where? Where is it all gone? Where is it? Oh, my God, my God! I've forgotten everything, I've forgotten . . . it's muddled in my head. . . . I don't remember what in Italian *window* is, or the ceiling there. . . . I'm forgetting everything, every day forgetting, and life slips away and will never return, never, we'll never go to Moscow. . . . I can see we'll never go.

OLGA: Darling, darling. . . .

IRINA (*Restraining herself*): Oh, I'm miserable. . . . I can't work and won't work. I'm sick of it, sick of it! I was a telegraph operator, and now have a place with the Town Board, and hate and despise everything they give me to do. . . . I'm going on twenty-four and have already been working a long time, and my brain's drying up, I'm getting thin, losing my looks, getting old, and there's nothing, nothing—no satisfaction of any kind—and time is passing, and it all seems to be moving away from any real, beautiful life, all moving away farther and farther into some abyss. . . . I'm in despair, and how I'm alive, how it is I haven't killed myself, I can't understand. . . .

OLGA: Don't cry, my own little girl, don't cry. . . .

IRINA: I am not crying, not crying. . . . I'm sick of it. . . . Now look—I am not crying any more. I'm sick of it. . . . I'm sick of it!

OLGA: Darling, I'm telling you as a sister, as a friend, if you want my advice, marry the Baron!

(IRINA *weeps silently*.)

OLGA: Why, you respect him, you value him highly. It's true he's not good-looking, but he's so decent and clean. . . . Why, one doesn't marry for love but to do

one's duty. At least, I think so, and I would marry
without being in love. At any rate I'd marry anyone
who proposed to me so long as he was an honorable
man. I'd marry even an old man. . . .

IRINA: I kept expecting us to move to Moscow; there
I'd meet my real beloved, I dreamed of him, loved
him. But it turned out just foolishness, just foolishness! . . .

OLGA (*Embracing her sister*): My dear, lovely sister, I
understand it all; when Baron Nikolai Lvovich left
the military service and came to see us in civilian
clothes, he seemed to me so homely that I even cried.
He asked, "Why are you crying?" How could I tell
him! But if God should grant he married you, I'd be
happy. Now, that's different, quite different!

(NATASHA *crosses the stage from the right door to
the left, without speaking, a candle in her hand.*)

MASHA (*Sitting up*): She walks as if she had been the
one to start the fire.

OLGA: Masha, you are silly! The silliest one in our family is you. Forgive me, please.

(*A pause.*)

MASHA: I want to confess, my dear sisters. I'm tired in
my soul. I'll confess to you and then to nobody else,
never. . . . I'll say it this minute. (*Quietly*) It's my
secret, but you must know everything. . . . I can't be
silent. . . . . (*A pause*) I love, love . . . I love that
man. . . . You just saw him. . . . Well, there it is. In
one word, I love Vershinin. . . .

OLGA (*Going behind her screen*): Stop that. At any rate
I'm not hearing.

MASHA: What is there to do about it? (*Clutching her
head*) At first he seemed to me strange, then I felt

sorry for him. . . . Then I began to love him . . . began to love him with his voice, his words, his misfortunes, his two girls. . . .

OLGA (*Behind the screen*): I'm not hearing you at any rate. Whatever silly things you say, at any rate I'm not hearing you!

MASHA: Oh, Olya, you are silly. I love—such, that is to say, is my fate. That is to say my lot is such. . . . And he loves me. . . . All that is frightening. Yes? Is it wrong? (*Taking* IRINA *by the hand and drawing her to her*) Oh, my darling . . . how are we going to live our life, what's to become of us? . . . When one reads some novel, all this seems old and all of it so understandable, but when you fall in love yourself, you begin to see that nobody knows anything and everybody must decide for himself. . . . My darlings, my sisters. . . . I confessed to you, now I'll be silent. . . . I'll be now like Gogol's madman . . . silence . . . silence. . . .

(ANDREI *enters, followed by* FERAPONT.)

ANDREI (*Annoyed*): What do you want? I don't understand.

FERAPONT (*Standing in the door, impatiently*): Andrei Sergeevich, I have already told you ten times.

ANDREI: First, I am not Andrei Sergeevich to you but Your Excellency!

FERAPONT: The firemen, Your Excellentness, ask your permission to go to the river through your garden. As it is, they are driving round and round—it's pure punishment.

ANDREI: Very well. Tell them, very well. (FERAPONT *goes out*) That's enough of them. Where's Olga? (OLGA *comes out from behind the screen*) I've come to ask

you to give me the key to the cupboard. I've lost mine.
You have one of the little keys. (OLGA *gives him the
key without speaking.* IRINA *goes behind her screen;
a pause*) And what a tremendous fire! It's starting to
die down now. The devil take it, that Ferapont's
made me lose my temper. I said a stupid thing to him.
. . . Your Excellency. . . . (*A pause*) But why are
you silent, Olya? (*A pause*) It's high time to stop this
silliness and stop pouting for no reason at all. . . .
You are here, Masha, Irina's here, well, that's fine—
let's have it out once and for all. What have you got
against me? Now what?

OLGA: Let it rest, Andrusha. Tomorrow we'll have it
out. (*Anxiously*) What a night of torment!

ANDREI (*He is very much confused*): Don't be upset.
I ask you absolutely in cold blood: what have you got
against me? Speak right out.

VERSHININ'S VOICE: Tram-tum-tum!

MASHA (*Rising, in a loud voice*): Tra-ta-ta! (*To* OLGA)
Good-by Olya, God be with you! (*She goes behind
the screen, kisses* IRINA) Sleep well. . . . Good-by, Andrei. Go on away, they are tired. . . . Tomorrow you
will have it out. (*She goes out.*)

OLGA: Indeed, Andrusha, let's put it off till tomorrow.
. . . (*She goes behind her screen*) It's time to go to
sleep.

ANDREI: I'll just say it and go. Right away. . . . In the
first place, you have something against Natasha, my
wife, and that I have noticed from the very day of
my wedding. Natasha is a splendid, honest person,
straightforward, and honorable—in my opinion. I
love and respect my wife, understand, I respect her
and demand that others respect her too. I repeat, she

is an honest, honorable person, and all your dissatis-
factions, excuse me, are simply caprices. . . . (*A pause*)
In the second place, you seem to be angry because of
the fact that I am not a professor, don't occupy myself
with learning. But I serve in the Zemstvo, I am a
member of the District Board, and this service of
mine I consider just as sacred and lofty as service to
learning. I'm a member of the District Board and I'm
proud of it, if you want to know. . . . (*A pause*) In
the third place, I have something else to say . . . : I
mortgaged the house without asking your permission.
. . . Of that I am guilty, yes, and ask you to forgive
me. I was forced to it by debts. . . . Thirty-five thousand. . . . I don't play cards any more, gave it up
long ago, but the chief thing I can say in my own
justification, is that you—girls, as of the privileged sex,
you receive a pension, while I didn't have . . . my
earnings, so to speak. . . . (*A pause.*)

KULYGIN (*At the door*): Masha not here? (*Perturbed*)
But where is she? That's strange. . . . (*He goes out.*)

ANDREI: They don't listen. Natasha is a superior, honest
person. (*Walks up and down the stage in silence,
then stops*) When I married, I thought we should be
happy . . . everybody happy . . . but, my God . . . !
(*Crying*) My dear sisters, darling sisters, don't believe
me, don't believe . . . (*He goes out.*)

KULYGIN (*At the door, anxiously*): Where is Masha?
Masha's not here? What an astonishing business! (*He
goes out.*)

(*Fire-alarm; the stage is empty.*)

IRINA (*Behind the screen*): Olya! Who is that knocking
on the floor?

OLGA: It's the doctor, Ivan Romanovich. He's drunk.

IRINA: What a torn-up night! (*A pause*) Olya! (*Looking out from behind the screen*) Did you hear? They are taking the brigade from us, transferring it somewhere far away.

OLGA: That's only a rumor.

IRINA: We'll be left alone then. . . . Olya!

OLGA: Well?

IRINA: Darling, precious, I respect, I value the Baron, he's a marvelous person, I'll marry him, I consent, only let's go to Moscow! I beg you, let's go! There's nothing in the world better than Moscow! Let's go, Olya! Let's go!

Curtain

ACT FOUR

An old garden in front of the PROZOROFFS' *house. A long alley of fir trees, at the end of which a river is seen. On the other side of the river, a wood. To the right a terrace of the house and on it a table with bottles and glasses; you can see they have just been drinking champagne. Twelve o'clock noon. Now and then on their way from the street to the river, people cross the garden; four or five soldiers pass that way, walking fast.* TCHEBUTYKIN, *in an amiable mood, which does not leave him during the entire Act, sits in an easy chair, in the garden, waiting to be called; he wears a military cap and carries a stick.* IRINA, KULYGIN *with a decoration around his neck, with no mustache, and* TUSENBACH, *are standing on the terrace, saying good-by to* FEDOTIK *and* RODAY, *who are going down the steps; both officers are in campaign uniform.*

TUSENBACH (*Exchanging kisses with* FEDOTIK): You are a good fellow, we lived like good friends. (*Exchanging kisses with* RODAY) Once again. . . . Good-by, my dear boy. . . .

IRINA: Till we meet again.

FEDOTIK: It's not meet again, but good-by, we shall never meet again.

KULYGIN: Who knows! (*Wiping his eyes, smiling*) There, I'm beginning to cry too.

IRINA: Some day we'll run across each other.

FEDOTIK: In ten or fifteen years maybe? But by then we'll scarcely know each other, we'll greet each other coldly. . . . (*Taking a snapshot*) Stand still. . . . Once more, for the last time.

RODAY (*Embracing* TUSENBACH): We won't meet again. . . . (*Kissing* IRINA's *hand*) Thank you for everything, for everything!

FEDOTIK (*Vexed*): Oh, wait a little!

TUSENBACH: God grant we meet. Write us though. Without fail write.

RODAY (*Casting a glance around the garden*): Good-by, trees! (*Shouting*) Yoo hoo! (*A pause*) Good-by, echo!

KULYGIN: I am afraid you'll marry there in Poland. . . . The Polish wife will embrace you and say: "*Kochany!*" (*Laughing.*)

FEDOTIK (*Looking at his watch*): There's less than an hour left. Out of our battery only Solyony is going on the barge, we are with the rank and file. Three battery divisions are going today, tomorrow three more—and quiet and peace will reign in the town. . . .

TUSENBACH: And terrible boredom.

RODAY: And where is Maria Sergeevna?

KULYGIN: Masha is in the garden.

FEDOTIK: We must say good-by to her.

RODAY: Good-by, I must go or I'll be crying. . . . (*He hurriedly embraces* TUSENBACH *and* KULYGIN, *kisses* IRINA's *hand*) It was fine living here.

FEDOTIK (*To* KULYGIN): This is a memento for you. . . . A notebook with a pencil. . . . We'll go this way to the river. . . . (*They move off, both look back.*)

RODAY (*Shouts*): Yoo hoo!

KULYGIN (*Shouts*): Good-by!

    (*At the rear of the stage* FEDOTIK *and* RODAY *meet* MASHA *and bid her good-by. She walks away with them.*)

IRINA: They are gone. . . . (*Sitting down on the bottom step of the terrace.*)

TCHEBUTYKIN: And forgot to say good-by to me.

IRINA: And what about you?

TCHEBUTYKIN: And I forgot too somehow. Anyway I'll soon see them, I'm leaving tomorrow. Yes. . . . One more short day is left. In a year they will retire me, I'll come back here and live out my little span near you. Just one short year is left before my pension. (*He puts one newspaper in his pocket and takes out another*) I'll come here to you and change my life from the very roots. I'll become so quiet, right—right-minded, respectable.

IRINA: And you really should change your life, dovey. You should somehow.

TCHEBUTYKIN: Yes, I feel so. (*Singing softly*) Ta-ra-ra-boom-de-aye. . . . Sit on a curb I may. . . .

KULYGIN: You're incorrigible, Ivan Romanovich! You're incorrigible!

TCHEBUTYKIN: Now then, if you'd only teach me! Then I'd be reformed.

IRINA: Fyodor has shaved off his mustache. I can't bear to look at him.

KULYGIN: Why not?

TCHEBUTYKIN: I could say what your physiognomy looks like now, but I can't.

KULYGIN: Well! It's the accepted thing, it is *modus vivendi*. Our director shaved off his mustache, and as soon as I became inspector, I shaved clean too. Nobody likes it, but that's all the same to me. I am content. I may be with a mustache, or without a mustache, but I'm equally content. . . . (*Sitting down.*)

(*At the rear of the stage* ANDREI *passes, wheeling a baby-carriage with a child asleep in it.*)

IRINA: Ivan Romanovich, my own darling, I am terribly disturbed. You were on the boulevard yesterday, tell me what happened there?

TCHEBUTYKIN: What happened? Nothing. Fidlesticks. (*Reading the newspaper*) All the same!

KULYKIN: What they are saying is that Solyony and the Baron met yesterday on the boulevard near the theatre. . . .

TUSENBACH: Stop it! Well, what really. . . . (*With a wave of his hand he goes into the house.*)

KULYGIN: Near the theatre . . . Solyony began picking on the Baron, and he wouldn't tolerate it, he said something insulting. . . .

TCHEBUTYKIN: I don't know. It's all nonsense.

KULYGIN: In a certain theological seminary a teacher wrote on a composition paper, "Nonsense" and the pupil read "consensus"—thought it was written in Latin. (*Laughing*) Amazingly funny. It's said that Solyony is in love with Irina, and that he's begun to hate the Baron. . . . That's understandable. Irina is a very nice girl. She even resembles Masha, just as thoughtful. It's merely that you have a gentle character, Irina. Though Masha, too, has a very fine character. I love her, my Masha.

(*At the rear of the garden offstage:* "Yoo, hoo!")

IRINA (*Shivering*): Somehow everything frightens me today. (*A pause*) I have everything all ready, after dinner I'm sending off my things. The Baron and I are getting married tomorrow, and tomorrow we are leaving for the brickyard, and day after tomorrow I'll be at the school, a new life is beginning. Somehow God will help me! When I passed my teacher's examination I cried for pure joy . . . so happy. (*A pause*) The cart will soon be here for my things. . . .

KULYGIN: That's all very well, only somehow it's not serious. Just ideas—and very little seriousness. However, I wish you luck with all my heart.

TCHEBUTYKIN (*Tenderly*): My darling, my dear child. . . . My treasure. . . . You have gone far away. I can't catch up with you. I'm left behind, like a bird of passage that has grown old, that can't fly. Fly on, my dears, fly on and God be with you! (*A pause*) It's too bad, Fyodor Ilyich, you shaved off your mustache.

KULYGIN: That'll do from you! (*Sighing*) Well, today the officers are leaving and everything will go on again as of old. Whatever they may say, Masha is a good, honest woman and I love her very much and I am thankful for my fate. People's fate differs. . . . In the excise office here a certain Kozyroff works. He went to school with me, was expelled from the fifth class at high school because he just couldn't understand *ut consecutivum*. Now he is terribly poor, ill, and when we meet I say to him: "Greetings, *ut consecutivum!*" Yes, he says, that's it, *consecutivum* . . . and then coughs. . . . And here I am, all my life I've been successful, I am happy, I have the Order of Stanislav, Second Degree, and am teaching others myself now that *ut consecutivum*. Of course, I am a clever man, cleverer than many others, but happiness doesn't consist in that. . . .

(*In the house they are playing "The Maiden's Prayer" on the piano.*)

IRINA: And tomorrow evening I won't be hearing that "Maiden's Prayer" any more, and won't be meeting Protopopov. . . . (*A pause*) And Protopopov is sitting there in the drawing room now; he came again today. . . .

KULYGIN: The headmistress has not come yet?

IRINA: No. They have sent for her. If only you knew how hard it is for me to live here alone, without Olya. . . . She lives at the high school; she's the headmistress, busy all day long with her duties, and I'm alone, I am bored with nothing to do, and the very room I live in is hateful. . . . So I have made up my mind: If it isn't my lot to be in Moscow, then let it be so. That's my lot. There's nothing to be done. All is God's will, that's the truth. Nikolai Lvovich proposed to me. . . . Well, then? I thought it over and made up my mind. He is a good man, it is really amazing how good. . . .

And suddenly as if wings had grown on my soul, I grew happier, relieved, and felt once more the desire for work, work. . . . Except that something happened yesterday, there's something hidden that's hanging over me. . . .

TCHEBUTYKIN: Consensus. Nonsense.

NATASHA (*At the window*): The headmistress!

KULYGIN: The headmistress has arrived. Let's go. (*He goes with* IRINA *into the house.*)

TCHEBUTYKIN (*Reading the newspaper, softly singing to himself*): Ta-ra-ra-boom-de-aye. . . . Sit on the curb I may. . . .

> (MASHA *approaches; in the background* ANDREI *is seen pushing the baby-carriage.*)

MASHA: There he sits, all settled. . . .

TCHEBUTYKIN: And what?

MASHA (*Sitting down*): Nothing. . . . (*A pause*) Did you love my mother?

TCHEBUTYKIN: Very much.

MASHA: And did she love you?

TCHEBUTYKIN (*After a pause*): That I no longer remember.

MASHA: Is "mine" here? Our cook Marfa used to talk about her policeman like that: mine. Is "mine" here?

TCHEBUTYKIN: Not yet.

MASHA: When you get happiness in snatches, in bits, and you lose it, like me, little by little you harden, you grow bitter. (*Pointing to her breast*) Right here I'm boiling. . . . (*Looking at her brother* ANDREI *pushing the baby-carriage*) There's Andrei, our little brother. . . . All our hopes gone. . . . Once upon a time thousands of people were hoisting a bell, a lot of effort and money were spent, and then suddenly it fell and broke. Suddenly for neither one reason nor another. The same with Andrei.

ANDREI: And when will they finally quiet down in the house? Such noise!

TCHEBUTYKIN: Soon. (*Looking at his watch*) I have a very old watch, with chimes. . . . (*Winding the watch; it chimes*) The first, second, and fifth batteries are going at one o'clock sharp. (*A pause*) And I to-morrow.

ANDREI: For good?

TCHEBUTYKIN: I don't know. I might return in a year. Though the devil knows . . . it's all the same. . . .
     (*Somewhere far off a harp and violin are playing.*)

ANDREI: The town will be dead. As if they had covered it with a cowl. (*A pause*) Something happened yesterday near the theatre; everybody is talking about it, but I don't know what it was.

TCHEBUTYKIN: Nothing. Nonsense. Solyony began to pick on the Baron and he lost his temper and insulted him, and it got finally to the point where Solyony had to challenge him to a duel. (*Looks at his watch*) It's time now, I believe. At half-past twelve, in the State forest there, the one we see from here, beyond the river. . . . Piff—paff. (*Laughing*) Solyony imagines he is Lermontov and even writes verses. Now jokes are jokes, but it is the third duel for him.

MASHA: For whom?

TCHEBUTYKIN: For Solyony.

MASHA: And for the Baron?

TCHEBUTYKIN: What for the Baron?
     (*A pause.*)

MASHA: I'm all confused in the head. All the same, I say

it shouldn't be allowed. He might wound the Baron
or even kill him.

TCHEBUTYKIN: The Baron is a good man but one baron
more, one less—isn't it all the same? Let them! All the
same! (*Beyond the garden there are shouts:* "Yoo hoo."
Answering the shout) You can wait. (*To* MASHA)
That's Skvortzoff shouting, the second. He's sitting in
a boat.

(*A pause.*)

ANDREI: To my mind either to engage in a duel or to be
present at one even in the capacity of doctor, is simply
immoral.

TCHEBUTYKIN: That only seems so. . . . We are not
here, there is nothing in the world, we don't exist, but
it only seems that we exist. . . . And isn't it all the
same!

MASHA: Just like that . . . all day long they talk, talk.
. . . (*Going*) To live in such a climate, be afraid it will
snow any minute, and still to have these conversations
—(*Stopping*) I'm not going into the house, I can't. . . .
When Vershinin comes let me know— (*She goes down
the alley*) And the birds of passage are flying already.
. . . (*Looking up*) Swans or geese. . . . My dear ones,
my happy ones—! (*She goes out.*)

ANDREI: Our house will be empty. The officers will go,
you will go, my sister will be married, and I'll be left
alone in the house.

TCHEBUTYKIN: And your wife?

(FERAPONT *enters with some papers.*)

ANDREI: A wife is a wife. She is honest, decent, well—
kind, but along with all that there's something in her
that reduces her to the level of some sort of petty,
blind, coarse animal. In any case, she's not a human

being. I say this to you as to a friend, the only man I can open my soul to. I love Natasha, it's true, but at times she seems to me amazingly vulgar, and then I lose my wits, I don't understand, what for or why, I love her so or, at least, did love. . . .

TCHEBUTYKIN [*Getting up*]: Brother, I'm going away tomorrow, we may never see each other again, so here is my advice to you. You know, put on your hat, take a walking-stick in your hands and be off— Be off, and go, go without looking back. And the farther you get the better.

(SOLYONY *walks by at the rear of the stage with two officers; seeing* TCHEBUTYKIN *he turns toward him; the officers walk on.*)

SOLYONY: Doctor, it's time! Half-past twelve. (*Greeting* ANDREI.)

TCHEBUTYKIN: Directly. I've had enough of you all. (*To* ANDREI) If anybody asks for me, Andrusha, say that I— directly . . . (*Sighing*) Oho-ho-ho—

SOLYONY (*Starting off with* TCHEBUTYKIN): Quick as a flash the bear made a dash— Why are you grunting, old man?

TCHEBUTYKIN: Get out!

SOLYONY: How's your health?

TCHEBUTYKIN (*Angrily*): Smooth as butter.

SOLYONY: The old man is needlessly upset. I'll indulge myself a little, I'll only wing him like a snipe. (*Takes out the perfume and sprinkles it on his hands*) There, I've poured a whole bottle out today and they still smell. My hands smell of a corpse. (*A pause*) So . . . Do you remember the poem? "And, rebellious, he seeks the storm, as if in storms were peace." . . .

TCHEBUTYKIN: Yes. Quick as a flash, the bear made a dash! (*He goes out with* SOLYONY.)

    (*Shouts are heard:* "Yoo hoo!" ANDREI *and* FERAPONT *enter.*)

FERAPONT: The papers to sign. . . .

ANDREI (*Nervously*): Leave me alone! Leave me! I beg of you! (*He walks away with the baby-carriage.*)

FERAPONT: But that's what papers are for, so they can be signed. (*He goes to the rear of the stage.*)

    (*Enter* IRINA *and* TUSENBACH, TUSENBACH *in a straw hat,* KULYGIN *crosses the stage, calling* "Ah-oo, Masha, Ah-oo.")

TUSENBACH: That seems to be the only man in town who's glad the officers are leaving.

IRINA: That's understandable. (*A pause*) Our town will be empty now.

TUSENBACH: Dear, I'll come right back.

IRINA: Where are you going?

TUSENBACH: I have to go to town, then . . . to see my comrades off.

IRINA: It's not true. . . . Nikolai, why are you so distraught today? (*A pause*) What happened yesterday near the theatre?

TUSENBACH (*With an impatient gesture*): In an hour I'll be back and will be with you again. (*Kissing her hand*) My beloved. . . . (*Looking into her face*) It's five years now I've loved you, and somehow I can't get used to it, and you seem always more beautiful to me. What lovely, wonderful hair! What eyes! I'll take you away tomorrow, we will work, we'll be rich, my dreams will come true. You shall be happy. Only there is one thing, one thing: You don't love me.

IRINA: That's not in my power! I'll be your wife, faithful
and obedient, but it's not love, what is there to do!
(*Crying*) I have never been in love—not once in my
life. Oh, I've dreamed so of love, I've dreamed of it a
long time now, day and night, but my soul is like
some fine piano that's locked and the key is lost. (*A
pause*) You have a restless look.

TUSENBACH: I haven't slept all night. There is nothing
in my life so terrible that it could frighten me, and only
that lost key tortures my soul—won't let me sleep. Say
something to me. (*A pause*) Say something to me. . . .

IRINA: What? What shall I say? What?

TUSENBACH: Something.

IRINA: That's enough! That's enough!

      (*A pause.*)

TUSENBACH: What nothings sometimes in life, what foolish trifles will take on meaning suddenly, for no reason at all. You laugh at them as you've always done,
you consider them nothings, and yet you go on and feel
that you haven't the strength to stop. Oh, let's not talk
about that! I feel gay. I see these firs, maples, birches
now as if I were seeing them for the first time and
they are all looking at me curiously and waiting. What
beautiful trees and what a beautiful life there should be
under them! (*A shout:* "Yoo hoo!") I must go. It's
time. . . . There's a tree that's dead, but it still waves
with the others in the wind. So it seems to me even if I
die, I'll still share in life somehow or other. Good-by,
my dearest. . . . (*Kissing her hands*) The papers you
gave me are lying on my table, under the calendar.

IRINA: But I'm going with you.

TUSENBACH (*Alarmed*): No, no! (*Going quickly, stopping in the alley*) Irina!

IRINA: What?

TUSENBACH (*Not knowing what to say*): I didn't drink any coffee today. Tell them, so that they'll make me some. . . . (*He goes quickly out.*)

> (IRINA *stands thinking, then goes to the rear of the stage and sits down in the swing.* ANDREI *comes in with the baby-carriage;* FERAPONT *appears.*)

FERAPONT: But Andrei Sergeevich, the papers aren't mine, they are official. I didn't think them up.

ANDREI: Oh, where is it, where is gone my past, when I was young and gay and clever, when my dreams and thoughts were full of grace, and the present and future bright with hope? Why is it that when we have barely begun to live we grow dull, gray, uninteresting, lazy, indifferent, useless, unhappy. . . . Our town has been in existence now for two hundred years, a hundred thousand people living in it, and there's not one who's not just like the others, not one that's outstanding either in the past or in the present, not one scholar, not one artist, not one who's even faintly remarkable, and would arouse envy or any passionate desire to imitate him. They just eat, drink, sleep, and then die. . . . Others are born and they, too, eat, drink, sleep and to keep from sinking into the torpor of boredom, vary their lives with foul gossip, vodka, cards, chicanery, and the wives deceive the husbands, while the husbands lie, pretend not to see anything, hear anything, and an unavoidably banal influence weighs on the children, and the divine spark dies in them and they become just as pitiful, identical corpses as their fathers and mothers were. . . . (*To* FERAPONT, *crossly*) What do you want?

FERAPONT: Hey? Papers to sign.

ANDREI: I've had enough of you.

FERAPONT (*Handing over the paper*): Just now the door-
man from the State Chamber was saying . . . It appears he says, this winter in Petersburg there was a
frost of two hundred degrees.

ANDREI: The present is hateful, but on the other hand,
when I think of the future— Oh, how good it is! I begin
to feel so easy, so free; and in the distance a light
dawns, I see freedom, I see how my children and I are
freed from idleness, from kvass, from goose with cab-
bage, from naps after dinner, from despicable sloth. . . .

FERAPONT: Two thousand people were frozen, it appears.
The people, they say, were horrified. It was either in
Petersburg, or it was in Moscow—I can't remember.

ANDREI (*Seized with a tender feeling*): My dear sisters,
my wonderful sisters (*Tearfully*) Masha, my sister.
. . .

NATASHA (*In the window*): Who is it talking so loud
out here? Is it you, Andrusha? You will wake up Sofie.
*Il ne faut pas faire du bruit, la Sofie est dormie déjà.
Vous êtes un ours.* (*Getting angry*) If you want to talk,
give the carriage and child to somebody else. Ferapont,
take the carriage from your master.

FERAPONT: Yes, ma'am. (*He takes the carriage.*)

ANDREI (*Embarrassed*): I'm speaking low.

NATASHA (*Behind the window, caressing her child*):
Bobik! Mischievous Bobik! Naughty Bobik!

ANDREI (*Glancing through the papers*): Very well, I'll
look through them and sign what's necessary, and you
can take them back to the Board. . . . (*He goes into
the house, reading the papers;* FERAPONT *pushes the
baby-carriage toward the rear of the garden.*)

NATASHA (*Behind the window*): Bobik, what is your Ma-

ma's name? Darling, darling! And who is this? This is
Aunt Olya. Say to Auntie: "How do you do, Olya!"

(*Some wandering musicians, a man and a girl, begin to play a violin and a harp;* VERSHININ, OLGA
and ANFISA *emerge from the house, and listen
quietly for a moment.* IRINA *joins them.*)

OLGA: Our garden's like a lot opening into several streets,
they walk and drive through it. Nurse, give these musicians something!

ANFISA (*Giving money to the musicians*): Good-by, my
dear souls! (*The musicians bow and go away*) Hard
lives they have! When you're full you don't play.
(*To* IRINA) Good morning, Irisha! (*Kissing her*) M-m-
m-m, child, how I live! How I live! At the high school
in a Government apartment, with Olyushka—God has
granted me that for my old age. Not since I was born,
sinner that I am, have I lived so. . . . A large apartment, the Government's, and a whole room for me and
a little bed. All the Government's. I wake up in the
night and—Oh Lord, Mother of God, there's nobody
happier than I am.

VERSHININ (*Looking at his watch*): We are going now,
Olga Sergeevna. It's time. (*A pause*) I wish you everything, everything. . . . Where's Maria Sergeevna?

IRINA: She's somewhere in the garden. I'll go look for her.

VERSHININ: Kindly, I'm in a hurry.

ANFISA: I'll go, too, and look for her. (*Calling*) Mashenka.
Ah, oo-oo! (*Going away with* IRINA *to the rear of the
garden*) Ah, oo-oo! Ah, oo-oo!

VERSHININ: Everything has its end. And here we are parting. (*Looking at his watch*) The town gave our company a sort of lunch, we drank champagne, the Mayor
made a speech, I ate and listened, but in my heart I was

here with you all—(*Looking around the garden*) I've grown used to you. . . .

OLGA: Are we ever to see each other again?

VERSHININ: Most likely not. (*A pause*) My wife and my two girls are leaving here in about two months; please, if anything happens, if anything is needed. . . .

OLGA: Yes, yes, of course. Be sure of that. (*A pause*) By tomorrow there won't be an officer in town; it will all be a memory and for us, of course, a new life will begin. . . . (*A pause*) Everything turns out not as we'd like to have it. I didn't want to be a headmistress and yet I became one. Which means we are not to be in Moscow.

VERSHININ: Well. . . . Thank you for everything. Forgive me, if anything was not quite. . . . Much, much too much, I've talked—forgive me for that, too, don't bear me any grudge.

OLGA (*Wiping her eyes*): Now why doesn't Masha come. . . .

VERSHININ: What else can I say to you as we part? What shall I philosophize about? . . . (*Laughing*) Life is difficult. It presents itself to many of us as blank and hopeless, and yet, one must admit, it gets always clearer and easier, and the day is not far off, apparently, when it will be wholly bright. (*Looking at his watch*) It's time for me to go, it's time! Once humanity was occupied with wars, filling its whole existence with marches, invasions, conquests, whereas now all of that is outlived, leaving behind it an enormous empty space which so far there is nothing to fill; humanity is searching passionately and, of course, will find it. Ah, if only it were quicker! (*A pause*) You know, if culture were added to industry and industry to culture. . . . (*Looking at his watch*) However, it's time for me. . . .

OLGA: There she comes.

(MASHA *enters.*)

VERSHININ: I came to say good-by. . . .

(OLGA *moves a little away so as not to disturb their farewell.*)

MASHA (*Looking into his face*): Good-by. . . . (*A long kiss*)

OLGA: Now, now. . . .

(MASHA *sobs violently.*)

VERSHININ: Write to me. . . . Don't forget me! Let me go . . . it's time. . . . Olga Sergeevna, take her, I'm all ready—it's time . . . late— (*Deeply moved, he kisses* OLGA'S *hand, then embraces* MASHA *again and goes quickly out.*)

OLGA: There, Masha! Stop, darling! . . .

(KULYGIN *enters.*)

KULYGIN (*Embarrassed*): No matter, let her cry, let her. . . . My good Masha, my kind Masha. . . . You are my wife and I am happy whatever happens. . . . I don't complain. . . . I don't make you a single reproach. And here's Olga to witness. . . . We'll begin to live again as we used to, and I won't say one word to you, not a breath. . . .

MASHA (*Stifling her sobs*): By the curved seashore a green oak, a golden chain upon that oak. . . . A golden chain upon that oak. . . . I'm going out of my mind. . . . By the curved seashore . . . a green oak.
. . .

OLGA: Be calm, Masha. . . . Be calm. . . . Give her some water.

MASHA: I am not crying any more.

KULYGIN: She is not crying now. . . . She's good. . . .
(*A shot is heard, faintly, from a distance.*)

MASHA: By the curved seashore a green oak, a golden
chain upon that oak. . . . The cat's green . . . the
oak's green. . . . I am mixing it up. . . . (*Taking a
drink of water*) My life is a failure. I don't want
anything now. I'll soon be calm. It's all the same. . . .
What does it mean: "By the curved seashore"? Why
does this word keep running through my head? My
thoughts are all mixed up.

(IRINA *enters.*)

OLGA: Be calm, Masha. Now, that's a good girl. . . .
Let's go in. . . .

MASHA (*Angrily*): I'm not going in there. (*Sobbing,
but checking herself at once*) I don't go in the house
any more, so I won't do it now.

IRINA: Let's sit down together just quietly. Well, tomorrow I'm going away. . . .

(*A pause.*)

KULYGIN: In the third grade yesterday I took this mustache and beard from a boy, see— (*Putting on the
mustache and beard*) I look like the German
teacher. . . . (*Laughing*) Isn't that so? Funny, these
boys. . . .

MASHA: Really you do look like your German.

OLGA: (*Laughing*): Yes.

(MASHA *weeps.*)

IRINA: There, Masha!

KULYGIN: A lot like. . . .

(NATASHA *enters.*)

NATASHA (*To the maid*): What? Protopopov will sit
with Sofotchka, Mikhail Ivanovich, and let Andrei
Sergeevich wheel Bobik. There's so much bother

with children. . . . (*To* IRINA) Irina, you are going away tomorrow—it's such a pity! Stay at least another week. (*Seeing* KULYGIN *she gives a shriek; he laughs and takes off the mustache and beard.*) Why, look at you, you scared me! (*To* IRINA) I am used to you and do you think parting with you will be easy for me? I'll give orders to put Andrei in your room, with his violin—let him saw away there!—and in his room we'll put Sofotchka. Marvelous, wonderful child! What a girl! Today she looked at me with such eyes, and—"Mama!"

KULYGIN: Beautiful child, that's true.

NATASHA: And so tomorrow I'll be all alone here. (*Sighing*) First of all, I'll give orders to chop down this alley of fir trees, then this maple here. . . . In the evening it looks so ugly. . . . (*To* IRINA) Dear, that belt doesn't suit you at all. . . . It's in very poor taste. You need something light. . . . And I'll order flowers planted, everywhere, flowers, and there'll be a fragrance . . . (*Severely*) What's a fork doing here on the bench? (*She goes into the house, to the maid.*) What's a fork doing here on the bench, I'd like to know? (*Shouting*) Shut up!

KULYGIN: She's off again!

(*Behind the scenes a band is playing a march; everybody listens.*)

OLGA: They are leaving.

(TCHEBUTYKIN *enters.*)

MASHA: Our friends are going. Well, then. . . . A pleasand journey to them! (*To her husband*) We must go home. . . . Where are my hat and cape?

KULYGIN: I carried them in the house . . . I'll get them right away.

OLGA: Yes, now we can all go home. It's time.

TCHEBUTYKIN: Olga Sergeevna!

OLGA: What? (*A pause*) What?

TCHEBUTYKIN: Nothing. . . . Don't know how to tell you. . . . (*Whispering in her ear*)

OLGA (*Alarmed*): It's not possible!

TCHEBUTYKIN: Yes. . . . What a story. . . . I'm tired, completely exhausted, don't want to talk any more. (*Irritably*) However, it's all the same!

MASHA: What happened?

OLGA (*Embracing* IRINA): It's a terrible day today. . . . I don't know how to tell you, my darling. . . .

IRINA: What? Say it quick. . . . What? For God's sake! (*Crying.*)

TCHEBUTYKIN: The Baron was killed just now in a duel.

IRINA (*Weeping quietly*): I knew, I knew. . . .

TCHEBUTYKIN (*Sitting down on a bench to the rear of the stage*): I'm tired. . . . (*Taking a newspaper out of his pocket*) Let them cry a little. . . . (*Singing softly*) Ta-ra-ra-boom-de-aye. . . . Sit on a curb I may. . . . As if it weren't all the same!

(*The three sisters stand with their arms around one another.*)

MASHA: Oh, how the music is playing! They are leaving us, one has gone entirely, entirely, forever. We'll be left alone to begin our life over again. We must live. . . . We must live. . . .

IRINA (*Putting her head on* OLGA's *breast*): The time will come when all will know why all this is, what these sufferings are for, there will be no secrets—but meanwhile we must live—must work, only work! Tomorrow I'm going away alone, I'll teach in the school and give my whole life to those who need it perhaps. It's autumn now; winter will soon come and cover everything with snow, and I'll work, work. . . .

OLGA (*Embracing both her sisters*): The music plays so gaily, bravely, and one wants to live. Oh, Lord! Time will pass and we shall be gone forever, they will forget us, they will forget our faces, voices, and how many of us there were, but our sufferings will turn into joy for those who will be living after us, happiness and peace will come on earth, and they will remember with some gentle word those who live now and will bless them. Oh, dear sisters, our life isn't over yet. We shall live! The music plays so gaily, so joyously, and it looks as if a little more and we shall know why we live, why we suffer. . . . If we only knew, if we only knew!

(*The music plays always softer and softer;* KULYGIN, *smiling and gay, brings the hat and cape,* ANDREI *is pushing the baby-carriage with Bobik in it.*)

TCHEBUTYKIN (*Singing softly*): Ta-ra-ra-boom-de-aye. . . . Sit on a curb I may. . . . (*Reading the newspaper*) It's all the same! It's all the same!

OLGA: If we only knew, if we only knew!

Curtain

The Cherry Orchard

CHARACTERS

RANEVSKAYA, LYUBOFF ANDREEVNA, *a landowner.*

ANYA, *her daughter, seventeen years old.*

VARYA, *her adopted daughter, twenty-four years old.*

GAYEFF, LEONID ANDREEVICH, *brother of Ranevskaya.*

LOPAHIN, YERMOLAY ALEXEEVICH, *a merchant.*

TROFIMOFF, PYOTR SERGEEVICH, *a student.*

SEMYONOFF-PISHTCHIK, BORIS BORISOVICH, *a landowner.*

CHARLOTTA IVANOVNA, *a governess.*

EPIHODOFF, SEMYON PANTELEEVICH, *a clerk.*

DUNYASHA, *a maid.*

FIERS, *a valet, an old man of eighty-seven.*

YASHA, *a young valet.*

A PASSERBY *or* STRANGER.

THE STATIONMASTER.

A POST-OFFICE CLERK.

Visitors, Servants.

The action takes place on the estate of L. A. Ranevskaya

ACT ONE

A room that is still called the nursery. One of the doors leads into ANYA's *room. Dawn, the sun will soon be rising. It is May, the cherry trees are in blossom but in the orchard it is cold, with a morning frost. The windows in the room are closed. Enter* DUNYASHA *with a candle and* LOPAHIN *with a book in his hand.*

LOPAHIN: The train got in, thank God! What time is it?

DUNYASHA: It's nearly two. (*Blows out his candle*) It's already daylight.

LOPAHIN: But how late was the train? Two hours at least. (*Yawning and stretching*) I'm a fine one, I am, look what a fool thing I did! I drove her on purpose just to meet them at the station, and then all of a sudden I'd overslept myself! Fell asleep in my chair. How provoking!—You could have waked me up.

DUNYASHA: I thought you had gone. (*Listening*) Listen, I think they are coming now.

LOPAHIN (*Listening*): No—No, there's the luggage and one thing and another. (*A pause*) Lyuboff Andreevna has been living abroad five years. I don't know what she is like now—She is a good woman. An easygoing, simple woman. I remember when I was a boy about fifteen, my father, who is at rest—in those days he ran a shop here in the village—hit me in the face with his fist, my nose was bleeding—We'd come to the yard together for something or other, and he was a little drunk. Lyuboff Andreevna, I can see her now, still so young, so slim, led me to the washbasin here in this very room, in the nursery. "Don't cry," she says, "little peasant, it will be well in time for your wedding"—(*A pause*) Yes, little peasant—My father was a peasant truly, and here I am in a white waistcoat and yellow shoes. Like a pig rooting in a pastry shop—I've got this rich, lots of money, but if you really stop and think of it, I'm just a peasant—(*Turning the pages of a book*) Here I was reading a book and didn't get a thing out of it. Reading and went to sleep. (*A pause*)

DUNYASHA: And all night long the dogs were not asleep, they know their masters are coming.

LOPAHIN: What is it, Dunyasha, you're so—

DUNYASHA: My hands are shaking. I'm going to faint.

LOPAHIN: You're just so delicate, Dunyasha. And all dressed up like a lady, and your hair all done up! Mustn't do that. Must know your place.

> (*Enter* EPIHODOFF, *with a bouquet: he wears a jacket and highly polished boots with a loud squeak. As he enters he drops the bouquet.*)

EPIHODOFF (*Picking up the bouquet*): Look, the gardener sent these, he says to put them in the dining room.

> (*Giving the bouquet to* DUNYASHA.)

LOPAHIN: And bring me some kvass.

DUNYASHA: Yes, sir. (*Goes out.*)

EPIHODOFF: There is a morning frost now, three degrees of frost (*Sighing*) and the cherries all in bloom. I cannot approve of our climate—I cannot. Our climate can never quite rise to the occasion. Listen, Yermolay Alexeevich, allow me to subtend, I bought myself, day before yesterday, some boots and they, I venture to assure you, squeak so that it is impossible. What could I grease them with?

LOPAHIN: Go on. You annoy me.

EPIHODOFF: Every day some misfortune happens to me. But I don't complain, I am used to it and I even smile.

(DUNYASHA *enters, serves* LOPAHIN *the kvass.*)

EPIHODOFF: I'm going. (*Stumbling over a chair and upsetting it*) There (*As if triumphant*) there, you see, pardon the expression, a circumstance like that, among others—It is simply quite remarkable. (*Goes out.*)

DUNYASHA: And I must tell you, Yermolay Alexeevich, that Epihodoff has proposed to me.

LOPAHIN: Ah!

DUNYASHA: I don't know really what to—He is a quiet man but sometimes when he starts talking, you can't understand a thing he means. It's all very nice, and full of feeling, but just doesn't make any sense. I sort of like him. He loves me madly. He's a man that's unfortunate, every day there's something or other. They tease him around here, call him twenty-two misfortunes—

LOPAHIN (*Cocking his ear*): Listen, I think they are coming—

DUNYASHA: They are coming! But what's the matter with me—I'm cold all over.

LOPAHIN: They're really coming. Let's go meet them. Will she recognize me? It's five years we haven't seen each other.

ᴅUNYASHA (*Excitedly*): I'm going to faint this very minute. Ah, I'm going to faint!

> (*Two carriages can be heard driving up to the house.* LOPAHIN *and* DUNYASHA *hurry out. The stage is empty. In the adjoining rooms a noise begins.* FIERS *hurries across the stage, leaning on a stick; he has been to meet* LYUBOFF ANDREEVNA, *and wears an old-fashioned livery and a high hat; he mutters something to himself, but you cannot understand a word of it. The noise offstage gets louder and louder. A voice: "Look! Let's go through here—"* LYUBOFF ANDREEVNA, ANYA *and* CHARLOTTA IVANOVNA, *with a little dog on a chain, all of them dressed for traveling,* VARYA, *in a coat and kerchief,* GAYEFF, SEMYONOFF-PISHTCHIK, LOPAHIN, DUNYASHA, *with a bundle and an umbrella, servants with pieces of luggage—all pass through the room.*)

ANYA: Let's go through here. Mama, do you remember what room this is?

LYUBOFF ANDREEVNA (*Happily, through her tears*): The nursery!

VARYA: How cold it is, my hands are stiff. (*To* LYUBOFF, ANDREEVNA) Your rooms, the white one and the violet, are just the same as ever, Mama.

LYUBOFF ANDREEVNA: The nursery, my dear beautiful room—I slept here when I was little— (*Crying*) And now I am like a child— (*Kisses her brother and* VARYA, *then her brother again*) And Varya is just the same as ever, looks like a nun. And I knew Dunyasha— (*Kisses* DUNYASHA.)

GAYEFF. The train was two hours late. How's that? How's that for good management?

CHARLOTTA (*To* PISHTCHIK): My dog he eats nuts too.

PISHTCHIK (*Astonished*): Think of that!

(*Everybody goes out except* ANYA *and* DUNYASHA.)

DUNYASHA: We waited so long— (*Taking off* ANYA's *coat and hat.*)

ANYA: I didn't sleep all four nights on the way. And now I feel so chilly.

DUNYASHA: It was Lent when you left, there was some snow then, there was frost, and now? My darling (*Laughing and kissing her*), I waited so long for you, my joy, my life—I'm telling you now, I can't keep from it another minute.

ANYA (*Wearily*): There we go again—

DUNYASHA: The clerk Epihodoff, proposed to me after Holy Week.

ANYA: You're always talking about the same thing— (*Arranging her hair*) I've lost all my hairpins— (*She is tired to the point of staggering.*)

DUNYASHA: I just don't know what to think. He loves me, loves me so!

ANYA: (*Looks in through her door, tenderly*) My room, my windows, it's just as if I had never been away. I'm home! Tomorrow morning I'll get up, I'll run into the orchard— Oh, if I only could go to sleep! I haven't slept all the way, I was tormented by anxiety.

DUNYASHA: Day before yesterday, Pyotr Sergeevich arrived.

ANYA (*Joyfully*): Petya!

DUNYASHA: He's asleep in the bathhouse, he lives there. I am afraid, he says, of being in the way. (*Taking her watch from her pocket and looking at it*) Somebody ought to wake him up. It's only that Varvara Mikhailovna told us not to. Don't you wake him up, she said

VARYA (*Enter* VARYA *with a bunch of keys at her belt*):
Dunyasha, coffee, quick—Mama is asking for coffee.

DUNYASHA: This minute. (*Goes out.*)

VARYA: Well, thank goodness, you've come back. You
are home again. (*Caressingly*) My darling is back! My
precious is back!

ANYA: I've had such a time.

VARYA: I can imagine!

ANYA: I left during Holy Week, it was cold then. Charlotta talked all the way and did her tricks. Why did you
fasten Charlotta on to me—?

VARYA: But you couldn't have traveled alone, darling;
not at seventeen!

ANYA: We arrived in Paris, it was cold there and snowing. I speak terrible French. Mama lived on the fifth
floor; I went to see her; there were some French people
in her room, ladies, an old priest with his prayer book,
and the place was full of tobacco smoke—very dreary.
Suddenly I began to feel sorry for Mama, so sorry, I
drew her to me, held her close and couldn't let her go.
Then Mama kept hugging me, crying—yes—

VARYA (*Tearfully*): Don't—oh, don't—

ANYA: Her villa near Mentone she had already sold, she
had nothing left, nothing. And I didn't have a kopeck
left. It was all we could do to get here. And Mama
doesn't understand! We sit down to dinner at a station
and she orders, insists on the most expensive things and
gives the waiters rouble tips. Charlotta does the same.
Yasha too demands his share; it's simply dreadful.
Mama has her butler, Yasha, we've brought him here—

VARYA: I saw the wretch.

ANYA: Well, how are things? Has the interest on the
mortgage been paid?

VARYA: How could we?

ANYA: Oh, my God, my God—!

VARYA: In August the estate is to be sold—

ANYA: My God—!

LOPAHIN (*Looking in through the door and mooing like a cow*): Moo-o-o— (*Goes away.*)

VARYA (*Tearfully*): I'd land him one like that— (*Shaking her fist.*)

ANYA (*Embracing* VARYA *gently*): Varya, has he proposed? (VARYA *shakes her head*) But he loves you— Why don't you have it out with him, what are you waiting for?

VARYA: I don't think anything will come of it for us. He is very busy, he hasn't any time for me—And doesn't notice me. God knows, it's painful for me to see him— Everybody talks about our marriage, everybody congratulates us, and the truth is, there's nothing to it—it's all like a dream— (*In a different tone*) You have a brooch looks like a bee.

ANYA (*Sadly*): Mama bought it. (*Going toward her room, speaking gaily, like a child*) And in Paris I went up in a balloon!

VARYA: My darling is back! My precious is back! (DUNYASHA *has returned with the coffee pot and is making coffee.* VARYA *is standing by the door*) Darling, I'm busy all day long with the house and I go around thinking things. If only you could be married to a rich man, I'd be more at peace too, I would go all by myself to a hermitage—then to Kiev—to Moscow, and I'd keep going like that from one holy place to another—I would go on and on. Heavenly!

ANYA: The birds are singing in the orchard. What time is it now?

VARYA. It must be after two. It's time you were asleep, darling. (*Going into* ANYA's *room*) Heavenly!

YASHA (YASHA *enters with a lap robe and a traveling bag. Crossing the stage airily*): May I go through here?

DUNYASHA: We'd hardly recognize you, Yasha; you've changed so abroad!

YASHA: Hm— And who are you?

DUNYASHA: When you left here, I was like that— (*Her hand so high from the floor*) I'm Dunyasha, Fyodor Kozoyedoff's daughter. You don't remember!

YASHA: Hm— You little peach!

(*Looking around before he embraces her; she shrieks and drops a saucer;* YASHA *hurries out.*)

VARYA (*At the door, in a vexed tone*): And what's going on here?

DUNYASHA (*Tearfully*): I broke a saucer—

VARYA: That's good luck.

ANYA (*Emerging from her room*): We ought to tell Mama beforehand: Petya is here—

VARYA: I told them not to wake him up.

ANYA (*Pensively*): Six years ago our father died, a month later our brother Grisha was drowned in the river, such a pretty little boy, just seven. Mama couldn't bear it, she went away, went away without ever looking back— (*Shuddering*) How I understand her, if she only knew I did. (*A pause*) and Petya Trofimoff was Grisha's tutor, he might remind—

FIERS (*Enter* FIERS; *he is in a jacket and white waistcoat. Going to the coffee urn, busy with it*): The mistress will have her breakfast here— (*Putting on white gloves*) Is the coffee ready? (*To* DUNYASHA, *sternly*) You! What about the cream?

DUNYASHA: Oh, my God— (*Hurrying out.*)

FIERS (*Busy at the coffee urn*): Oh, you good-for-nothing—! (*Muttering to himself*) Come back from Paris— And the master used to go to Paris by coach— (*Laughing.*)

VARYA: Fiers, what are you—?

FIERS: At your service. (*Joyfully*) My mistress is back! It's what I've been waiting for! Now I'm ready to die— (*Crying for joy.*)

> (LYUBOFF ANDREEVNA, GAYEFF *and* SEMYONOFF-PISH-TCHIK *enter;* SEMYONOFF-PISHTCHIK *is in a podyovka of fine cloth and sharovary.* GAYEFF *enters; he makes gestures with his hands and body as if he were playing billiards.*)

LYUBOFF ANDREEVNA: How is it? Let me remember— Yellow into the corner! Duplicate in the middle!

GAYEFF: I cut into the corner. Sister, you and I slept here in this very room once, and now I am fifty-one years old, strange as that may seem—

LOPAHIN: Yes, time passes.

GAYEFF: What?

LOPAHIN: Time, I say, passes.

GAYEFF: And it smells like patchouli here.

ANYA: I'm going to bed. Good night, Mama. (*Kissing her mother.*)

LYUBOFF ANDREEVNA: My sweet little child. (*Kissing her hands*) You're glad you are home? I still can't get myself together.

ANYA: Good-by, Uncle.

GAYEFF (*Kissing her face and hands*): God be with you. How like your mother you are! (*To his sister*) Lyuba, at her age you were exactly like her.

> (ANYA *shakes hands with* LOPAHIN *and* PISHTCHIK, *goes out and closes the door behind her.*)

LYUBOFF ANDREEVNA: She's very tired.

PISHTCHIK: It is a long trip, I imagine.

VARYA (*To* LOPAHIN *and* PISHTCHIK): Well, then, sirs? It's going on three o'clock, time for gentlemen to be going.

LYUBOFF ANDREEVNA (*Laughing*): The same old Varya. (*Drawing her to her and kissing her*) There, I'll drink my coffee, then we'll all go. (FIERS *puts a small cushion under her feet*) Thank you, my dear. I am used to coffee. Drink it day and night. Thank you, my dear old soul.

(*Kissing* FIERS.)

VARYA: I'll go see if all the things have come. (*Goes out.*)

LYUBOFF ANDREEVNA: Is it really me sitting here? (*Laughing*) I'd like to jump around and wave my arms. (*Covering her face with her hands*) But I may be dreaming! God knows I love my country, love it deeply, I couldn't look out of the car window, I just kept crying. (*Tearfully*) However, I must drink my coffee. Thank you, Fiers, thank you, my dear old friend. I'm so glad you're still alive.

FIERS: Day before yesterday.

GAYEFF: He doesn't hear well.

LOPAHIN: And I must leave right now. It's nearly five o'clock in the morning, for Kharkov. What a nuisance! I wanted to look at you—talk— You are as beautiful as ever.

PISHTCHIK (*Breathing heavily*): Even more beautiful— In your Paris clothes— It's a feast for the eyes—

LOPAHIN: Your brother, Leonid Andreevich here, says I'm a boor, a peasant money grubber, but that's all the same to me, absolutely. Let him say it. All I wish is you'd trust me as you used to, and your wonderful, touching eyes would look at me as they did. Merciful God! My father was a serf; belonged to your grand-father and your father; but you, your own self, you did so much for me once that I've forgotten all that and love you like my own kin—more than my kin.

LYUBOFF ANDREEVNA: I can't sit still—I can't. (*Jumping up and walking about in great excitement*) I'll never live through this happiness— Laugh at me, I'm silly— My own little bookcase—! (*Kissing the bookcase*) My little table!

GAYEFF: And in your absence the nurse here died.

LYUBOFF ANDREEVNA (*Sitting down and drinking cof-fee*): Yes, may she rest in Heaven! They wrote me.

GAYEFF: And Anastasy died. Cross-eyed Petrushka left me and lives in town now at the police officer's. (*Tak-ing out of his pocket a box of hard candy and sucking a piece.*)

PISHTCHIK: My daughter, Dashenka—sends you her greetings—

LOPAHIN: I want to tell you something very pleasant, cheerful. (*Glancing at his watch*) I'm going right away. There's no time for talking. Well, I'll make it two or three words. As you know, your cherry orchard is to be sold for your debts; the auction is set for August 22nd, but don't you worry, my dear, you just sleep in peace, there's a way out of it. Here's my plan. Please lis-ten to me. Your estate is only thirteen miles from town. They've run the railroad by it. Now if the cherry orchard and the land along the river were cut up into building lots and leased for summer cottages, you'd have at the very lowest twenty-five thousand roubles per year income.

GAYEFF: Excuse me, what rot!

LYUBOFF ANDREEVNA: I don't quite understand you, Yermolay Alexeevich.

LOPAHIN: At the very least you will get from the summer residents twenty-five roubles per year for a two-and-a-half acre lot and if you post a notice right off, I'll bet you anything that by autumn you won't have a single patch of land free, everything will be taken. In a word, my congratulations, you are saved. The location is wonderful, the river's so deep. Except, of course, it all needs to be tidied up, cleared— For instance, let's say, tear all the old buildings down and this house, which is no good any more, and cut down the old cherry orchard—

LYUBOFF ANDREEVNA: Cut down? My dear, forgive me, you don't understand at all. If there's one thing in the whole province that's interesting—not to say remarkable—it's our cherry orchard.

LOPAHIN: The only remarkable thing about this cherry orchard is that it's very big. There's a crop of cherries once every two years and even that's hard to get rid of. Nobody buys them.

GAYEFF: This orchard is even mentioned in the encyclopedia.

LOPAHIN (*Glancing at his watch*): If we don't cook up something and don't get somewhere, the cherry orchard and the entire estate will be sold at auction on the twenty-second of August. Do get it settled then! I swear here is no other way out. Not a one!

FIERS: There was a time, forty-fifty years ago when the cherries were dried, soaked, pickled, cooked into jam and it used to be—

GAYEFF: Keep quiet, Fiers.

FIERS: And it used to be that the dried cherries were shipped by the wagon-load to Moscow and to Kharkov. And the money there was! And the dried cherries were soft then, juicy, sweet, fragrant— They had a way of treating them then—

LYUBOFF ANDREEVNA: And where is that way now?

FIERS: They have forgotten it. Nobody remembers it.

PISHTCHIK (*To* LYUBOFF ANDREEVNA): What's happening in Paris? How is everything? Did you eat frogs?

LYUBOFF ANDREEVNA: I ate crocodiles.

PISHTCHIK: Think of it—!

LOPAHIN: Up to now in the country there have been only the gentry and the peasants, but now in summer the villa people too are coming in. All the towns, even the least big ones, are surrounded with cottages. In about twenty years very likely the summer resident will multiply enormously. He merely drinks tea on the porch now, but it might well happen that on this two-and-a-half acre lot of his, he'll go in for farming, and then your cherry orchard would be happy, rich, splendid—

GAYEFF (*Getting hot*): What rot!

(*Enter* VARYA *and* YASHA.)

VARYA: Here, Mama. Two telegrams for you. (*Choosing a key and opening the old bookcase noisily*) Here they are.

LYUBOFF ANDREEVNA: From Paris (*Tearing up the telegrams without reading them*) Paris, that's all over—

GAYEFF: Do you know how old this bookcase is, Lyuba? A week ago I pulled out the bottom drawer and looked, and there the figures were burned on it. The bookcase was made exactly a hundred years ago. How's that? Eh? You might celebrate its jubilee. It's an inanimate object, but all the same, be that as it may, it's a bookcase.

PISHTCHIK (*In astonishment*): A hundred years—! Think of it—!

GAYEFF: Yes—quite something— (*Shaking the bookcase*) Dear, honored bookcase! I saluted your existence, which for more than a hundred years has been directed toward the clear ideals of goodness and justice; your silent appeal to fruitful endeavor has not flagged in all the course of a hundred years, sustaining (*Tearfully*) through the generations of our family, our courage and our faith in a better future and nurturing in us ideals of goodness and of a social consciousness.

(*A pause.*)

LOPAHIN: Yes.

LYUBOFF ANDREEVNA: You're the same as ever, Lenya.

GAYEFF (*Slightly embarrassed*): Carom to the right into the corner pocket. I cut into the side pocket!

LOPAHIN (*Glancing at his watch*): Well, it's time for me to go.

YASHA (*Handing medicine to* LYUBOFF ANDREEVNA): Perhaps you'll take the pills now—

PISHTCHIK: You should never take medicaments, dear madam— They do neither harm nor good— Hand them here, dearest lady. (*He takes the pillbox, shakes the pills out into his palm, blows on them, puts them in his mouth and washes them down with kvass*) There! Now!

LYUBOFF ANDREEVNA (*Startled*): Why, you've lost your mind!

PISHTCHIK: I took all the pills.

LOPAHIN: Such a glutton!
    (*Everyone laughs.*)

FIERS: The gentleman stayed with us during Holy Week, he ate half a bucket of pickles— (*Muttering.*)

LYUBOFF ANDREEVNA: What is he muttering about?

VARYA: He's been muttering like that for three years. We're used to it.

YASHA: In his dotage.
    (CHARLOTTA IVANOVNA *in a white dress—she is very thin, her corset laced very tight—with a lorgnette at her belt, crosses the stage.*)

LOPAHIN: Excuse me, Charlotta Ivanovna, I haven't had a chance yet to welcome you. (*Trying to kiss her hand.*)

CHARLOTTA (*Drawing her hand away*): If I let you kiss my hand, 'twould be my elbow next, then my shoulder—

LOPAHIN: No luck for me today. (*Everyone laughs*) Charlotta Ivanovna, show us a trick!

CHARLOTTA: No. I want to go to bed. (*Exit.*)

LOPAHIN: In three weeks we shall see each other. (*Kissing* LYUBOFF ANDREEVNA's *hand*) Till then, good-by. It's time. (*To* GAYEFF) See you soon. (*Kissing* PISHT-CHIK) See you soon. (*Shaking* VARYA's *hand, then* FIERS' *and* YASHA's) I don't feel like going. (*To* LYUBOFF ANDREEVNA) If you think it over and make up your mind about the summer cottages, let me know and I'll arrange a loan of something like fifty thousand roubles. Think it over seriously.

VARYA (*Angrily*): Do go on, anyhow, will you!

LOPAHIN: I'm going, I'm going— (*Exit.*)

GAYEFF: Boor. However, pardon—Varya is going to marry him, it's Varya's little fiancé.

VARYA: Don't talk too much, Uncle.

LYUBOFF ANDREEVNA. Well, Varya, I should be very glad. He's a good man.

PISHTCHIK: A man, one must say truthfully—A most worthy—And my Dashenka—says also that—she says all sorts of things— (*Snoring but immediately waking up*) Nevertheless, dearest lady, oblige me—With a loan of two hundred and forty roubles— Tomorrow the interest on my mortgage has got to be paid—

VARYA (*Startled*): There's not any money, none at all.

LYUBOFF ANDREEVNA: Really, I haven't got anything.

PISHTCHIK: I'll find it, somehow. (*Laughing*) I never give up hope. There, I think to myself, all is lost, I am ruined and lo and behold—a railroad is put through my land and—they paid me. And then, just watch, something else will turn up—if not today, then tomorrow— Dashenka will win two hundred thousand— She has a ticket.

LYUBOFF ANDREEVNA: We've finished the coffee, now we can go to bed.

FIERS (*Brushing GAYEFF's clothes, reprovingly*): You put on the wrong trousers again. What am I going to do with you!

VARYA (*Softly*): Anya is asleep. (*Opening the window softly*) Already the sun's rising—it's not cold. Look, Mama! What beautiful trees! My Lord, what air! The starlings are singing!

GAYEFF (*Opening another window*): The orchard is all white. You haven't forgotten, Lyuba? That long lane there runs straight—as a strap stretched out. It glistens on moonlight nights. Do you remember? You haven't forgotten it?

LYUBOFF ANDREEVNA (*Looking out of the window on to the*

orchard): Oh, my childhood, my innocence! I slept in this nursery and looked out on the orchard from here, every morning happiness awoke with me, it was just as it is now, then, nothing has changed. (*Laughing with joy*) All, all white! Oh, my orchard! After a dark, rainy autumn and cold winter, you are young again and full of happiness. The heavenly angels have not deserted you— If I only could lift the weight from my breast, from my shoulders, if I could only forget my past!

GAYEFF: Yes, and the orchard will be sold for debt, strange as that may seem.

LYUBOFF ANDREEVNA: Look, our dear mother is walking through the orchard—In a white dress! (*Laughing happily*) It's she.

GAYEFF: Where?

VARYA: God be with you, Mama!

LYUBOFF ANDREEVNA: There's not anybody, it only seemed so. To the right, as you turn to the summerhouse, a little white tree is leaning there, looks like a woman— (*Enter* TROFIMOFF, *in a student's uniform, well worn, and glasses*) What a wonderful orchard! The white masses of blossoms, the sky all blue.

TROFIMOFF: Lyuboff Andreevna! (*She looks around at him*) I will just greet you and go immediately. (*Kissing her hand warmly*) I was told to wait until morning, but I hadn't the patience—

     (LYUBOFF ANDREEVNA *looks at him puzzled.*)

VARYA (*Tearfully*): This is Petya Trofimoff—

TROFIMOFF: Petya Trofimoff, the former tutor of your Grisha— Have I really changed so?

     (LYUBOFF ANDREEVNA *embraces him; and crying quietly.*)

GAYEFF (*Embarrassed*): There, there, Lyuba.

VARYA (*Crying*): I told you, Petya, to wait till tomorrow.

LYUBOFF ANDREEVNA: My Grisha—My boy—Grisha—Son—

VARYA: What can we do, Mama? It's God's will.

TROFIMOFF (*In a low voice tearfully*): There, there—

LYUBOFF ANDREEVNA (*Weeping softly*): My boy was lost, drowned— Why? Why, my friend? (*More quietly*) Anya is asleep there, and I am talking so loud—Making so much noise— But why, Petya? Why have you lost your looks? Why do you look so much older?

TROFIMOFF: A peasant woman on the train called me a mangy-looking gentleman.

LYUBOFF ANDREEVNA: You were a mere boy then, a charming young student, and now your hair's not very thick any more and you wear glasses. Are you really a student still? (*Going to the door.*)

TROFIMOFF: Very likely I'll be a perennial student.

LYUBOFF ANDREEVNA (*Kissing her brother, then* VARYA): Well, go to bed— You've grown older too, Leonid.

PISHTCHIK (*Following her*): So that's it, we are going to bed now. Oh, my gout! I'm staying here— I'd like, Lyuboff Andreevna, my soul, tomorrow morning— Two hundred and forty roubles—

GAYEFF: He's still at it.

PISHTCHIK: Two hundred and forty roubles— To pay interest on the mortgage.

LYUBOFF ANDREEVNA: I haven't any money, my dove.

PISHTCHIK: I'll pay it back, my dear— It's a trifling sum—

LYUBOFF ANDREEVNA: Oh, very well, Leonid will give— You give it to him, Leonid.

GAYEFF: Oh, certainly, I'll give it to him. Hold out your pockets.

LYUBOFF ANDREEVNA: What can we do, give it, he needs it— He'll pay it back.

>(LYUBOFF ANDREEVNA, TROFIMOFF, PISHTCHIK *and* FIERS *go out.* GAYEFF, VARYA *and* YASHA *remain.*)

GAYEFF: My sister hasn't yet lost her habit of throwing money away. (*To* YASHA) Get away, my good fellow, you smell like hens.

YASHA (*With a grin*): And you are just the same as you used to be, Leonid Andreevich.

GAYEFF: What? (*To* VARYA) What did he say?

VARYA (*To* YASHA): Your mother has come from the village, she's been sitting in the servants' hall ever since yesterday, she wants to see you—

YASHA: The devil take her!

VARYA: Ach, shameless creature!

YASHA: A lot I need her! She might have come tomorrow.

>(*Goes out.*)

VARYA: Mama is just the same as she was, she hasn't changed at all. If she could, she'd give away everything she has.

GAYEFF: Yes— If many remedies are prescribed for an illness, you may know the illness is incurable. I keep thinking, I wrack my brains, I have many remedies, a great many, and that means, really, I haven't any at all. It would be fine to inherit a fortune from somebody, it would be fine to marry off our Anya to a very rich man, it would be fine to go to Yaroslavl and try our luck with our old aunt, the Countess. Auntie is very, very rich.

VARYA (*Crying*): If God would only help us!

GAYEFF: Don't bawl! Auntie is very rich but she doesn't like us. To begin with, Sister married a lawyer, not a nobleman— (ANYA *apears at the door*) Married not a nobleman and behaved herself, you could say, not very virtuously. She is good, kind, nice, I love her very much, but no matter how much you allow for the extenuating circumstances, you must admit she's a depraved woman. You feel it in her slightest movement.

VARYA (*Whispering*): Anya is standing in the door there.

GAYEFF: What? (*A pause*) It's amazing, something got in my right eye. I am beginning to see poorly. And on Thursday, when I was in the District Court—

(ANYA *enters.*)

VARYA: But why aren't you asleep, Anya?

ANYA: I don't feel like sleeping. I can't.

GAYEFF: My little girl— (*Kissing* ANYA's *face and hands*) My child— (*Tearfully*) You are not my niece, you are my angel, you are everything to me. Believe me, believe—

ANYA: I believe you, Uncle. Everybody loves you, respects you— But dear Uncle, you must keep quiet, just keep quiet— What were you saying, just now, about my mother, about your own sister? What did you say that for?

GAYEFF: Yes, yes— (*Putting her hand up over his face*) Really, it's terrible! My God! Oh, God, save me! And today I made a speech to the bookcase— So silly! And it was only when I finished it that I could see it was silly.

VARYA: It's true, Uncle, you ought to keep quiet. Just keep quiet. That's all.

ANYA: If you kept quiet, you'd have more peace.

GAYEFF: I'll keep quiet. (*Kissing* ANYA's *and* VARYA's *hands*) I'll keep quiet. Only this, it's about business. On Thursday I was in the District Court; well, a few of us gathered around and a conversation began about this and that, about lots of things; apparently it will be possible to arrange a loan on a promissory note to pay the bank the interest due.

VARYA: If the Lord would only help us!

GAYEFF: Tuesday I shall go and talk it over again. (*To* VARYA) Don't bawl! (*To* ANYA) Your mother will talk to Lopahin; of course, he won't refuse her . . . And as soon as you rest up, you will go to Yaroslavl to your great-aunt, the Countess. There, that's how we will move from three directions, and the business is in the bag. We'll pay the interest. I am convinced of that— (*Putting a hard candy in his mouth*) On my honor I'll swear, by anything you like, that the estate shall not be sold! (*Excitedly*) By my happiness, I swear! Here's my hand, call me a worthless, dishonorable man, if I allow it to come up for auction! With all my soul I swear it!

ANYA (*A quieter mood returns to her; she is happy*): How good you are, Uncle, how clever! (*Embracing her uncle*) I feel easy now! I feel easy! I'm happy!

FIERS (FIERS *enters, reproachfully*): Leonid Andreevich, have you no fear of God! When are you going to bed?

GAYEFF: Right away, right away. You may go, Fiers. For this once I'll undress myself. Well, children, beddy bye— More details tomorrow, and now, go to bed (*Kissing* ANYA *and* VARYA) I am a man of the eighties— It is a period that's not admired, but I can say, nevertheless, that I've suffered no little for my convictions in the course of my life. It is not for nothing that the peasant loves me. One must know the peasant! One must know from what—

ANYA: Again, Uncle!

VARYA: You, Uncle dear, keep quiet.

FIERS (*Angrily*): Leonid Andreevich!

GAYEFF: I'm coming, I'm coming— Go to bed. A double bank into the side pocket! A clean shot—
(*Goes out,* FIERS *hobbling after him.*)

ANYA: I feel easy now. I don't feel like going to Yaroslavl; I don't like Great-aunt, but still I feel easy. Thanks to Uncle. (*Sits down.*)

VARYA: I must get to sleep. I'm going. And there was unpleasantness here during your absence. In the old servants' quarters, as you know, live only the old servants: Yephemushka, Polya, Yevstignay, well, and Karp. They began to let every sort of creature spend the night with them—I didn't say anything. But then I hear they've spread the rumor that I'd given orders to feed them nothing but beans. Out of stinginess, you see— And all that from Yevstignay— Very well, I think to myself. If that's the way it is, I think to myself, then you just wait. I call in Yevstignay— (*Yawning*) He comes— How is it, I say, that you, Yevstignay— You're such a fool— (*Glancing at* ANYA) Anitchka!—(*A pause*) Asleep! (*Takes* ANYA *by her arm*) Let's go to bed— Come on!— (*Leading her*) My little darling fell asleep! Come on— (*They go. Far away beyond the orchard a shepherd is playing on a pipe.* TROFIMOFF *walks across the stage and, seeing* VARYA *and* ANYA, *stops*) Shh— She is asleep—asleep— Let's go, dear.

ANYA (*Softly, half dreaming*): I'm so tired— All the bells!—Uncle—dear— And Mama and Uncle— Varya.

VARYA: Come on, my dear, come on. (*They go into* ANYA's *room.*)

TROFIMOFF (*Tenderly*): My little sun! My spring!

Curtain

ACT TWO

A field. An old chapel, long abandoned, with crooked walls, near it a well, big stones that apparently were once tombstones, and an old bench. A road to the estate of GAYEFF *can be seen. On one side poplars rise, casting their shadows, the cherry orchard begins there. In the distance a row of telegraph poles; and far, far away, faintly traced on the horizon, is a large town, visible only in the clearest weather. The sun will soon be down.* CHARLOTTA, YASHA *and* DUNYASHA *are sitting on the bench;* EPIHODOFF *is standing near and playing the guitar; everyone sits lost in thought.* CHARLOTTA *wears an old peak cap* (fourrage); *she has taken a rifle from off her shoulders and is adjusting the buckle on the strap.*

CHARLOTTA (*Pensively*): I have no proper passport, I don't know how old I am—it always seems to me I'm very young. When I was a little girl, my father and mother traveled from fair to fair and gave performances, very good ones. And I did *salto mortale* and different tricks. And when Papa and Mama died, a German lady took me to live with her and began teaching me. Good. I grew up. And became a governess. But where I came from and who I am I don't know— Who my parents were, perhaps they weren't even married—I don't know. (*Taking a cucumber out of her pocket and beginning to eat it*) I don't know a thing. (*A pause*) I'd like so much to talk but there's not anybody. I haven't anybody.

EPIHODOFF (*Playing the guitar and singing*): "What care I for the noisy world, what care I for friends and foes."—How pleasant it is to play the mandolin!

DUNYASHA: That's a guitar, not a mandolin. (*Looking into a little mirror and powdering her face.*)

EPIHODOFF: For a madman who is in love this is a mandolin— (*Singing*) "If only my heart were warm with the fire of requited love. "

(YASHA *sings with him.*)

CHARLOTTA: How dreadfully these people sing— Phooey! Like jackals.

DUNYASHA (*To* YASHA): All the same what happiness to have been abroad.

YASHA: Yes, of course. I cannot disagree with you. (*Yawning and then lighting a cigar.*)

EPIHODOFF: That's easily understood. Abroad everything long since attained its complete development.

YASHA: That's obvious.

EPIHODOFF: I am a cultured man. I read all kinds of remarkable books, but the trouble is I cannot discover my own inclinations, whether to live or to shoot myself, but nevertheless, I always carry a revolver on me. Here it is—(*Showing a revolver.*)

CHARLOTTA: That's done. Now I am going. (*Slinging the*

rifle over her shoulder) You are a very clever man, Epihodoff, and a very terrible one; the women must love you madly. Brrrr-r-r-r! (*Going*) These clever people are all so silly, I haven't anybody to talk with. I'm always alone, alone, I have nobody and— Who I am, why I am, is unknown— (*Goes out without hurrying.*)

EPIHODOFF: Strictly speaking, not touching on other subjects, I must state about myself, in passing, that fate treats me mercilessly, as a storm does a small ship. If, let us suppose, I am mistaken, then why, to mention one instance, do I wake up this morning, look and there on my chest is a spider of terrific size — There, like that. (*Showing the size with both hands*) And also I take some kvass to drink and in it I find something in the highest degree indecent, such as a cockroach. (*A pause*) Have you read Buckle? (*A pause*) I desire to trouble you, Avdotya Feodorovna, with a couple of words.

DUNYASHA: Speak.

EPIHODOFF: I have a desire to speak with you alone— (*Sighing.*)

DUNYASHA (*Embarrassed*): Very well— But bring me my cape first—by the cupboard— It's rather damp here—

EPIHODOFF: Very well—I'll fetch it— Now I know what I should do with my revolver—(*Takes the guitar and goes out playing.*)

YASHA: Twenty-two misfortunes! Between us he's a stupid man, it must be said. (*Yawning.*)

DUNYASHA: God forbid he should shoot himself. (*A pause*) I've grown so uneasy, I'm always fretting. I was only a girl when I was taken into the master's

house, and now I've lost the habit of simple living—
and here are my hands white, white as a lady's. I've
become so delicate, fragile, ladylike, afraid of everything—Frightfully so. And, Yasha, if you deceive me,
I don't know what will happen to my nerves.

YASHA (*Kissing her*): You little cucumber! Of course
every girl must behave properly. What I dislike above
everything is for a girl to conduct herself badly.

DUNYASHA: I have come to love you passionately, you are
educated, you can discuss anything. (*A pause.*)

YASHA (*Yawning*): Yes, sir—To my mind it is like this:
If a girl loves someone, it means she is immoral. (*A
pause*) It is pleasant to smoke a cigar in the clear air
—(*Listening*) They are coming here— It is the ladies
and gentlemen—

(DUNYASHA *impulsively embraces him.*)

YASHA: Go to the house, as though you had been to
bathe in the river, go by this path, otherwise, they
might meet you and suspect me of making a rendez-
vous with you. That I cannot tolerate.

DUNYASHA (*With a little cough*): Your cigar has given
me the headache. (*Goes out.*)

(YASHA *remains, sitting near the chapel.* LYUBOFF
ANDREEVNA, GAYEFF *and* LOPAHIN *enter.*)

LOPAHIN: We must decide definitely, time doesn't wait.
Why, the matter's quite simple. Are you willing to
lease your land for summer cottages or are you not?
Answer in one word, yes or no? Just one word!

LYUBOFF ANDREEVNA: Who is it smokes those disgusting
cigars out here—? (*Sitting down.*)

GAYEFF: The railroad running so near is a great con-
venience. (*Sitting down*) We made a trip to town
and lunched there— Yellow in the side pocket! Per-

haps I should go in the house first and play one
game—

LYUBOFF ANDREEVNA: You'll have time.

LOPAHIN: Just one word! (*Imploringly*) Do give me
your answer!

GAYEFF (*Yawning*): What?

LYUBOFF ANDREEVNA (*Looking in her purse*): Yesterday
there was lots of money in it. Today there's very little. My poor Varya! For the sake of economy she
feeds everybody milk soup, and in the kitchen the old
people get nothing but beans, and here I spend
money—senselessly— (*Dropping her purse and scattering gold coins*) There they go scattering! (*She is
vexed.*)

YASHA: Allow me, I'll pick them up in a second. (*Picking up the coins*)

LYUBOFF ANDREEVNA: If you will, Yasha. And why did
I go in town for lunch—? Your restaurant with its
music is trashy, the tablecloths smell of soap— Why
drink so much, Lyonya? Why eat so much? Why
talk so much? Today in the restaurant you were talking a lot again, and all of it beside the point. About
the seventies, about the decadents. And to whom?
Talking to waiters about the decadents!

LOPAHIN: Yes.

GAYEFF (*Waving his hand*): I am incorrigible, that's evident— (*To* YASHA *irritably*) What is it?—You are forever swirling around in front of us?

YASHA (*Laughing*): I cannot hear your voice without
laughing.

GAYEFF (*To his sister*): Either I or he—

LYUBOFF ANDREEVNA: Go away, Yasha. Go on—

YASHA (*Giving* LYUBOFF ANDREEVNA *her purse*): I am

going right away. (*Barely suppressing his laughter*)
This minute. (*Goes out.*)

LOPAHIN: The rich Deriganoff intends to buy your estate. They say he is coming personally to the auction.

LYUBOFF ANDREEVNA: And where did you hear that?

LOPAHIN: In town they are saying it.

GAYEFF: Our Yaroslavl aunt promised to send us something, but when and how much she will send, nobody knows—

LOPAHIN: How much will she send? A hundred thousand? Two hundred?

LYUBOFF ANDREEVNA: Well—maybe ten, fifteen thousand
—we'd be thankful for that.

LOPAHIN: Excuse me, but such light-minded people as
you are, such odd, unbusinesslike people, I never saw.
You are told in plain Russian that your estate is being
sold up and you just don't seem to take it in.

LYUBOFF ANDREEVNA: But what are we to do? Tell us
what?

LOPAHIN: I tell you every day. Every day I tell you the
same thing. Both the cherry orchard and the land
have got to be leased for summer cottages, it has to be
done right now, quick— The auction is right under
your noses. Do understand! Once you finally decide
that there are to be summer cottages, you will get all
the money you want, and then you'll be saved.

LYUBOFF ANDREEVNA: Summer cottages and summer
residents—it is so trivial, excuse me.

GAYEFF: I absolutely agree with you.

LOPAHIN: I'll either burst out crying, or scream, or faint.
I can't bear it! You are torturing me! (*To* GAYEFF)
You're a perfect old woman!

GAYEFF: What?

LOPAHIN: A perfect old woman! (*About to go.*)

LYUBOFF ANDREEVNA (*Alarmed*): No, don't go, stay, my lamb, I beg you. Perhaps we will think of something!

LOPAHIN: What is there to think about?

LYUBOFF ANDREEVNA: Don't go, I beg you. With you here it is more cheerful anyhow— (*A pause*) I keep waiting for something, as if the house were about to tumble down on our heads.

GAYEFF (*Deep in thought*): Double into the corner pocket— Bank into the wide pocket—

LYUBOFF ANDREEVNA: We have sinned so much—

LOPAHIN: What sins have you—?

GAYEFF (*Puts a hard candy into his mouth*): They say I've eaten my fortune up in hard candies— (*Laughing.*)

LYUBOFF ANDREEVNA: Oh, my sins—I've always thrown money around like mad, recklessly, and I married a man who accumulated nothing but debts. My husband died from champagne—he drank fearfully—and to my misfortune I fell in love with another man. I lived with him, and just at that time—it was my first punishment—a blow over the head: right here in the river my boy was drowned and I went abroad—went away for good, never to return, never to see this river again—I shut my eyes, ran away, beside myself, and he after me—mercilessly, brutally. I bought a villa near Mentone, because he fell ill there, and for three years I knew no rest day or night, the sick man exhausted me, my soul dried up. And last year when the villa was sold for debts, I went to Paris and there he robbed me of everything, threw me over, took up with another woman; I tried to poison myself—so stupid, so shameful— And suddenly I was seized with longing for Russia, for my own country, for my little girl— (*Wiping away her tears*) Lord, Lord, have mercy, forgive me my sins! Don't punish me any more! (*Getting a telegram out of her pocket*) I got this today from Paris, he asks forgiveness, begs me to return— (*Tears up the telegram*) That sounds like music somewhere.

(*Listening.*)

GAYEFF: It is our famous Jewish orchestra. You remember, four violins, a flute and double bass.

LYUBOFF ANDREEVNA: Does it still exist? We ought to get hold of it sometime and give a party.

LOPAHIN (*Listening*): Can't hear it— (*Singing softly*) "And for money the Germans will frenchify a Russian." (*Laughing*) What a play I saw yesterday at the theatre, very funny!

LYUBOFF ANDREEVNA: And most likely there was nothing funny about it. You shouldn't look at plays, but look oftener at yourselves. How gray all your lives are, what a lot of idle things you say!

LOPAHIN: That's true. It must be said frankly this life of ours is idiotic— (*A pause*) My father was a peasant, an idiot, he understood nothing, he taught me nothing, he just beat me in his drunken fits and always with a stick. At bottom I am just as big a dolt and idiot as he was. I wasn't taught anything, my handwriting is vile, I write like a pig—I am ashamed for people to see it.

LYUBOFF ANDREEVNA: You ought to get married, my friend.

LOPAHIN: Yes—That's true.

LYUBOFF ANDREEVNA: To our Varya, perhaps. She is a good girl.

LOPAHIN: Yes.

LYUBOFF ANDREEVNA: She comes from simple people, and she works all day long, but the main thing is she loves you. And you, too, have liked her a long time.

LOPAHIN: Why not? I am not against it— She's a good girl. (*A pause.*)

GAYEFF: They are offering me a position in a bank. Six thousand a year— Have you heard that?

LYUBOFF ANDREEVNA: Not you! You stay where you are—

FIERS (FIERS *enters, bringing an overcoat. To* GAYEFF): Pray, Sir, put this on, it's damp.

GAYEFF (*Putting on the overcoat*): You're a pest, old man.

FIERS: That's all right— This morning you went off without letting me know. (*Looking him over.*)

LYUBOFF ANDREEVNA: How old you've grown, Fiers!

FIERS: At your service.

LOPAHIN: She says you've grown very old!

FIERS: I've lived a long time. They were planning to marry me off before your papa was born. (*Laughing*) And at the time the serfs were freed I was already the head footman. I didn't want to be freed then, I stayed with the masters—(*A pause*) And I remember, everybody was happy, but what they were happy about they didn't know themselves.

LOPAHIN: In the old days it was fine. At least they flogged.

FIERS (*Not hearing*): But, of course. The peasants stuck to the masters, the masters stuck to the peasants, and now everything is all smashed up, you can't tell about anything.

GAYEFF: Keep still, Fiers. Tomorrow I must go to town. They have promised to introduce me to a certain general who might make us a loan.

LOPAHIN: Nothing will come of it. And you can rest assured you won't pay the interest.

LYUBOFF ANDREEVNA: He's just raving on. There aren't any such generals.

(TROFIMOFF, ANYA *and* VARYA *enter.*)

GAYEFF: Here they come.

ANYA: There is Mama sitting there.

LYUBOFF ANDREEVNA (*Tenderly*): Come, come—My darlings—(*Embracing* ANYA *and* VARYA) If you only knew how I love you both! Come sit by me—there—like that.

(*Everybody sits down.*)

LOPAHIN: Our perennial student is always strolling with the young ladies.

TROFIMOFF: It's none of your business.

LOPAHIN: He will soon be fifty and he's still a student.

TROFIMOFF: Stop your stupid jokes.

LOPAHIN: But why are you so peevish, you queer duck?

TROFIMOFF: Don't you pester me.

LOPAHIN (*Laughing*): Permit me to ask you, what do you make of me?

TROFIMOFF: Yermolay Alexeevich, I make this of you: you are a rich man, you'll soon be a millionaire. Just as it is in the metabolism of nature, a wild beast is needed to eat up everything that comes his way; so you, too, are needed.

(*Everyone laughs.*)

VARYA: Petya, you'd better tell us about the planets.

LYUMOFF ANDREEVNA: No, let's go on with yesterday's conversation.

TROFIMOFF: What was it about?

GAYEFF: About the proud man.

TROFIMOFF: We talked a long time yesterday, but didn't get anywhere. In a proud man, in your sense of the word, there is something mystical. Maybe you are right, from your standpoint, but if we are to discuss it in simple terms, without whimsy, then what pride can there be, is there any sense in it, if man physiologically is poorly constructed, if in the great majority he is crude, unintelligent, profoundly miserable. One must stop admiring oneself. One must only work.

GAYEFF: All the same, you will die.

TROFIMOFF: Who knows? And what does it mean—you will die? Man may have a hundred senses, and when he dies only the five that are known to us may perish, and the remaining ninety-five go on living.

LYUBOFF ANDREEVNA: How clever you are, Petya!

LOPAHIN (*Ironically*): Terribly!

TROFIMOFF: Humanity goes forward, perfecting its powers. Everything that's unattainable now will some day become familiar, understandable; it is only that one must work and must help with all one's might those who seek the truth. With us in Russia so far only a very few work. The great majority of the intelligentsia that I know are looking for nothing, doing nothing, and as yet have no capacity for work. They call themselves intelligentsia, are free and easy with the servants, treat the peasants like animals, educate themselves poorly, read nothing seriously, do absolutely nothing; about science they just talk and about art they understand very little. Every one of them is serious, all have stern faces; they all talk of nothing but important things, philosophize, and all the time everybody can see that the workmen eat abominably, sleep without any pillows, thirty or forty to a room, and everywhere there are bedbugs, stench, dampness, moral uncleanness— And apparently with us, all the fine talk is only to divert the attention of ourselves and of others. Show me where we have the day nurseries they are always talking so much about, where are the reading rooms? They only write of these in novels, for the truth is there are not any at all. There is only filth, vulgarity, orientalism— I am afraid of very serious faces and dislike them. I'm afraid of serious conversations. Rather than that let's just keep still.

LOPAHIN: You know I get up before five o'clock in the morning and work from morning till night. Well, I always have money, my own and other people's, on hand, and I see what the people around me are. One has only to start doing something to find out how few honest and decent people there are. At times when I can't go to sleep, I think: Lord, thou gavest us immense forests, unbounded fields and the widest horizons, and living in the midst of them we should indeed be giants—

LYUBOFF ANDREEVNA: You feel the need for giants— They are good only in fairy tales, anywhere else they only frighten us.

(*At the back of the stage* EPIHODOFF *passes by, playing the guitar.*)

LYUBOFF ANDREEVNA (*Lost in thought*): Epihodoff is coming—

ANYA (*Lost in thought*): Epihodoff is coming.

GAYEFF: The sun has set, ladies and gentlemen.

TROFIMOFF: Yes.

GAYEFF (*Not loud and as if he were declaiming*): Oh, Nature, wonderful, you gleam with eternal radiance, beautiful and indifferent, you, whom we call Mother, combine in yourself both life and death, you give life and you take it away.

VARYA (*Beseechingly*): Uncle!

ANYA: Uncle, you're doing it again!

TROFIMOFF: You'd better bank the yellow into the side pocket.

GAYEFF: I'll be quiet, quiet.

> (*All sit absorbed in their thoughts. There is only the silence.* FIERS *is heard muttering to himself softly. Suddenly a distant sound is heard, as if from the sky, like the sound of a snapped string, dying away, mournful.*)

LYUBOFF ANDREEVNA: What's that?

LOPAHIN: I don't know. Somewhere far off in a mine shaft a bucket fell. But somewhere very far off.

GAYEFF: And it may be some bird—like a heron.

TROFIMOFF: Or an owl—

LYUBOFF ANDREEVNA (*Shivering*): It's unpleasant, somehow. (*A pause.*)

FIERS: Before the disaster it was like that. The owl hooted and the samovar hummed without stopping, both.

GAYEFF: Before what disaster?

FIERS: Before the emancipation.

> (*A pause.*)

LYUBOFF ANDREEVNA: You know, my friends, let's go. Twilight is falling. (*To* ANYA) You have tears in your eyes— What is it, my dear little girl? (*Embracing her.*)

ANYA: It's just that, Mama. It's nothing.

TROFIMOFF: Somebody is coming.

(*A* STRANGER *appears in a shabby white cap, and an overcoat; he is a little drunk.*)

THE STRANGER: Allow me to ask you, can I go straight through here to the station?

GAYEFF: You can. Go by that road.

THE STRANGER: I am heartily grateful to you. (*Coughing*) The weather is splendid— (*Declaiming*) Brother of mine, suffering brother— Go out to the Volga, whose moans— (*To* VARYA) Mademoiselle, grant a hungry Russian man some thirty kopecks—

(VARYA *is frightened and gives a shriek.*)

LOPAHIN (*Angrily*): There's a limit to everything.

LYUBOFF ANDREEVNA (*Flustered*): Take this— Here's this for you— (*Searching in her purse*) No silver— It's all the same, here's a gold piece for you—

THE STRANGER: I am heartily grateful to you. (*Goes out. Laughter.*)

VARYA (*Frightened*): I'm going—I'm going— Oh, Mama, you poor little Mama! There's nothing in the house for people to eat, and you gave him a gold piece.

LYUBOFF ANDREEVNA: What is to be done with me, so silly? I shall give you all I have in the house. Yermolay Alexeevich, you will lend me some this once more!—

LOPAHIN: Agreed.

LYUBOFF ANDREEVNA: Let's go, ladies and gentlemen, it's time. And here, Varya, we have definitely made a match for you, I congratulate you.

VARYA (*Through her tears*): Mama, that's not something to joke about.

LOPAHIN: Achmelia, get thee to a nunnery.

GAYEFF: And my hands are trembling; it is a long time since I have played billiards.

LOPAHIN: Achmelia, Oh nymph, in thine orisons be all my sins remember'd—

LYUBOFF ANDREEVNA: Let's go, my dear friends, it will soon be suppertime.

VARYA: He frightened me. My heart is thumping so!

LOPAHIN: I remind you, ladies and gentlemen: August 22nd the cherry orchard will be auctioned off. Think about that!—Think!—

(*All go out except* TROFIMOFF *and* ANYA.)

ANYA (*Laughing*): My thanks to the stranger, he frightened Varya, now we are alone.

TROFIMOFF: Varya is afraid we might begin to love each other and all day long she won't leave us to ourselves. With her narrow mind she cannot understand that we are above love. To sidestep the petty and illusory, which prevent our being free and happy, that is the aim and meaning of our life. Forward! We march on irresistibly toward the bright star that burns there in the distance. Forward! Do not fall behind, friends!

ANYA (*Extending her arms upward*): How well you talk! (*A pause*) It's wonderful here today!

TROFIMOFF: Yes, the weather is marvelous.

ANYA: What have you done to me, Petya, why don't I love the cherry orchard any longer the way I used to? I loved it so tenderly, it seemed to me there was not a better place on earth than our orchard.

TROFIMOFF: All Russia is our orchard. The earth is immense and beautiful, and on it are many wonderful places. (*A pause*) Just think, Anya: your grandfather, great-grandfather and all your ancestors were slave owners, in possession of living souls, and can you doubt that from every cherry in the orchard, from every leaf, from every trunk, human beings are looking at you, can it be that you don't hear their voices? To possess living souls, well, that depraved all of you who lived before and who are living now, so that your mother and you, and your uncle no longer notice that you live by debt, at somebody else's expense, at the expense of those very people whom you wouldn't let past your front door— We are at least two hundred years behind the times, we have as yet absolutely nothing, we have no definite attitude toward the past, we only philosophize, complain of our sadness or drink vodka. Why, it is quite clear that to begin to live in the present we must first atone for our past, must be done with it; and we can atone for it only through suffering, only through uncommon, incessant labor. Understand that, Anya.

ANYA: The house we live in ceased to be ours long ago, and I'll go away, I give you my word.

TROFIMOFF: If you have the household keys, throw them in the well and go away. Be free as the wind.

ANYA (*Transported*): How well you said that!

TROFIMOFF: Believe me, Anya, believe me! I am not thirty yet, I am young, I am still a student, but I have already borne so much! Every winter I am hungry, sick, anxious, poor as a beggar, and—where has destiny not chased me, where haven't I been! And yet, my soul has always, every minute, day and night, been full of inexplicable premonitions. I have a premonition of happiness, Anya, I see it already—

ANYA (*Pensively*): The moon is rising.

> (EPIHODOFF *is heard playing on the guitar, always the same sad song. The moon rises. Somewhere near the poplars* VARYA *is looking for* ANYA *and calling:* "*Anya! Where are you?*")

TROFIMOFF: Yes, the moon is rising. (*A pause*) Here is happiness, here it comes, comes always nearer and nearer, I hear its footsteps now. And if we shall not see it, shall not come to know it, what does that matter? Others will see it!

VARYA (*Off*): Anya! Where are you?

TROFIMOFF: Again, that Varya! (*Angrily*) It's scandalous!

ANYA: Well, let's go to the river. It's lovely there.

TROFIMOFF: Let's go. (*They go out.*)

VARYA (*Off*): Anya! Anya!

Curtain

ACT THREE

The drawing room, separated by an arch from the ball-room. A chandelier is lighted. A Jewish orchestra is play-ing—the same that was mentioned in Act Two. Evening. In the ballroom they are dancing grand rond. The voice of SEMYONOFF-PISHTCHIK: "*Promenade à une paire!*" *They enter the drawing room; in the first couple are* PISHTCHIK *and* CHARLOTTA IVANOVNA; *in the second,* TROFIMOFF *and* LYUBOFF ANDREEVNA; *in the third,* ANYA *with the* POST-OFFICE CLERK; *in the fourth,* VARYA *with the* STATION-

MASTER, *et cetera*—VARYA *is crying softly and wipes away her tears while she is dancing.* DUNYASHA *is in the last couple through the drawing room,* PISHTCHIK *shouts:* "Grand rond, balancez!" *and* "Les Cavaliers à genoux et remerciez vos dames!"

FIERS *in a frock coat goes by with seltzer water on a tray.* PISHTCHIK *and* TROFIMOFF *come into the drawing room.*

PISHTCHIK: I am full-blooded, I have had two strokes already, and dancing is hard for me, but as they say, if you are in a pack of dogs, you may bark and bark, but you must still wag your tail. At that, I have the health of a horse. My dear father—he was a great joker— may be dwell in Heaven—used to talk as if our ancient line, the Semyonoff-Pishtchiks, were descended from the very horse that Caligula made a Senator— (*Sitting down*) But here's my trouble: I haven't any money. A hungry dog believes in nothing but meat— (*Snoring but waking at once*) And the same way with me—I can't talk about anything but money.

TROFIMOFF: Well, to tell you the truth, there is something of a horse about your figure.

PISHTCHIK: Well—a horse is a fine animal— You can sell a horse—

> (*The sound of playing billiards comes from the next room.* VARYA *appears under the arch to the ballroom.*)

TROFIMOFF (*Teasing*): Madam Lopahin! Madam Lopahin!

VARYA (*Angrily*): A mangy-looking gentleman!

TROFIMOFF: Yes, I am a mangy-looking gentleman, and proud of it!

VARYA (*In bitter thought*): Here we have gone and

hired musicians and what are we going to pay them with?

(*Goes out.*)

TROFIMOFF (*To* PISHTCHIK): If the energy you have wasted in the course of your life trying to find money to pay the interest had gone into something else, you could very likely have turned the world upside down before you were done with it.

PISHTCHIK: Nietzsche—the philosopher—the greatest—the most celebrated—a man of tremendous mind—says in his works that one may make counterfeit money.

TROFIMOFF: And have you read Nietzsche?

PISHTCHIK: Well—Dashenka told me. And I'm in such a state now that I could make counterfeit money my-self— Day after tomorrow three hundred and ten roubles must be paid—one hundred and thirty I've on hand— (*Feeling in his pockets, alarmed*) The money is gone! I have lost the money! (*Tearfully*) Where is the money? (*Joyfully*) Here it is, inside the lining—I was in quite a sweat—

(LYUBOFF ANDREEVNA *and* CHARLOTTA IVANOVNA *come in.*)

LYUBOFF ANDREEVNA (*Humming lazginka, a Georgian dance*): Why does Leonid take so long? What's he do-ing in town? (*To* DUNYASHA) Dunyasha, offer the mu-sicians some tea—

TROFIMOFF: In all probability the auction did not take place.

LYUBOFF ANDREEVNA: And the musicians came at an un-fortunate moment and we planned the ball at an un-fortunate moment— Well, it doesn't matter. (*Sitting down and singing softly.*)

CHARLOTTA (*Gives* PISHTCHIK *a deck of cards*): Here is a deck of cards for you, think of some one card.

PISHTCHIK: I have thought of one.

CHARLOTTA: Now, shuffle the deck. Very good. Hand it here; oh, my dear Monsieur Pishtchik. *Ein, zwei, drei!* Now look for it, it's in your coat pocket—

PISHTCHIK (*Getting a card out of his coat pocket*): The eight of spades, that's absolutely right! (*Amazed*) Fancy that!

CHARLOTTA (*Holding a deck of cards in her palm; to* TROFIMOFF): Tell me quick now, which card is on top?

TROFIMOFF: What is it? Well—the Queen of Spades.

CHARLOTTA: Right! (*To* PISHTCHIK) Well? Which card's on top?

PISHTCHIK: The Ace of Hearts.

CHARLOTTA: Right! (*Strikes the deck against her palm; the deck of cards disappears*) And what beautiful weather we are having today!

> (*A mysterious feminine voice answers her, as if from under the floor: "Oh, yes. The weather is splendid, madame." "You are so nice, you're my ideal—" The voice: "Madame, you too please me greatly."*)

THE STATIONMASTER (*Applauding*): Madam Ventriloquist, bravo!

PISHTCHIK (*Amazed*): Fancy that! Most charming Charlotta Ivanovna—I am simply in love with you.

CHARLOTTA: In love? (*Shrugging her shoulders*) Is it possible that you can love? *Guter menschaber schlachter musikant.*

TROFIMOFF (*Slapping* PISHTCHIK *on the shoulder*): You horse, you—

CHARLOTTA: I beg your attention, one more trick. (*Taking a lap robe from the chair*) Here is a very fine lap robe—I want to sell it— (*Shaking it out*) Wouldn't somebody like to buy it?

PISHTCHIK (*Amazed*): Fancy that!

CHARLOTTA: *Ein, zwei, drei!*
    (*She quickly raises the lowered robe, behind it stands* ANYA, *who curtseys, runs to her mother, embraces her and runs back into the ballroom amid the general delight.*)

LYUBOFF ANDREEVNA (*Applauding*): Bravo, bravo—!

CHARLOTTA: Now again! *Ein, zwei, drei!*
    (*Lifting the robe: behind it stands* VARYA, *she bows.*)

PISHTCHIK (*Amazed*): Fancy that!

CHARLOTTA: That's all. (*Throwing the robe at* PISHTCHIK, *curtseying and running into the ballroom.*)

PISHTCHIK (*Hurrying after her*): You little rascal— What a girl! What a girl! (*Goes out.*)

LYUBOFF ANDREEVNA: And Leonid is not here yet. What he's doing in town so long, I don't understand! Everything is finished there, either the estate is sold by now, or the auction didn't take place. Why keep it from us so long?

VARYA (*Trying to comfort her*): Uncle has bought it, I am sure of that.

TROFIMOFF (*Mockingly*): Yes.

VARYA: Great-aunt sent him power of attorney to buy it in her name and transfer the debt. She did this for Anya. And I feel certain, God willing, that Uncle will buy it.

LYUBOFF ANDREEVNA: Our Yaroslavl great-aunt has sent fifteen thousand to buy the estate in her name— She doesn't trust us, but that wouldn't be enough to pay the interest even— (*Covering her face with her hands*) Today my fate will be decided, my fate—

TROFIMOFF (*Teasing* VARYA): Madam Lopahin!

VARYA (*Angrily*): Perennial student! You have already been expelled from the University twice.

LYUBOFF ANDREEVNA: But why are you angry, Varya? He teases you about Lopahin, what of it? Marry Lopahin if you want to, he is a good man, interesting. If you don't want to, don't marry him; darling, nobody is making you do it.

VARYA: I look at this matter seriously, Mama, one must speak straight out. He's a good man, I like him.

LYUBOFF ANDREEVNA: Then marry him. What there is to wait for I don't understand!

VARYA: But I can't propose to him myself, Mama. It's two years now; everyone has been talking to me about him, everyone talks, and he either remains silent or jokes. I understand. He's getting rich, he's busy with his own affairs, and has no time for me. If there were money, ever so little, even a hundred roubles, I would drop everything, and go far away. I'd go to a nunnery.

TROFIMOFF: How saintly!

VARYA (*To* TROFIMOFF): A student should be intelligent! (*In a low voice, tearfully*) How homely you have grown, Petya, how old you've got. (*To* LYUBOFF ANDREEVNA, *no longer crying*) It is just that I can't live without working, Mama. I must be doing something every minute.

YASHA (YASHA *enters. Barely restraining his laughter*): Epihodoff has broken a billiard cue!— (*Goes out.*)

VARYA: But why is Epihodoff here? Who allowed him

to play billiards? I don't understand these people—
(*Goes out.*)

LYUBOFF ANDREEVNA: Don't tease her, Petya; you can
see she has troubles enough without that.

TROFIMOFF: She is just too zealous. Sticking her nose
into things that are none of her business. All summer
she gave us no peace, neither me nor Anya; she was
afraid a romance would spring up between us. What
business is that of hers? And besides I haven't
shown any signs of it. I am so remote from triviality.
We are above love!

LYUBOFF ANDREEVNA: Well, then, I must be beneath
love. (*Very anxiously*) Why isn't Leonid here? Just
to tell us whether the estate is sold or not? Calamity
seems to me so incredible that I don't know what to
think, I'm lost—I could scream this minute—I could
do something insane. Save me, Petya. Say something, do say. . . .

TROFIMOFF: Whether the estate is sold today or is not
sold—is it not the same? There is no turning back,
the path is all grown over. Calm yourself, my dear, all
that was over long ago. One mustn't deceive oneself,
one must for once at least in one's life look truth
straight in the eye.

LYUBOFF ANDREEVNA: What truth? You see where the
truth is and where the untruth is, but as for me, it's as
if I had lost my sight, I see nothing. You boldly decide all important questions, but tell me, my dear
boy, isn't that because you are young and haven't had
time yet to suffer through any one of your problems?
You look boldly ahead, and isn't that because you
don't see and don't expect anything terrible, since life
is still hidden from your young eyes? You are

braver, more honest, more profound than we are, but stop and think, be magnanimous, have a little mercy on me, just a little. Why, I was born here. My father and mother lived here and my grandfather. I love this house, I can't imagine my life without the cherry orchard and if it is very necessary to sell it, then sell me along with the orchard— (*Embracing* TROFIMOFF *and kissing him on the forehead.*) Why, my son was drowned here—(*Crying*) Have mercy on me, good, kind man.

TROFIMOFF: You know I sympathize with you from the bottom of my heart.

LYUBOFF ANDREEVNA: But that should be said differently, differently—(*Taking out her handkerchief; a telegram falls on the floor*) My heart is heavy today, you can't imagine how heavy. It is too noisy for me here, my soul trembles at every sound, I tremble all over and yet I can't go off to myself, when I am alone the silence frightens me. Don't blame me, Petya—I love you as one of my own. I should gladly have given you Anya's hand, I assure you, only, my dear, you must study and finish your course. You do nothing. Fate simply flings you about from place to place, and that's so strange— Isn't that so? Yes? And you must do something about your beard, to make it grow somehow— (*Laughing*) You look funny!

TROFIMOFF (*Picking up the telegram*): I do not desire to be beautiful.

LYUBOFF ANDREEVNA: This telegram is from Paris. I get one every day. Yesterday and today too. That wild man has fallen ill again, something is wrong again with him— He asks forgiveness, begs me to come, and really I ought to make a trip to Paris and stay

awhile near him. Your face looks stern, Petya, but
what is there to do, my dear, what am I to do, he is
ill, he is alone, unhappy and who will look after him
there, who will keep him from doing the wrong
thing, who will give him his medicine on time? And
what is there to hide or keep still about? I love him,
that's plain. I love him, love him— It's a stone about
my neck, I'm sinking to the bottom with it, but I love
that stone and live without it I cannot. (*Pressing*
TROFIMOFF's *hand*) Don't think harshly of me, Petya,
don't say anything to me, don't—

TROFIMOFF (*Tearfully*): Forgive my frankness, for God's
sake! Why, he picked your bones.

LYUBOFF ANDREEVNA: No, no, no, you must not talk like
that. (*Stopping her ears.*)

TROFIMOFF: But he is a scoundrel, only you, you are the
only one that doesn't know it. He is a petty scoundrel, a nonentity—

LYUBOFF ANDREEVNA (*Angry but controlling herself*):
You are twenty-six years old or twenty-seven, but you
are still a schoolboy in the second grade!

TROFIMOFF: Very well!

LYUBOFF ANDREEVNA: You should be a man—at your age
you should understand people who love. And you
yourself should love someone—you should fall in
love! (*Angrily*) Yes, yes! And there is no purity in
you; you are simply smug, a ridiculous crank, a
freak—

TROFIMOFF (*Horrified*): What is she saying!

LYUBOFF ANDREEVNA: "I am above love!" You are not
above love, Petya, you are, as our Fiers would say, just
a good-for-nothing. Imagine, at your age, not having a
mistress—!

TROFIMOFF (*Horrified*): This is terrible! What is she saying! (*Goes quickly into the ballroom, clutching his head*) This is horrible—I can't bear it, I am going— (*Goes out but immediately returns*) All is over between us. (*Goes out into the hall.*)

LYUBOFF ANDREEVNA (*Shouting after him*): Petya, wait! You funny creature, I was joking! Petya! (*In the hall you hear someone running up the stairs and suddenly falling back down with a crash. You hear* ANYA *and* VARYA *scream but immediately you hear laughter*) What's that?

ANYA (ANYA *runs in. Laughing*): Petya fell down the stairs! (*Runs out.*)

LYUBOFF ANDREEVNA: What a funny boy that Petya is—! (*The* STATIONMASTER *stops in the center of the ballroom and begins to recite "The Sinner" by A. Tolstoi. They listen to him but he has recited only a few lines when the strains of a waltz are heard from the hall and the recitation is broken off. They all dance.* TROFIMOFF, ANYA, VARYA *and* LYUBOFF ANDREEVNA *come in from the hall*) But, Petya—but, dear soul—I beg your forgiveness— Let's go dance.

> (*She dances with* TROFIMOFF. ANYA *and* VARYA *dance.* FIERS *enters, leaving his stick by the side door.* YASHA *also comes into the drawing room and watches the dancers.*)

YASHA: What is it, Grandpa?

FIERS: I don't feel very well. In the old days there were generals, barons, admirals dancing at our parties, and now we send for the post-office clerk and the stationmaster, and even they are none too anxious to come. Somehow I've grown feeble. The old master, the grandfather, treated everybody with sealing-wax for all sicknesses. I take sealing-wax every day, have done so for twenty-odd years or more; it may be due to that that I'm alive.

YASHA: You are tiresome, Grandpa. (*Yawning*) Why don't you go off and die?

FIERS: Aw, you—good-for-nothing!— (*Muttering.*)
(TROFIMOFF *and* LYUBOFF ANDREEVNA *dance in the ballroom and then in the drawing room.*)

LYUBOFF ANDREEVNA: *Merci.* I'll sit down awhile—
(*Sitting down*) I'm tired.

ANYA (ANYA *enters. Agitated*): And just now in the kitchen some man was saying that the cherry orchard had been sold today.

LYUBOFF ANDREEVNA: Sold to whom?

ANYA: He didn't say who to. He's gone.
(*Dancing with* TROFIMOFF, *they pass into the ballroom.*)

YASHA: It was some old man babbling there. A stranger.

FIERS: And Leonid Andreevich is still not here, he has not arrived. The overcoat he has on is light, midseason—let's hope he won't catch cold. Ach, these young things!

LYUBOFF ANDREEVNA: I shall die this minute. Go, Yasha, find out who it was sold to.

YASHA: But he's been gone a long time, the old fellow.
(*Laughing.*)

LYUBOFF ANDREEVNA (*With some annoyance*): Well, what are you laughing at? What are you so amused at?

YASHA: Epihodoff is just too funny. An empty-headed man. Twenty-two misfortunes!

LYUBOFF ANDREEVNA: Fiers, if the estate is sold, where will you go?

FIERS: Wherever you say, there I'll go.

LYUBOFF ANDREEVNA: Why do you look like that? Aren't you well? You know you ought to go to bed—

FIERS: Yes—(*With a sneer*) I go to bed and without me who's going to serve, who'll take care of things? I'm the only one in the whole house.

YASHA (*To* LYUBOFF ANDREEVNA): Lyuboff Andreevna, let me ask a favor of you, do be so kind! If you ever go back to Paris, take me with you, please do! It's impossible for me to stay here. (*Looking around him, and speaking in a low voice*) Why talk about it? You can see for yourself it's an uncivilized country, an immoral people and not only that, there's the boredom of it. The food they give us in that kitchen is abominable and there's that Fiers, too, walking about and muttering all kinds of words that are out of place. Take me with you, be so kind!

PISHTCHIK (PISHTCHIK *enters*): Allow me to ask you— for a little waltz, most beautiful lady— (LYUBOFF ANDREEVNA *goes with him*) Charming lady, I must borrow a hundred and eighty roubles from you— will borrow— (*Dancing*) a hundred and eighty roubles— (*They pass into the ballroom.*)

YASHA (*Singing low*): "Wilt thou know the unrest in my soul!"

(*In the ballroom a figure in a gray top hat and checked trousers waves both hands and jumps about; there are shouts of "Bravo, Charlotta Ivanovna!"*)

DUNYASHA (*Stopping to powder her face*): The young lady orders me to dance—there are a lot of gentlemen and very few ladies—but dancing makes my head swim and my heart thump. Fiers Nikolaevich, the

post-office clerk said something to me just now that
took my breath away.

(*The music plays more softly.*)

FIERS: What did he say to you?

DUNYASHA: You are like a flower, he says.

YASHA (*Yawning*): What ignorance—! (*Goes out.*)

DUNYASHA: Like a flower—I am such a sensitive girl, I
love tender words awfully.

FIERS: You'll be getting your head turned.

(EPIHODOFF *enters.*)

EPIHODOFF: Avdotya Feodorovna, you don't want to see
me— It's as if I were some sort of insect. (*Sighing*)
Ach, life!

DUNYASHA: What do you want?

EPIHODOFF: Undoubtedly you may be right. (*Sighing*)
But of course, if one considers it from a given point
of view, then you, I will allow myself so to express it,
forgive my frankness, absolutely led me into a state of
mind. I know my fate, every day some misfortune
happens to me, but I have long since become accus-
tomed to that, and so I look on my misfortunes with
a smile. You gave me your word and, although I—

DUNYASHA: I beg you, we'll talk later on, but leave me
now in peace. I'm in a dream now. (*Playing with her
fan.*)

EPIHODOFF: I have a something wrong happens every
day—I will allow myself so to express it—I just smile,
I even laugh.

VARYA (VARYA *enters from the ballroom*): You are not
gone yet, Semyon? What a really disrespectful man
you are! (*To* DUNYASHA) Get out of here, Dunyasha.
(*To* EPIHODOFF) You either play billiards and break

a cue or you walk about the drawing room like a guest.

EPIHODOFF: Allow me to tell you, you cannot make any demands on me.

VARYA: I'm not making any demands on you, I'm talking to you. All you know is to walk from place to place but not do any work. We keep a clerk, but what for, nobody knows.

EPIHODOFF (*Offended*): Whether I work, whether I walk, whether I eat, or whether I play billiards are matters to be discussed only by people of understanding and my seniors.

VARYA: You dare to say that to me! (*Flying into a temper*) You dare? So I don't understand anything? Get out of here! This minute!

EPIHODOFF (*Alarmed*): I beg you to express yourself in a delicate manner.

VARYA (*Beside herself*): This very minute, get out of here! Get out! (*He goes to the door; she follows him*) Twenty-two misfortunes! Don't you dare breathe in here! Don't let me set eyes on you! (EPIHODOFF *has gone out, but his voice comes from outside the door: "I shall complain about you."*) Ah, you are coming back? (*Grabbing the stick that* FIERS *put by the door*) Come on, come—come on, I'll show you— Ah, you are coming? You are coming? Take that then—!

　　(*She swings the stick, at the very moment when* LOPAHIN *is coming in.*)

LOPAHIN: Most humbly, I thank you.

VARYA (*Angrily and ironically*): I beg your pardon!

LOPAHIN: It's nothing at all. I humbly thank you for the pleasant treat.

VARYA: It isn't worth your thanks. (*Moving away, then looking back and asking gently*) I haven't hurt you?

LOPAHIN: No, it's nothing. There's a great bump coming though.

(*Voices in the ballroom: "Lopahin has come back." "Yermolay Alexeevich!"*)

PISHTCHIK (*Enters*): See what we see, hear what we hear—! (*He and* LOPAHIN *kiss one another*) You smell slightly of cognac, my dear, my good old chap. And we are amusing ourselves here too.

LYUBOFF ANDREEVNA (LYUBOFF ANDREEVNA *enters*) Is that you, Yermolay Alexeevich? Why were you so long? Where is Leonid?

LOPAHIN: Leonid Andreevich got back when I did, he's coming.

LYUBOFF ANDREEVNA (*Agitated*): Well, what? Was there an auction? Do speak!

LOPAHIN (*Embarrassed, afraid of showing the joy he feels*): The auction was over by four o'clock— We were late for the train, had to wait till half-past nine. (*Sighing heavily*) Ugh, my head's swimming a bit!

(GAYEFF *enters; with his right hand he carries his purchases, with his left he wipes away his tears.*)

LYUBOFF ANDREEVNA: Lyona, what? Lyona, eh? (*Impatiently, with tears in her eyes*) Quick, for God's sake—

GAYEFF (*Not answering her, merely waving his hand; to* FIERS, *crying*): Here, take it— There are anchovies, some Kertch herrings— I haven't eaten anything all day— What I have suffered! (*The door into the billiard room is open; you hear the balls clicking and* YASHA's *voice: "Seven and eighteen!"* GAYEFF's *expression changes, he is no longer crying*) I'm terribly tired. You help me change, Fiers. (*Goes to his room through the ballroom,* FIERS *behind him.*)

PISHTCHIK: What happened at the auction? Go on, tell us!

LYUBOFF ANDREEVNA: Is the cherry orchard sold?

LOPAHIN: It's sold.

LYUBOFF ANDREEVNA: Who bought it?

LOPAHIN: I bought it. (*A pause.* LYUBOFF ANDREEVNA *is overcome. She would have fallen had she not been standing near the chair and table.* VARYA *takes the keys from her belt, throws them on the floor in the middle of the drawing room and goes out*) I bought it. Kindly wait a moment, ladies and gentlemen, everything is muddled up in my head, I can't speak— (*Laughing*) We arrived at the auction, Deriganoff was already there. Leonid Andreevich had only fifteen thousand and Deriganoff right off bids thirty over and above indebtedness. I see how things are, I match him with forty thousand. He forty-five. I fifty-five. That is to say he raises it by fives, I by tens.— So it ended. Over and above the indebtedness, I bid up to ninety thousand, it was knocked down to me. The cherry orchard is mine now. Mine! (*Guffawing*) My God, Lord, the cherry orchard is mine! Tell me I'm drunk, out of my head, that I'm imagining all this— (*Stamps his feet*) Don't laugh at me! If only my father and grandfather could rise from their graves and see this whole business, see how their Yermolay, beaten, half-illiterate Yermolay, who used to run around barefoot in winter, how that very Yermolay has bought an estate that nothing in the world can beat. I bought the estate where grandfather and father were slaves, where you wouldn't even let me in the kitchen. I am asleep, it's only some dream of mine, it only seems so to me— That's nothing but the fruit of your imagination, covered with the darkness of the unknown— (*Picking up the keys, with a gentle smile*) She threw down the keys, wants to show she is not mistress any more— (*Jingling the keys*) Well, it's all the same. (*The orchestra is heard tuning up*) Hey, musicians, play, I want to hear you! Come on, everybody, and see how Yermolay Lopahin will swing the ax in the cherry orchard, how the trees will fall to the ground! We are going to build villas and our grandsons and great-grandsons will see a new life here— Music, play! (*The music is playing.* LYUBOFF ANDREEVNA *has sunk into a chair, crying bitterly.* LOPAHIN *reproachfully*) Why, then, didn't you listen to me? My poor dear, it can't be undone now. (*With tears*) Oh, if this could all be over soon, if somehow our awkward, unhappy life would be changed!

PISHTCHIK (*Taking him by the arm, in a low voice*): She is crying. Come on in the ballroom, let her be by herself— Come on— (*Taking him by the arm and leading him into the ballroom.*)

LOPAHIN: What's the matter? Music, there, play up! (*Sarcastically*) Everything is to be as I want it! Here comes the new squire, the owner of the cherry orchard. (*Quite accidentally, he bumps into the little table, and very nearly upsets the candelabra*) I can pay for everything!

(*Goes out with* PISHTCHIK. *There is nobody left either in the ballroom or the drawing room but* LYUBOFF ANDREEVNA, *who sits all huddled up and crying bitterly. The music plays softly.* ANYA *and* TROFIMOFF *enter hurriedly.* ANYA *comes up to her mother and kneels in front of her.* TROFIMOFF *remains at the ballroom door.*)

ANYA: Mama—! Mama, you are crying? My dear, kind, good Mama, my beautiful, I love you—I bless you. The cherry orchard is sold, it's not ours any more, that's true, true; but don't cry, Mama, you've your life still left you, you've your good, pure heart ahead of you— Come with me, come on, darling, away from here, come on— We will plant a new orchard, finer than this one, you'll see it, you'll understand; and joy, quiet, deep joy will sink into your heart, like the sun at evening, and you'll smile, Mama! Come, darling, come on!

Curtain

ACT FOUR

The same setting as in Act One. There are neither curtains on the windows nor are there any pictures on the walls. Only a little furniture remains piled up in one corner as if for sale. A sense of emptiness is felt. Near the outer door, at the rear of the stage, is a pile of suitcases, traveling bags, and so on. The door on the left is open, and through it VARYA's *and* ANYA's *voices are heard.* LOPAHIN *is standing waiting.* YASHA *is holding a tray with glasses of champagne. In the hall* EPIHODOFF *is tying up a box, offstage at the rear there is a hum. It is the peasants who have come to say good-by.* GAYEFF's *voice: "Thanks, brothers, thank you."*

YASHA: The simple folk have come to say good-by. I am of the opinion, Yermolay Alexeevich, that the people are kind enough but don't understand anything. (*The hum subsides.* LYUBOFF ANDREEVNA *enters through the hall with* GAYEFF; *she is not crying, but is pale, her face quivers, she is not able to speak.*)

GAYEFF: You gave them your purse, Lyuba. Mustn't do that! Mustn't do that!

LYUBOFF ANDREEVNA: I couldn't help it! I couldn't help it!

(*Both go out.*)

LOPAHIN (*Calling through the door after them*): Please, I humbly beg you! A little glass at parting. I didn't think to bring some from town, and at the station I found just one bottle. Please! (*A pause*) Well, then, ladies and gentlemen! You don't want it? (*Moving away from the door*) If I'd known that, I wouldn't have bought it. Well, then I won't drink any either. (YASHA *carefully sets the tray down on a chair*) At least, you have some, Yasha.

YASHA: To those who are departing! Pleasant days to those who stay behind! (*Drinking*) This champagne is not the real stuff, I can assure you.

LOPAHIN: Eight roubles a bottle. (*A pause*) It's devilish cold in here.

YASHA: They didn't heat up today, we are leaving anyway. (*Laughing.*)

LOPAHIN: What are you laughing about?

YASHA: For joy.

LOPAHIN: Outside it's October, but it's sunny and still, like summer. Good for building. (*Looking at his watch, then through the door*) Ladies and gentlemen, bear in mind we have forty-six minutes in all till train time! Which means you have to go to the station in twenty minutes. Hurry up a little.

TROFIMOFF (*In an overcoat, entering from outside*): Seems to me it is time to go. The carriages are ready. The devil knows where my rubbers are. They've disappeared. (*In the door*) Anya, my rubbers are not here! I can't find them.

LOPAHIN: And I have to go to Harkoff. I'm going on the same train with you. I'm going to live in Harkoff all winter. I've been dilly-dallying along with you, I'm tired of doing nothing. I can't be without work, look, I don't know what to do with my hands here, see, they are dangling somehow, as if they didn't belong to me.

TROFIMOFF: We are leaving right away, and you'll set about your useful labors again.

LOPAHIN: Here, drink a glass.

TROFIMOFF: I shan't.

LOPAHIN: It's to Moscow now?

TROFIMOFF: Yes. I'll see them off to town, and tomorrow to Moscow.

LOPAHIN: Yes— Maybe the professors are not giving their lectures. I imagine they are waiting till you arrive.

TROFIMOFF: That's none of your business.

LOPAHIN: How many years is it you've been studying at the University?

TROFIMOFF: Think of something newer. This is old and flat. (*Looking for his rubbers*) You know, perhaps, we shall not see each other again; therefore, permit me to give you one piece of advice at parting! Don't wave your arms! Cure yourself of that habit—of arm waving. And also of building summer cottages, figuring that the summer residents will in time become individual landowners; figuring like that is arm waving too— Just the same, however, I like you. You have delicate soft fingers like an artist, you have a delicate soft heart—

LOPAHIN (*Embracing him*): Good-by, my dear boy. Thanks for everything. If you need it, take some money from me for the trip.

TROFIMOFF: Why should I? There's no need for it.

LOPAHIN: But you haven't any!

TROFIMOFF: I have. Thank you. I got some for a translation. Here it is in my pocket. (*Anxiously*) But my rubbers are gone.

VARYA (*From another room*): Take your nasty things! (*Throws a pair of rubbers on to the stage.*)

TROFIMOFF: But what are you angry about, Varya? Hm— Why, these are not my rubbers.

LOPAHIN: In the spring I planted twenty-seven hundred acres of poppies and now I've made forty thousand clear. And when my poppies were in bloom, what a picture it was! So look, as I say, I've made forty thousand, which means I'm offering you a loan because I can afford to. Why turn up your nose? I'm a peasant —I speak straight out.

TROFIMOFF: Your father was a peasant, mine—an apothecary—and from that absolutely nothing follows. (LOPAHIN *takes out his wallet*) Leave it alone, leave it alone— If you gave me two hundred thousand even, I wouldn't take it. I am a free man. And everything that you all value so highly and dearly, both rich man and beggars, has not the slightest power over me, it's like a mere feather floating in the air. I can get along without you, I can pass you by, I am strong and proud. Humanity is moving toward the loftiest truth, toward the loftiest happiness that is possible on earth and I am in the front ranks.

LOPAHIN: Will you get there?

TROFIMOFF: I'll get there. (*A pause*) I'll get there, or I'll show the others the way to get there.

> (*In the distance is heard the sound of an ax on a tree.*)

LOPAHIN: Well, good-by, my dear boy. It's time to go. We turn up our noses at one another, but life keeps on passing. When I work a long time without stopping, my thoughts are clearer, and it seems as if I, too, know what I exist for, and, brother, how many people are there in Russia who exist, nobody knows for what! Well, all the same, it's not that that keeps things circulating. Leonid Andreevich, they say, has accepted a position—he'll be in a bank, six thousand a year—the only thing is he won't stay there, he's very lazy—

ANYA (*In the doorway*): Mama begs of you until she's gone, not to cut down the orchard.

TROFIMOFF: Honestly, haven't you enough tact to— (*Goes out through the hall.*)

LOPAHIN: Right away, right away— What people, really!

> (*Goes out after him.*)

ANYA: Has Fiers been sent to the hospital?

YASHA: I told them to this morning. They must have sent him.

ANYA (*To* EPIHODOFF, *who is passing through the room*): Semyon Panteleevich, please inquire whether or not they have taken Fiers to the hospital.

YASHA (*Huffily*): This morning, I told Igor. Why ask ten times over!

EPIHODOFF: The venerable Fiers, according to my conclusive opinion, is not worth mending, he ought to join his forefathers. And I can only envy him. (*Putting a suitcase on a hatbox and crushing it*) Well, there you are, of course. I knew it. (*Goes out.*)

YASHA (*Mockingly*): Twenty-two misfortunes—

VARYA (*On the other side of the door*): Have they taken Fiers to the hospital?

ANYA: They have.

VARYA: Then why didn't they take the letter to the doctor?

ANYA: We must send it on after them— (*Goes out.*)

VARYA (*From the next room*): Where is Yasha? Tell him his mother has come, she wants to say good-by to him.

YASHA (*Waving his hand*): They merely try my patience. (DUNYASHA *has been busying herself with the luggage; now when* YASHA *is left alone, she goes up to him.*)

DUNYASHA: If you'd only look at me once, Yasha. You are going away—leaving me— (*Crying and throwing herself on his neck.*)

YASHA: Why are you crying? (*Drinking champagne*) In six days I'll be in Paris again. Tomorrow we will board the express train and dash off out of sight; somehow, I can't believe it. *Vive la France!* It doesn't suit me here—I can't live here— Can't help that. I've seen enough ignorance—enough for me. (*Drinking champagne*) Why do you cry? Behave yourself properly, then you won't be crying.

DUNYASHA (*Powdering her face, looking into a small mirror*): Send me a letter from Paris. I loved you, Yasha, you know, loved you so! I am a tender creature, Yasha!

YASHA: They are coming here. (*Bustling about near the suitcases, humming low.*)

(LYUBOFF ANDREEVNA, GAYEFF, ANYA and CHARLOTTA IVANOVNA *enter.*)

GAYEFF: We should be going. There is very little time left. (*Looking at* YASHA) Who is it smells like herring!

LYUBOFF ANDREEVNA: In about ten minutes let's be in the carriage— (*Glancing around the room*) Good-by, dear house, old Grandfather. Winter will pass, spring will be here, but you won't be here any longer, they'll tear you down. How much these walls have seen! (*Kissing her daughter warmly*) My treasure, you are beaming, your eyes are dancing like two diamonds. Are you happy? Very?

ANYA: Very! It's the beginning of a new life, Mama!

GAYEFF (*Gaily*): Yes, indeed, everything is fine now. Before the sale of the cherry orchard, we all were troubled, distressed, and then when the question was settled definitely, irrevocably, we all calmed down and were even cheerful— I'm a bank official. I am a financier now— Yellow ball into the side pocket, anyway, Lyuba, you look better, no doubt about that.

LYUBOFF ANDREEVNA: Yes. My nerves are better, that's true. (*They hand her her hat and coat*) I sleep well. Carry out my things, Yasha. It's time. (*To* ANYA) My little girl, we shall see each other again soon— I am going to Paris, I shall live there on the money your Yaroslavl great-aunt sent for the purchase of the estate

—long live Great-aunt! But that money won't last long.

ANYA: Mama, you'll come back soon, soon— Isn't that so? I'll prepare myself, pass the examination at high school, and then I'll work, I will help you. We'll read all sorts of books together. Mama, isn't that so? (*Kissing her mother's hands*) We'll read in the autumn evenings, read lots of books, and a new, wonderful world will open up before us— (*Daydreaming*) Mama, do come—

LYUBOFF ANDREEVNA: I'll come, my precious. (*Embracing her daughter.*)

    (LOPAHIN *enters with* CHARLOTTA *who is softly humming a song.*)

GAYEFF: Lucky Charlotta: she's singing!

CHARLOTTA (*Taking a bundle that looks like a baby wrapped up*) My baby, bye, bye— (*A baby's cry is heard: Ooah, ooah—!*) Hush, my darling, my dear little boy. (*Ooah, ooah—!*) I am so sorry for you! (*Throwing the bundle back*) Will you please find me a position? I cannot go on like this.

LOPAHIN: We will find something, Charlotta Ivanovna, don't worry.

GAYEFF: Everybody is dropping us, Varya is going away. —All of a sudden we are not needed.

CHARLOTTA: I have no place in town to live. I must go away. (*Humming*) It's all the same—

    (PISHTCHIK *enters.*)

LOPAHIN: The freak of nature—!

PISHTCHIK (*Out of breath*): Ugh, let me catch my breath—I'm exhausted— My honored friends— Give me some water—

GAYEFF: After money, I suppose? This humble servant will flee from sin! (*Goes out.*)

PISHTCHIK: It's a long time since I was here— Most beautiful lady— (*To* LOPAHIN) You here—? Glad to see you—a man of the greatest intellect— Here— Take it— (*Giving* LOPAHIN *some money*) Four hundred roubles— That leaves eight hundred and forty I still owe you—

LOPAHIN (*With astonishment, shrugging his shoulders*): I must be dreaming. But where did you get it?

PISHTCHIK: Wait—I'm hot— Most extraordinary event. Some Englishmen came and found on my land some kind of white clay— (*To* LYUBOFF ANDREEVNA) And four hundred for you—Beautiful lady—Wonderful lady— (*Handing over the money*) The rest later. (*Taking a drink of water*) Just now a young man was saying on the train that some great philosopher recommends jumping off roofs—"Jump!" he says, and "therein lies the whole problem." (*With astonishment*) You don't say! Water!

LOPAHIN: And what Englishmen were they?

PISHTCHIK: I leased them the parcel of land with the clay for twenty-four years— And now, excuse me, I haven't time—I must run along—I'm going to Znoykoff's—To Kardamonoff's— I owe everybody— (*Drinking*) I wish you well—I'll drop in on Thursday—

LYUBOFF ANDREEVNA: We are moving to town right away, and tomorrow I'm going abroad—

PISHTCHIK: What? (*Alarmed*) Why to town? That's why I see furniture—Suitcases— Well, no matter— (*Tearfully*) No matter— Men of the greatest minds —those Englishmen— No matter— Good luck! God

will help you— No matter— Everything in this
world comes to an end—(*Kissing* LYUBOFF ANDRE-
EVNA's *hand*) And should the report reach you that
my end has come, think of that well-known horse
and say: "There was once on earth a so and so—
Semyonoff Pishtchik— The kingdom of Heaven be
his." Most remarkable weather—yes— (*Going out
greatly disconcerted, but immediately returning and
speaking from the door*) Dashenka sends her greetings!

    (*Goes out.*)

LYUBOFF ANDREEVNA: And now we can go. I am leaving with two worries. First, that Fiers is sick. (*Glanc-
at her watch*) We still have five minutes—

ANYA: Mama, Fiers has already been sent to the hospital. Yasha sent him off this morning.

LYUBOFF ANDREEVNA: My second worry—is Varya. She
is used to getting up early and working, and now
without any work she is like a fish out of water. She
has grown thin, pale and cries all the time, poor
thing— (*A pause*) You know this, Yermolay Alexeevich: I dreamed—of marrying her to you. And there
was every sign of your getting married. (*Whispering
to* ANYA, *who beckons to* CHARLOTTA; *both go out*)
She loves you, you are fond of her, and I don't know,
don't know why it is you seem to avoid each other—I
don't understand it!

LOPAHIN: I don't understand it either, I must confess.
It's all strange somehow— If there's still time, I am
ready right now even— Let's finish it up—and *basta,*
but without you I feel I won't propose.

LYUBOFF ANDREEVNA: But that's excellent. Surely it takes
only a minute. I'll call her at once.

LOPAHIN: And to fit the occasion there's the champagne. (*Looking at the glasses*) Empty, somebody has already drunk them. (YASHA *coughs*) That's what's called lapping it up—

LYUBOFF ANDREEVNA (*Vivaciously*): Splendid! We'll go out— Yasha, *allez!* I'll call her— (*Through the door*) Varya, drop everything and come here. Come on! (*Goes out with* YASHA.)

LOPAHIN (*Looking at his watch*): Yes—
    (*A pause. Behind the door you hear smothered laughter, whispering, finally* VARYA *enters.*)

VARYA (*Looking at the luggage a long time*): That's strange, I just can't find it—

LOPAHIN: What are you looking for?

VARYA: I packed it myself and don't remember where. (*A pause.*)

LOPAHIN: Where do you expect to go now, Varvara Mikhailovna?

VARYA: I? To Regulin's. I agreed to go there to look after the house— As a sort of housekeeper.

LOPAHIN: That's in Yashnevo? It's nigh on to seventy miles. (*A pause*) And here ends life in this house—

VARYA (*Examining the luggage*): But where is it? Either I put it in the trunk, perhaps— Yes, life in this house is ended—it won't be any more—

LOPAHIN: And I am going to Harkoff now—By the next train. I've a lot to do. And I am leaving Epihodoff—on the ground here—I've hired him.

VARYA: Well!

LOPAHIN: Last year at this time it had already been snowing, if you remember, and now it's quiet, it's sunny. It's only that it's cold, about three degrees of frost.

VARYA: I haven't noticed. (*A pause*) And besides our thermometer is broken— (*A pause. A voice from the yard through the door*) Yermolay Alexeevich—

LOPAHIN (*As if he had been expecting this call for a long time*): This minute! (*Goes out quickly.*)

 (VARYA, *sitting on the floor, putting her head on a bundle of clothes, sobs quietly. The door opens,* LYUBOFF ANDREEVNA *enters cautiously.*)

VARYA (*She is not crying any longer, and has wiped her eyes*): Yes, it's time, Mama. I can get to Regulin's today, if we are just not too late for the train— (*Through the door*) Anya, put your things on!

 (ANYA, *then* GAYEFF *and* CHARLOTTA IVANOVNA *enter.* GAYEFF *has on a warm overcoat, with a hood. The servants gather, also the drivers.* EPIHODOFF *busies himself with the luggage*) Now we can be on our way.

ANYA (*Joyfully*): On our way!

GAYEFF: My friends, my dear, kind friends! Leaving this house forever, can I remain silent, can I restrain myself from expressing, as we say, farewell, those feelings that fill now my whole being—

ANYA (*Beseechingly*): Uncle!

VARYA: Dear Uncle, don't!

GAYEFF (*Dejectedly*): Bank the yellow into the side pocket— I am silent—

 (TROFIMOFF *and then* LOPAHIN *enter.*)

TROFIMOFF: Well, ladies and gentlemen, it's time to go!

LOPAHIN: Epihodoff, my coat!

LYUBOFF ANDREEVNA: I'll sit here just a minute more. It's as if I had never seen before what the walls in this house are like, what kind of ceilings, and now I look at them greedily, with such tender love—

GAYEFF: I remember when I was six years old, on Trinity Day, I sat in this window and watched my father going to Church—

LYUBOFF ANDREEVNA: Are all the things taken out?

LOPAHIN: Everything, I think. (*Putting on his overcoat. To* EPIHODOFF) Epihodoff, you see that everything is in order.

EPIHODOFF (*Talking in a hoarse voice*): Don't worry, Yermolay Alexeevich!

LOPAHIN: Why is your voice like that?

EPIHODOFF: Just drank some water, swallowed something.

YASHA (*With contempt*): The ignorance—

LYUBOFF ANDREEVNA: We are going and there won't be a soul left here—

LOPAHIN: Till spring.

VARYA (*She pulls an umbrella out from a bundle, it looks as if she were going to hit someone;* LOPAHIN *pretends to be frightened*) What do you, what do you— I never thought of it.

TROFIMOFF: Ladies and gentlemen, let's get in the carriages— It's time! The train is coming any minute.

VARYA: Petya, here they are, your rubbers, by the suitcase. (*Tearfully*) And how dirty yours are, how old—!

TROFIMOFF (*Putting on the rubbers*): Let's go, ladies and gentlemen!

GAYEFF (*Greatly embarrassed, afraid he will cry*): The train— The station— Cross into the side, combination off the white into the corner—

LYUBOFF ANDREEVNA: Let's go!

LOPAHIN: Everybody here? Nobody there? (*Locking the side door on the left*) Things are stored here, it must be locked up, let's go!

ANYA: Good-by, house! Good-by, the old life!

TROFIMOFF: Long live the new life!

(Goes out with ANYA. VARYA casts a glance around the room and, without hurrying, goes out. YASHA and CHARLOTTA, with her dog, go out.)

LOPAHIN: And so, till spring. Out, ladies and gentle men— Till we meet. *(Goes out.)*

(LYUBOFF ANDREEVNA and GAYEFF are left alone. As if they had been waiting for this, they throw themselves on one another's necks sobbing, but smothering their sobs as if afraid of being heard.)

GAYEFF *(In despair)*: Oh, Sister, Sister—

LYUBOFF ANDREEVNA: Oh, my dear, my lovely, beautiful orchard! My life, my youth, my happiness, good-by!

ANYA *(ANYA's voice, gaily, appealingly)* Mama—!

TROFIMOFF *(TROFIMOFF's voice, gaily, excitedly)*: Aaooch!

LYUBOFF ANDREEVNA: For the last time, just to look at the walls, at the window— My dear mother used to love to walk around in this room—

GAYEFF: Oh, Sister, Sister—!

ANYA *(ANYA's voice)*: Mama—!

TROFIMOFF *(TROFIMOFF's voice)*: Aaooch—!

LYUBOFF ANDREEVNA: We are coming! *(They go out.)*

(The stage is empty. You hear the keys locking all the doors, then the carriages drive off. It grows quiet. In the silence you hear the dull thud of an ax on a tree, a lonely, mournful sound. Footsteps are heard. From the door on the right FIERS appears. He is dressed as usual, in a jacket and a white waistcoat, slippers on his feet. He is sick.)

FIERS *(Going to the door and trying the knob)*: Locked. They've gone. *(Sitting down on the sofa)* They forgot about me— No matter— I'll sit here awhile—

And Leonid Andreevich, for sure, didn't put on his fur coat, he went off with his topcoat— (*Sighing anxiously*) And I didn't see to it— The young saplings! (*He mutters something that cannot be understood*) Life has gone by, as if I hadn't lived at all— (*Lying down*) I'll lie down awhile— You haven't got any strength, nothing is left, nothing— Ach, you—good-for-nothing— (*He lies still.*)

(*There is a far-off sound as if out of the sky, the sound of a snapped string, dying away, sad. A stillness falls, and there is only the thud of an ax on a tree, far away in the orchard.*)

Curtain